The Working Mother's Complete Handbook

GLORIA NORRIS
JO ANN MILLER

The Working Mother's Complete Handbook

A SUNRISE BOOK E.P. DUTTON/NEW YORK

Grateful acknowledgment is made to the following for permission to quote from previously published material:

Baby and Child Care, by Benjamin Spock, M.D. Copyright © 1945, 1946, 1957, 1968, 1976 by Benjamin Spock, M.D. Reprinted by permission of Pocket Books, a Simon and Schuster division of Gulf & Western Corporation.

Co-Parenting: Sharing Your Child Equally, by Miriam Galper. Copyright © 1978 by Running Press. Reprinted courtesy of Running Press.

Everything a Woman Needs to Know to Get Paid What She's Worth, by Caroline Bird. Copyright © 1973 by Caroline Bird. Reprinted by permission of the David McKay Co., Inc.

How Was School Today, Dear? Copyright © 1977 by Sara Ann Friedman. Published by Reader's Digest Press.

"Some Theoretical Considerations on the Problem of Mother-Child Separation," by Margaret Mead, which apppeared in the *American Journal of Orthopsychiatry,* Volume 24, Number 3, July 1954. Reprinted, with permission, from the *American Journal of Orthopsychiatry*: Copyright 1954 by the American Orthopsychiatric Association, Inc.

The Day Care Book: The Why, What, and How of Community Day Care, by Vicki Breitbart. Copyright © 1974 by Vicki Breitbart. Reprinted by permission of Alfred A. Knopf, Inc.

The Future of Motherhood, by Jessie Bernard. Copyright © 1974, used by permission of The Dial Press.

Working It Out, © by Sara Ruddick and Pamela Daniels. Reprinted by permission of Pantheon Books, a Division of Random House, Inc.

Working Mothers: An Evaluative Review of the Consequences for Wife, Husband, and Child, by Lois Wladis Hoffman and F. Ivan Nye. Copyright © 1974 by Jossey-Bass, Inc., Publishers. Reprinted by permission of Jossey-Bass, Inc.

Worlds of Pain: Life in the Working-Class Family, by Lillian Breslow Rubin, pp. 169, 170. © 1976 by Lillian Breslow Rubin. Basic Books, Inc. Publishers, New York.

To Mary Ella, Jasie and Sylvia

To Lou, Michael and Nicholas

Contents

A Word on Words

The use throughout this book of "working mother" is something of a misnomer, of course. All mothers work. We might have said more precisely the "wage-earning" mother. But since working mother has come to mean, in public and private usage, the woman who holds a job outside the home, we have stuck to this instantly recognizable term.

As for pronouns, we have alternated "he" and "she" arbitrarily throughout when what we have to say can apply to children of both sexes. Because the people who care for children while their parents are at work—housekeepers, baby-sitters, day-care teachers—are most often women, we have chosen to refer to these caregivers with the feminine pronoun. We hope we have managed to avoid cumbersome language without offending the growing body of dedicated male caregivers we have met. We can only hope that in future editions of this book, the concept of men caring for children will have taken hold so firmly that we will have to revise our language to reflect a new reality.

Acknowledgments

Many people helped us in creating this book. Our thanks go, first of all, to the busy women who so generously shared with us their feelings and experiences as working mothers. We are grateful to them for their candor and good humor, and for the many good ideas that we hope will inspire women everywhere.

We would like to thank Stella Chess, M.D., who found time in a heavy schedule to give us the benefit of her expert clinical knowledge of the children of working mothers.

Felice Schwartz, President of Catalyst, graciously contributed valuable information on careers for women. So, too, did Anne Close, Personnel Manager of Book-of-the-Month Club. Helen Barer gave us excellent food preparation ideas for which we are most appreciative.

Our thanks to Roberta Gordon, Lynn Weinberg, and Betsy Kovacs, who posed for our pictures, and to Henri Gueron, who took them. Among the many women who helped us reach mothers in their communities, Ernestine Wiseman was indispensable.

Our editor at E. P. Dutton, Nancy Crawford, provided sound guidance and support, for which we are most grateful.

Finally, we would like to thank each other for a collaboration that has been stimulating, rewarding, and, most of all, fun.

—G. N. and J. A. M.

I am grateful to my children, Michael and Nicholas, for displaying admirable patience and understanding during the many hours that I disappeared to "work on the book about mommies who work." Lou

Miller was equally tolerant of an absentee wife. To him goes my gratitude, not only for his love and encouragement, but for cheerfully sharing in every aspect of raising our sons. This book could not have been written without his help.

My housekeeper, Helen Plowden, has been a mother to my children —and to me. Her devotion and warmth have helped me be that rarest of creatures, a guilt-free working mother.

I am grateful to Nancy Hechinger, Helen Barer, and Susan Moore for sharing over the years their personal feelings about careers and families.

My very special thanks to Fran Castan and Marcia Rosen for believing I could do it.

—J. A. M.

Preface
HOW WRITING THIS BOOK
CHANGED US

When we began interviewing women for this book, we did not have any
hard and fixed convictions about the wisdom of mothers working. We
only knew that more women were taking jobs while their children were
small and that some were managing pretty well. But we also knew, from
our own experience, how tough it is to cope—the fatigue, the tug from
two worlds, and that constant nagging question in the back of the head:
Is it really okay to work and mother? We thought that a book sharing
these dark moments, along with ways that some mothers are working
out their hectic lives, would be helpful.

But our ideas changed as we interviewed over 150 women all across
the country, including mothers who work for the money and those for
whom working is a choice. From Boston to Memphis, from California to
New Jersey, we spoke to women holding all kinds of jobs—as stockbroker, hairdresser, teacher, factory worker, librarian, judge, professor,
film producer, computer programmer, boutique owner, accountant, secretary. And we listened to these women speak in similar terms about
similar experiences. Yes, they talked about doubts and guilt. But they
also told us about how they were coping. About the pleasure and sense
of self they got from working and earning a paycheck. About real benefits that were flowing to their children . . . and how their husbands
were sharing parenting in rewarding ways they never would have had
their wives been home full-time. Clearly, working mothers have more
up moments than we'd realized.

We delved into the newest studies on childcare and the effect of
surrogate mothers and day care—for example, in the fascinating work of
Harvard psychologist Dr. Jerome Kagan—and found much data to reassure mothers. Many women passionately recalled the depression and

isolation they'd felt before taking a job—and that drove us in a new direction we'd not intended, examining the historic changes in the institution of mothering and how being the perfect, full-time mother, as defined by some childcare experts, has created enormous strains on mothers and families. We organized rap groups of married and single working mothers and discovered the magical release that women sharing their common problems could offer each other. Most of all, exploring the lives, energies, and deep concern of working mothers for their children convinced us that not only can working mothers succeed, they *are* succeeding. And this despite little or no help from business firms or government in meeting the crying needs of families in which the mother holds a job.

As the cost of living rises, driving more women into the work force; as more divorced mothers take jobs to make ends meet; as women who are trained for better jobs opt not to take twenty years out of their working lives; the working mother is becoming as much a norm as the mother who stays at home. (Indeed, in some circles, the pressure for a woman to be "doing something" is already creating an unwholesome pressure on those women who do prefer to stay at home.) We are urgently concerned that more public support—for good childcare and for more flexible work schedules, to name only two glaring problems—be extended to American families in which the mother must or chooses to work. After seeing, close up, a number of working mothers who are valiantly managing on their own, we believe that with a bit of help, both mothers and families can thrive when the mother works.

The Working Mother's Complete Handbook

Chapter One
WHY DO MOTHERS WORK?

Once upon a time, the family script was simple. Nancy, with two years of college, and Joe, proud new recipient of a B.S., were married in June, attended by six bridesmaids in yellow frocks. Nancy did a brief stint in an office until the first of their 2.5 children was born, then retreated to the new suburban house she and Joe proudly staked a down payment on, a new tract house in a new community inhabited by young parents who were carbon copies of themselves. Producing right on schedule the next of her 2.5 children, Nancy busily occupied her days with changing diapers, reading *Pat-the-Bunny*, mopping up milk spills, soothing cries, and meeting the commuter train. Joe, who departed on the 7:22 in the morning and returned on the 7:03, devoted himself to advancing in the business world. He saw the children mostly on weekends, and discharged his fatherly duties by playing ball with his son and daughter on Sunday.

Then something happened. The last addition to Nancy and Joe's 2.5 children arrived and found no room to put its head in a house packed to the rafters with the growing family. Joe took out a new mortgage and added a couple of rooms, but it wasn't long before the weekly rises at the grocery store, the mushrooming property taxes, and the children's needs for costly things like orthodontia and summer camp caused an embarrassing budget crisis. Nancy took a job—"just temporary, until we catch up"—and hired a neighbor to keep an eye on the older children after school and care for the new baby. When Nancy got a promotion, the family celebrated her raise by buying a new refrigerator and an outdoor jungle gym for the children. Arrives on the scene: Joe's mother, who is aghast at the spectacle of a strange woman "bringing up" her grandchildren.

This is a scandal, she declares. No stranger with unknown values brought up Joe. No other hand served up the cookies and fruit after school. Stricken, she offers to contribute a monthly sum to relieve Nancy of the sacrifice of working. And then, something really happened. Nancy decided she didn't want to stop working.

Nancy's experience is being shared by women all over America. The number of working mothers has jumped *tenfold* since the beginning of World War II, creating what the U.S. Department of Labor—hardly given to overstatement—simply calls "the most significant change in the labor force in our history." Back in 1940, only a tiny percentage—about 9 percent—of women who had children at home held jobs. By 1955, at the height of the "feminine mystique," when the average American family ballooned to four children and women were supposedly busily retreating to the home, the percentage of working mothers tripled, unnoticed, to 27 percent. *Today, the percentage of mothers working outstrips the overall rate of women working in this country.* Half of all the mothers in this country—about fifteen million women—now work, and every expert predicts the rate will keep right on rising in the 1980s. Already the school-age child is more likely to have a mother who works than not, for 56 percent of mothers with children over six hold jobs outside the home.

Without much guidance from experts, this shift is altering how our children are reared, how marriages work, and how we think of ourselves. These changes profoundly affect our roles as women—changes that Columbia University economist Eli Ginsberg assesses "will have an even greater impact than the rise of Communism and the development of nuclear energy." The rise in working women, he adds, "is the single most important phenomenon of the century."

WHO WORKS AND WHY?

While some alarmists try to tie this revolution in women's working patterns to misguided feminist ideology, the truth is mothers are going to work for a variety of reasons: for personal fulfillment . . . from their fear that taking a lengthy break from their field will leave them unable to return . . . from their desire to be a contributing member of their families. And many, if not the majority, of us are working for the same reason men do: Our families need the money.

Changing economic realities are altering life for us all. Two out of three single mothers work, as many an ex-husband's check stretches too thin to support two establishments. And since only about 20 percent of single mothers regularly collect child support, the odds are that a single mother's paycheck is *fully* supporting her children.

With inflation now an accepted part of life, many two-parent middle-income and even high-income families can no longer afford a satisfactory life-style without Mom's salary. In the case of one out of ten married working mothers, her wages mean the difference between her family living below the poverty level and enjoying a more comfortable existence.

Mothers who are working because their families definitely *need* the money generally feel less guilty about leaving home (though they share the same problems of juggling two jobs at once). But mothers like Nancy who don't *absolutely* have to work face a load of guilt—imposed on them not only from others but from within themselves.

For according to many childcare experts and the average American, the ideal mother is an exclusive, full-time mother. She is the sole care-taker of her child. And mothering is her major activity. Yet as we interviewed women all over the country, from highly educated women to high school dropouts, we found pervasive signs that this exclusive, intensive mothering produces strains. Mothers tend to blame these strains on their own inadequacies as nurturers. But with remarkably similar words, all kinds of women told of common problems: isolation, physical fatigue, lack of identity, and even a galling sense of failure as a mother when they stayed home full-time with their children.

Gail, a thirty-one-year-old Denver health administrator who is married to a lawyer, is typical. She had just finished a cozy evening bath with her two-year-old daughter, whom she brought curly-haired and damp to join her seven-year-old brother on the floor of a cheerfully scattered living room. Gail began motherhood with the high enthusiasm and fuzzy expectations—typified by Pampers ads that show a glowing, peignoir-clad mother ecstatically nuzzling a beaming baby—with which most young women embark on the commitment of motherhood.

"I was so excited when I got the positive rabbit test that I resigned from my teaching job the same day—even though it would have been months before I really needed to leave," remembers Gail, wearing blue jeans, her long, brunette hair pulled into a chic roll on top of her head. "I planned to nurse and be a terrific mother. My role model was my mother-in-law, who had raised four terrific sons and found time to do important volunteer work as well. And besides, my husband's baby doctor had been Dr. Spock himself! I was definitely planning to stay home, breast-feed, and be a perfect, sensitive mother."

After her son was born, like so many women before her, Gail found the real experience of motherhood light-years from her expectations, stressful and isolating in ways she never had imagined.

"The doctor told me, 'Establish that physical bond, don't let anyone else pick him up,' and I didn't dare. I literally didn't think I could leave him for an hour."

After about six months of intensive mothering, Gail discovered a change in herself. Her husband came home and announced a treat: He was taking her out to a party with his office mates to celebrate winning a case. "I was in absolute terror for the next few days. I kept saying to myself: 'What am I going to say, I just have nothing to say, I'm a totally uninteresting person.' I was appalled at how a person with a strong sense of herself could deteriorate so quickly. I had thought I'd catch up on my reading while I was at home, but what happened was I couldn't read a word. I couldn't think of anything but children. I had even enrolled for a course in child psychology at the college nearby, but I never went to a single class."

Gail's husband was puzzled by her behavior and offered little sympathy. "I'd always been the outgoing one, the one who loved parties. My husband just couldn't fathom it when I would cry at the drop of a hat, or pour out that I felt worthless and had no self-identity anymore. By the time Jonathan got to be a year old, I felt so lonely I couldn't stand it, although I loved the baby terribly. And I was so worn down by the routine—this all-day all-night feed the baby, wash the dishes, go to the park, feed the baby, put the baby to sleep, do the wash, feed the baby—that I cried all the time. I couldn't even eat a meal with my husband anymore. I would hold the baby and eat bites my husband cut up for me on his plate. I hated myself and felt guilty at the same time. I couldn't understand how anyone could love her baby the way I did and still hate the routine. There were these tiny spaces of bliss and the rest of the time I felt like a prisoner."

Gail stops to admire two runny watercolors her son and daughter hold up. "Eventually, I made the decision to go to graduate school, which was a turning point for me. Jonathan managed just fine with the baby-sitter we'd hired, and after graduation, I took a job. My work is rewarding, and now we're all happier."

Gail's freedom to recognize her isolation and boredom marks the rending of the veil of sacredness that swathes motherhood. But by no means is every mother able to acknowledge her feelings and act on them as swiftly as Gail did.

Barbara, a forty-two-year-old married psychologist who lives in the Midwest, recalls her fourteen years at home, a painful odyssey that finally led her to return to work six years ago. A thoughtful woman who listens closely in a way that encourages her clients to talk, Barbara enjoys her work and has advanced rapidly in her profession. What were the fourteen years like?

"I met my husband in 1958—he was in mathematics and I was in psychology—when everyone wanted to live in the suburbs and TV sitcoms were pounding home the image of mothers happily serving their families. Both Al and I thought I would continue to work, though, and I got a job doing psychological testing at the university where he began teaching. But when our daughter was born, his feelings about my working became more ambivalent than he let on. I hired a dependable but not terribly bright woman to take care of Maggie, but every morning Al would call me at my office and say, 'Do you think Maggie's all right? She was crying for you when I left.' I felt so guilty I would shake at my desk for an hour.

"So when I got pregnant again, I quit. In a way, Al sabotaged me." But Barbara tried to be a good mother. "It was a big change. Instead of conferring with the head psychiatrist over test scores, I spent a lot of time ferrying the kids to the doctor and asking him what to do. Instead of running psychological tests, I was down on the floor making endless Play Doh creations with the kids. Or making my two thousandth child's snack. I would wash the kitchen walls and the high chair and the table three times a day. When you're home, you're always doing these things nobody notices and you don't even know why. And whenever you clean, the kids are always two steps behind you destroying everything you do.

"Gradually nothing I did seemed important anymore—except I kept doing it, what we call in psychology getting trapped in the secondary gains. You've forgotten what you started out to do, and keep doing the activity that was supposed to lead you to it. For the first time in my life, I started to get fat and frumpy and I became terribly jealous of Al's work. We weren't equals like we had been. He had moved up the ranks regularly at the unversity and even had a book to write. We all organized our lives around Al's book, but I desperately needed something just for me. So as the children got older, I switched from being their physical servicer to being their social servicer, the family organizer and facilitator, managing all their dates and lessons. I made elaborate plans for my daughter—sleep-over parties and arrangements to pick up girl friends for her to play with. I had to be on tap and free because if she wanted to go anywhere I had to drive her."

Barbara's moment of truth came unexpectedly. "I tried the conventional wisdom at that time, which was that mothers needed to take an hour off now and then, and enrolled in pottery lessons. But it was such a pretense of busywork that I never even finished the course. Then I became a compulsive shopper. The climax came one afternoon when I was riding the escalator in the local department store. I looked down at all those aimless women shopping and shopping and I actually shrieked, 'What am I doing here every week? I don't even have anything I need to shop for.' "

Painfully, after several weeks of arguing with Al, Barbara made her choice to go back to graduate school as the first step to rebuilding her professional life. In the six years since, her children have not only adjusted to Barbara's career but developed on their own. "They've taken charge of their own social lives more—and I discovered they do it much better than I." As for Barbara herself, "It's been an explosion of growth for me. I just wish I hadn't wasted all those years staying home—for the wrong reasons."

Susan, a slim, red-haired store buyer with three sons who is married to an Atlanta businessman, had always dreamed of being a mother. "For as long as I can remember, I've been a maternal kind of person. Children and animals have always just gravitated to me. My ideal was to have children and live in the suburbs—complete with a beautiful lawn, a blue station wagon, and a brown dog. I thought I would feel fulfilled and successful. But when my first two boys were small, even though my mother was near me to back me up, I still had black moments when I felt I just wasn't making it. I felt such guilt about my children's eating habits. I thought it all depended on me being there to feed them their carrots, and that if I left it to Mother, it might not go right. Toilet training was the same. Only *I* could do it exactly right. Every time one of the boys babbled, I felt I had to be there to babble back."

But then Susan's husband transferred five hundred miles south to Atlanta, uprooting the family. "The kids were now starting to run around on their own, and things got even worse. If I didn't stay on the alert every second, one of them would jump out the window. I couldn't go to the bathroom without one of them hanging onto me. I couldn't talk on the phone—they would scream the minute I picked up the receiver. All these men who talk about the glory of motherhood should spend a few rainy days with a houseful of kids running the television, asking for a drink of water two hundred times a day, interrupting whatever you're doing, breaking things, asking you questions—and try to keep their sanity. Try as you will, you're not the mother you want to be; you turn into this snarling, screaming Mommy. And you feel like such a failure."

Susan tried to sum it up. "You never have one moment to yourself, but you never feel you get one single thing done." She shakes her head; that's not what she means exactly. "It's that when your children are small, you can sort of respond, it's like an emergency. But when they get older, you discover that childhood is a long, gray, upward slope. So many days *nothing* happens. You feel your mind is rotting and you look in vain for some effect you're having on them, and all you can see is whining and power struggles and they want to eat you up."

Martha, who won a Woodrow Wilson scholarship and studied Greek literature in England before marrying and raising her two daughters in a restored Massachusetts farmhouse, sees a deeper reason behind such frustration. "What's hardest is that mothering brings absolutely no rewards to the ego. Nobody ever says, 'You did good mothering today.' Nobody ever gives you a raise or a new title. That's inherent in mothering. You don't just put X time in and expect X rewards back."

Martha grows more heated. "But the real reason is that *no one values this job*. Only on a very abstract basis. Oh, men pay lip service. They all declare that being a wife and mother is wonderful, they love you for it. But they themselves will not pay money for this job, and women absorb that from men, they take the cue, they think this job is second-rate. In our society, you just don't make it unless you have power and money."

Gloria, a young black mother who has a two-year-old and who enjoys her work as a paralegal, has come to the same conclusion. "Money is the way our society decides our worth. I suppose we should all say how awful that is, but the truth is I accept those values, too. Spending my time tutoring underprivileged kids for no pay might be more socially useful than keeping the traffic-offense records, but I wouldn't feel as good about myself as I do earning a paycheck. And my husband wouldn't respect me as much."

Gail, Barbara, Susan, Martha, and Gloria are all conscientious mothers. All love their children and are eager to fulfill their needs. Yet they discovered that in their single-minded efforts to meet all their children's needs, something crucial was missing in their lives. Again and again, women tried to explain the feeling, usually settling for "no identity." Fran, mother of twins and married to a doctor, said it:

"I've always been a reasonably self-confident person, but after marriage and motherhood, I sank into this depressed state, feeling that I was no one, a nothing person. Everywhere I went I was introduced as 'the twins' mother.' At school functions, it was 'This is Mrs. Frank, the twins' mother.' Among John's business friends, it was 'Here's Mrs. Frank, John's wife, the twins' mother.' I would cringe and think, God, am I so uninteresting that that's all people know me for—giving birth to twins and marrying John? And then I'd think, they're right, I have no self, no identity."

HOW MOTHERING HAS CHANGED

Most of us, living in greatly heightened awareness of women's potential created by the women's movement, like to think we've come a long way in the two decades since Betty Friedan's *The Feminine Mystique* exposed "the problem that has no name"—that anxiety that women suffered trying to fulfill themselves solely through their husbands and children. But despite the new images we see for women as more of us win equal pay and recognition, we often discover we haven't really veered from traditional ways of seeing ourselves as mothers. We are still surprised and feel guilty when we grow restless in the traditional role of motherhood. Why *should* rearing children, the giving and receiving of love—surely one of the basic human drives—make a mother feel like the family doormat? Why *shouldn't* being a mother be a satisfying and fulfilling career as it was for earlier generations of women?

The answers lie tangled in a knot of historical, economical, and psychological changes which have added strains to mothering that would make the job unrecognizable to our great-grandmothers. Never before have we demanded so much of mothers. Yet never before have we given so little support to them.

For motherhood, modern American-style, has been transformed by the death of the family economic unit, by the new demands that child-care experts have foisted on the mother to be the sole shaper of her child's happiness, and by the loss of the extended family, a loss that deprives young mothers of traditional family help in child-rearing, leaving them with the heavy strain of twenty-four-hour, unrelieved childcare.

Singly, each of these new conditions of motherhood would profoundly affect how mothers perform. Collectively, they have changed motherhood into what sociologist Jessie Bernard labels "a new and unique invention." Bernard, who has spent over thirty years charting the changing roles of women as wives and mothers, adds that the new motherhood—with its demands that a mother be the *only* caretaker of her child and also that mothering be her *only* occupation—may be the worst of all possible approaches to caring for our children.

WHAT HAPPENED TO MOTHER'S WAGES?

The loss of identity that women complain of is not imaginary but rooted in economic fact. Until the Industrial Revolution in the eighteenth century, the housewife was part and parcel of the family economic unit. At the same time she was raising a large family of children, she also grew the family's food, preserved it, and cooked it. She made the family's clothes, created household goods from soap to bedsteads, and made other items for sale or barter, all essential to her family's survival. She was both nurturer and provider. But when the production of goods switched from the home to the factory, the mother lost half her role and consequently half her importance. What followed was a profound shift in how women were viewed and valued. Factory owners, piling up great fortunes in the new industrial economy, now wanted the status of being able to afford an idle wife, a wife who need do nothing more taxing than manage the servants and stitch dainty needlepoint.

Not surprisingly, in this Victorian age of idle wives, the myth of the "weaker sex" bloomed. And while women were revered as weak and delicate, they became more dependent on their husbands financially and emotionally. Victorians might spin a heady cocoon of extravagant sentiment about the figure of wife and mother, eulogizing her as an angel, a bloodless Madonna, a saintly guardian of the sacred temple of home. Yet the fact remained that her life and experience had narrowed, her role reduced to devoting herself to childcare and her family's psychological needs. Mother had become a specialist. But unlike other specialists in the industrial age, she was paid in the uncashable coin of sentiment, gratitude, and verbal praise. As sociologist Nils Newton sums up: "Women *lost* status, not gained it from the Industrial Revolution."

The robbing of woman's role as productive worker did not go unnoticed. In America in 1942, sociologist Ferdinand Lundberg and psychoanalyst Marynia Farnham pondered women's discontent in their influential book *Modern Woman: The Lost Sex*. Mothers were bound to be unhappy having only half of their former role, no longer being an integral part of the economic support systems of their families. But society needed mothers to nurture children. How could they be persuaded to stay at home and concentrate on this task, especially when women were being given educations equal to those of men? Lundberg and Farnham's solution was to glorify motherhood, to imbue it with awesome new responsibility. To bolster their case, they offered psychological interpretations that defined woman's innate nature as dependent and submissive. The newly educated woman only *thought* she wanted to be independent; in fact, she could only be happy serving others.

Lundberg and Farnham's thesis that the real fulfillment of women comes through serving others was widely quoted. It became the keystone in the arch of the feminine mystique—that combination of myth and shrewd advertising strategy that persuaded a generation of women in the fifties to stay at home.

Yet even the constant hammering home of this message in magazines, movies, and popular thought could not disguise to women the fact that no economic value was placed on their supposedly essential labors. Just as today, lack of pay for a mother-housewife's endless labors still undermines the sense of worth a woman might feel as she performs the repetitive work of childcare.

A MOTHER'S JOB IS NEVER DONE

But mother's lack of wage-earning work hardly leaves her with hours of free time to study, be creative, or do what she pleases. While Whirlpool washers and microwave ovens, packaged cookie rolls and polyester everything have supposedly shrunk the hours she must devote to housekeeping, the pressure to be a 24-hour mother, to be emotionally available to her children every second of the day, has introduced psychological strains that can be as stressful as an 18-hour day of hard labor.

In the past, when a mother had many jobs to do, she didn't dream that all her time and energy should be devoted to her children. Backed up by child-rearing theories that put her firmly in the driver's seat, she felt confident about postponing her children's demands when discipline demanded it. But thanks to the child-centered theories of the last forty years, a mother in our age of Psychological Awareness is judged by how effectively she responds to the "needs" of her child.

And being sensitive to a child's needs can often mean that a mother becomes a servant to her child. An American mama today anxiously performs a dizzying range of services for her children—from chauffeuring

---

DR. SPOCK CHANGES HIS MIND

1946, 1st Edition of Baby and Child Care:

It doesn't make sense to let mothers go to work making dresses in a factory or tapping typewriters in an office, and have them pay other people to do a poorer job of bringing up their children. . . . The important thing for a mother to realize is that the younger the child, the more necessary it is for him to have a steady, loving person taking care of him. In most cases, the mother is the best one to give him this feeling of "belonging," safely and surely. . . . If a mother realizes clearly how vital this kind of care is to a small child, it may make it easier for her to decide that the extra money she might earn, or the satisfaction she might receive from an outside job, is not important after all.

1971, Newsweek Magazine:

Women should have as much choice as men as to where their place will be. . . . If a mother wants an uninterrupted career, it is up to the two parents to decide, without prejudice, how to divide the child care or get part-time assistance from a grandmother or a suitable sitter. I admit my sexism in having presumably assumed that the mother would be the one who would limit her outside work at least to part-time until her children are three.

1976, Revised Edition of Baby and Child Care:

Parents who know that they need a career or a certain kind of work for fulfillment should not simply give it up for their children. . . . Both parents have an equal right to a career if they want one, it seems to me, and an equal obligation to share in the care of their child. . . .

endless after-school activities to spending hours shopping for the perfect pair of Pumas for her son to accompanying her eight-year-old daughter to gymnastics class and worriedly taking notes on the routines so she can help her daughter rehearse. Critics have accused her of smother-love, but, for most of us, drawing a line between what mother should and shouldn't do is nearly impossible. With Freudian childcare experts at her elbow, reminding her of the life-long importance of the mother-baby bond, a mother treads an anxious path. Uncertain just *what* is expected of her, she rushes to do all until she drops.

The often naive interpretation of Freudian psychology has convinced mothers they have powers enough to maim their children for life and that assumption can frighten even the most secure woman. Convinced that her every action can cause her children life-long anxiety, bowel problems, neurosis, and inability to love, she finds that getting through a morning of bathing, feeding, and diapering is fraught with psychological mine fields. Mother is required, as a young mother overwhelmed with feelings of inadequacy moaned, "to be a combination of Earth Mother and child-development expert."

But while a mother is strained by new demands to be everything to her child, one of her key supports has vanished. With the rise of the nuclear family—one father, one mother, and the children isolated in one home—the historical support of the extended family has disappeared.

In times past, a mother could always snatch an hour of rest and relief from the insatiable demands of a child, secure while a trusted aunt, grandmother, uncle, or neighbor relieved her. Now locked in the lonely self-sufficiency of the nuclear family, in suburban house or apartment hundreds of miles from kin, a young mother must bear the physical and psychological strains of child-rearing alone—strains that most pediatricians, experts, and mothers themselves have ignored.

Adjusting to the treadmill of constant childcare is something women are just assuming to be magically able to do. As Norman, an otherwise sensitive man and father of five, smugly reasoned about his wife's efficient care of a succession of babies, "She's biologically equipped to get up off and on all night. It would kill me, but she's gone without sleep every night with all the babies and goes on the next day like nothing disturbed her. I'd be destroyed." (Needless to say, Norman doesn't allow himself to be.) "And all that noise, too. It drives me crazy when I'm home. But she can handle it. Women's hormones are different from men's."

Okay, motherhood is tough—a job with no monetary compensation, scattered ego rewards, and the hardest schedule in the world. But many people will argue that mothers don't take on their maternal duties expecting traditional job rewards. What *do* we expect to get from motherhood? Certainly not the title of Vice-President in Charge of Mothering and a salary of $36,000 a year. But all mothers *do* expect to gain a sense of identity from their work. And a woman who spends say, ages twenty-four to thirty-nine as a full-time mother is earning her identity—her source of who she is and her worth, how competent she is, and the meaning of her life—just as surely as being a plumber or bank teller or junior executive or district attorney or successful salesman gives identity to her husband. What exactly *does* she get for her services?

OCCUPATION: MOTHER; PAY: GRATITUDE

Her hours are straightforward: seven days a week, twenty-four hours a day. Her pay is room and board. When the baby is young, she functions in a sleep-starved state, seldom getting a full night of uninterrupted sleep—a biological stress that is often used as a technique to brainwash political prisoners. In this state of stress, she is bombarded regularly with high-decibel infant crying, urgent and anxiety-provoking, but uncontrollable. Later will come the perpetual noise of small children breaking her favorite objects, demanding her attention, and crying that Mommy do something *right now.*

Unrelieved from a regimen of constant demands and interruptions, the women whose exclusive function is that of mother is appalled when, unable to get her child to stop crying, despite weary days and hours of playing, walking, and cooing, she has the urge to smack this creature who seems to be fighting her out of sheer perversity. Guilt over being that miserable failure—the bad mother—is then piled onto her burden of loneliness and fatigue.

Her work environment confines her to socializing with others of her kind: other mothers whose experience does not enlarge hers but reflects her own unvarying days. Should she attempt to tear herself away for a little relaxation or grooming, she'll have to negotiate it. And she'd better be very firm in her mind about her own need if she's to win that.

Advancement in her chosen career as a mother is unknown, and the only "paycheck" acknowledging her usefulness and importance she re-

ceives usually comes once a year on the second Sunday in May—Mother's Day—when she's served a precarious breakfast in bed by her children and presented with a pair of underpants that don't fit her because she's gained fifteen pounds while serving as family cook.

In years to come, when the children need her less, her experience equips her for no other gainful employment (except possibly as unpaid baby-sitter to her grandchildren). Once she's past her prime, she is entitled to no pensions or future security, except what she might receive from the gratitude of her children. But woe betide her should she try to collect on gratitude by reminding them of her past contributions to their welfare. She'll be universally condemned as a guilt-provoking mother.

Analyzed in the blank terms of a job description, no other occupation in our society compares to a mother's in time consumed, physical stress, contradictory demands, or emotional commitment. The closest analogy is probably the physician—yet the rewards of the two professions couldn't be more opposite. The doctor routinely works to physical exhaustion, but he earns the highest average income of any paid employee —not to mention prestige, control over others, plus a diversity of experience seldom matched in business. For his devotion in time, body, and spirit, he earns the very best our world can give him in self-esteem, money, power, and intellectual stimulation. The housewife-mother, who devotes equal energy to her enterprise, gets low status, the tyrannical expectations of those she is devoting her energies to, and absolutely no financial security.

Mothers everywhere might agree that the work they put into their jobs and the compensation they get back are not equitable. But, they guiltily rush on, tough as it is, all these sacrifices are simply *in the nature of motherhood.* Fair or not, once a child springs to life in her womb, a mother feels bound to follow through on her responsibility for exclusive care of the child.

Astonishing as it may seem to those of us who are firmly caught up in trying to be Supermom, studies from other cultures suggest that this exclusive focusing on mothering is *not* the best way to raise children. In fact, the contrary may be true. Drawing on well-documented evidence of how mothers in different cultures handle childcare, Jessie Bernard says:

"The way we institutionalize motherhood in our society—assigning sole responsibility for childcare to the mother, cutting her off from the easy help of others in an isolated household, requiring round-the-clock tender loving care and making such *her exclusive activity*—is not only new and unique, but not even good for women . . . or for children. It may, in fact, be the worst. It is as though we had selected the worst features of all the ways motherhood is structured around the world and combined them to produce our current design."

In many societies (such as the Nyansongo of Kenya; the Alors; the Mixtecans of Mexico; the village folk of Taira, Okinawa; the Rajputs of Kuala Lumpur), other members of the extended family relieve the mother during the day: She does not have the physically and emotionally exhausting task of round-the-clock care. The baby quickly becomes accustomed to being cared for part of the day by his brothers and sisters, grandmother, neighbors, father, or grandfather. They are part of his world, just as his mother is.

Surely these mothers who care for their children fewer hours and share the responsibility for their upbringing will be less caring? Researchers find just the opposite. Leigh Minturn and William Lambert conclude in *Mothers of Six Cultures* that mothers who spend a high proportion of their time caring for children are more changeable in expressing warmth than those in other cultures and more likely to show hostilities unrelated to their children's behavior. Another study, conducted by James Prescott and Carol McKay, of forty-five cultures found a relationship between a high incidence of isolated mother-child households and lack of physical affection and even the inflicting of pain on the child by the mother. Far from producing a stable, loving mother, these findings suggest that the exclusive mother is more unstable in her emotional reactions to her child and is, in fact, more apt to show negative emotions.

Anthropologist Margaret Mead echoes this view, warning us against the unnatural—and unnecessary—insistence on a mother's constant presence. "The continuing relationship of the child to its need for care by human beings is being hopelessly confused in the growing insistence that child and biological mother or mother surrogate, must never be separated, that all separation, even for a few days is inevitably damaging. . . ." Mead continues, "On the contrary, cross cultural studies suggest that adjustment is most facilitated if the child is cared for by many warm friendly people."

In our nuclear families, the mother shouldering all childcare herself may be subjected to strains that make it impossible for her to do her best by her children. Or as Jessie Bernard concludes: "The two requirements we build into the role of mother—full-time care of children and sole responsibility for them—seem to be incompatible with one another, even mutually exclusive."

OTHER REASONS MOTHERS WORK

Hearing this grim description of a mother's lot, many women still shake their heads. "*I* didn't go to work because it was so bad at home," they will say. And certainly, not only discontent with exclusive mothering but also a number of other economic and social changes are drawing mothers into the office.

One of the most powerful of all is *the changing job market.* American businesses now need and are wooing women workers. In the past twenty years, jobs in manufacturing—a traditional male preserve—have remained stagnant while the clerical and service industries—which favor women workers—have mushroomed more than 100 percent and will go on booming in our technological society, assuring a continuing large demand for women employees.

This fact changed the life plans of Sharon, a twenty-four-year-old Stockton, California, office worker who handles long-distance sales for an international paper company. "I intended to stay home and I just loved the first three months of taking care of my son. But my old boss called me one day desperate to have me come back for three weeks because he hadn't been able to find anyone as good as I was. As it turned out, our family expenses had been more than we'd expected, and it worked out real well with my next-door neighbor keeping the baby. I enjoyed being back doing something I was good at and when my boss offered me a nice raise I decided it would be best for my husband and our baby to keep on working."

For many another woman, the decision to join the work force comes after *looking ahead and fearing empty-nest depression.* Gwen, a thirty-eight-year-old mother of five married to a doctor, three years ago accepted an important political post as transportation chief in her ecologically aware town, where she has pioneered bus service. "Nothing in the world could have made me leave my children when they were small. But the truth is, now that the youngest is eleven, they really don't need me hovering around constantly. I'm afraid of getting to that awful point where I need the children more than they need me. In a few years, they'll be gone. I don't want to be one of those leftover mothers who's begging her nineteen-year-old son to come home for the weekend."

The longer life spans women enjoy now, coupled with the fewer children they have, leave a far larger proportion of their lives child-free. A woman who bears the last of her two children when she's twenty-five will still be under forty, with half of her adult life ahead of her, by the time the youngest is reasonably self-sufficient. Waiting to return to work until your nest is empty is risky, and many a mother wants to avoid the crisis of finding herself with no job skills after twenty years away from work.

Another powerful reason many women choose to work while raising their children was pointed out to us by Ursula, a thirty-two-year-old stockbroker: "I've never heard anyone talk about this, but in all the jobs I've held, from my high school job as grocery store checkout clerk to my professional job now, I've gotten a deep satisfaction from being part of a team of people working together, being part of a work force. I think it's a basic instinct of humans—to work cooperatively and know you can pull your weight with the rest.

"The people I've worked with weren't necessarily people I'd be great friends with away from work. But their respect is very important to me. It gives me an important part of my identity to know I'm *needed* on the team and people are counting on me to do my job. I think to be a productive, competent worker is something we all want and need."

Many women cite their *identity as part of a working team* when they speak of their pleasure in their jobs. "At work, I'm not just the house doormat, I'm respected and needed," said a department store saleswoman.

"Getting the others to work with you so we get the job done together is very, very important to my self-esteem," says an office manager of a typing pool.

"I missed the office camaraderie terribly when I took two years off," says a bank teller. "I got very lonely; I needed to be working with others."

Feeling competent as a worker and having a worker identity are rewards we seldom talk about. But we think the instinct to work together with other people toward tangible results, the race to perform against deadlines—whether that deadline is a sales conference or a 5 P.M. wrap-up of the day's typing—the testing of our competence and skills we get from working with others *is* a basic need. This confirmation of our importance makes us feel part of our larger society. And for many women who have devoted themselves exclusively to mothering, depriving themselves of these rewards has seemed too big a price to pay.

PINK-COLLAR WORKERS TOO?

Work pleasure—the sense of satisfaction and the personal and financial rewards that come from having a meaningful, enjoyable job—sounds persuasive when you look at women who work as managers, lawyers, teachers, doctors, store buyers, scientists, researchers, editors—professionals with careers that give them some control over their work. But what about waitresses, beauty-salon hairdressers, factory workers, pool typists, and the whole wide world of pink-collar, lower-paying jobs, where most working mothers pick up their paychecks?

The fact is that many blue-collar mothers share the pleasure in working experienced by their middle-class sisters. In *Worlds of Pain*, psychologist Lillian Rubin's sensitive exploration of working-class life, one of her typical interviewees, a thirty-one-year-old factory worker, mother of five children, says:

"I really love going to work. I guess it's because it gets me away from home. It's not that I don't love my home; I do. But you get awfully tired of just keeping house and doing those housewifely things. . . . You know when I was home . . . I had that old housewife's syndrome, where you either crawl in bed after the kids go to school or sit and watch TV by the hour. I was just dying of boredom and the more bored I got, the less I did. I finally knew I had to do something about it, so I took this course in upholstery."

Typists, hairdressers, and factory workers also told Rubin about the ego satisfactions, the pride in making money that their jobs gave them.

Rubin concludes that most women find the work world a satisfying place, at least when compared to the world of the housewife. "Although many of these women are pushed into the job market by economic necessity," she says, "they often stay in it for a variety of reasons. . . . They take pride in doing a good job, in feeling competent. They are glad to get some relief from the routines of housewifery and mothering small children. They are pleased to earn some money to feel more independent, more as if they have some ability to control their lives."

FINDING NEW SOLUTIONS

So, for reasons that range from boredom to need for two paychecks to support a family, from career necessity to a vague need to "get back to the office," women who have children are holding jobs outside the home. They are combining the joys and duties of motherhood with the joys and duties of a job.

Many of us are finding that juggling act difficult. Partly because jobs remain rigidly keyed to what employers consider business needs (inflexible eight-hour days, jobs performed only by one person). Partly, too, because many of us are doubtful about whether we are wise to leave our children during the day, about whether we're being selfish and uncaring mothers. Partly because housekeeping and childcare remain chiefly our responsibility as mothers. And, in part, because, without models to follow, deciding on each day's priorities, deciding what must be done each day and what to leave undone leaves us feeling uncertain and guilty.

Yet many women—determined and inventive—*are* hammering out new solutions, and we want to share them with you. How can you stay in touch with your child when you're putting in ten hours a day at the office? Can you work out a flexible job schedule to take some pressure off yourself? How can you pace your career, finding ways to give your children time at crucial periods, without losing all the status you've worked for in the job market? What happens when fathers mother? And when wives work? And how can you make your family a sharing family, in which kids and father pull their weight?

Being a working mother is sure to change your perspective on a lot of things. We hope the feelings and solutions that women offer in this book can help make that change of perspective easier for you.

BOOKS THAT MAY HELP

The Growth and Development of Mothers, Angela B. McBride (Harper & Row, 1973). An impassioned examination of the needs of *mothers* (surrise! we do have needs, too) and how we have been programmed to believe that motherhood skills develop automatically. McBride deals fearlessly with the rage, guilt, and ambivalence that mothers routinely feel toward their children. She shows how mothers do not drop full-blown off trees, but develop along with their children, with age and experience.

Mother's Day Is Over, Shirley Radl (Charterhouse, 1973). Radl attacks the apple-pie myth of motherhood and exposes the forces—including "experts" and simple-minded TV-mother images—that make mothering even more difficult than it need be. Radl is wonderful for crystalizing the frazzled nerves, convictions of failure, and marital strains that are part and parcel of being a mother.

Mother's Day, Robert Miner (Putnam's, 1978). What happens when a man becomes a mother? In a novel that flashes nuggets of truth on every page, Miner writes of a single father quickly going berserk as he tries to cope with two children, a madhouse day-care center, and the children's seemingly endless round of Pampers, whining, and neediness.

Mothering, Elaine Heffner (Doubleday, 1978). A psychologist maps the syndrome of guilt and self-doubt that a generation of male childcare experts has created among mothers. Heffner plots a child-rearing approach that encourages mothers to feel confident about their own abilities to recognize and fill their children's physical and emotional needs.

The Feminine Mystique, Betty Friedan (Dell, reprinted 1974). Still says it all, brilliantly exposing the mix of psychoanalytic distortion, advertisers' need to create housewife-consumers, and popular myth that told women their only fulfillment lay in husband, children, and the home.

The Future of Motherhood, Jessie Bernard (Dial, 1974). Drawing on thirty years of study of the changing roles of women, this is a rich, full examination of how American motherhood came to be what it is and how it is changing.

Working Mothers, Jean Curtis (Doubleday, 1976). Warm and incisive looks at the problems of working mothers—from sex on the job to childcare arrangements—and how women are coping.

Your Family

Chapter Two
CHILDCARE AT HOME— MARY POPPINS AND OTHER POSSIBILITIES

Once you take a job, the first—and maybe most crucial—decision you will make is: how will my child be taken care of? Experts and mothers agree that *the success of a working mother hinges on how satisfactorily she manages to arrange for surrogate childcare.*

For many women, first thoughts fly to getting childcare in their homes. "I want my son to be taken care of at home; he's only three and he needs the comfort of his own toys, his own bed to nap in," insists Natalie, the manager of a boutique on Chicago's fashionable Near North Side. And says Millie, a pediatric nurse at a large Philadelphia hospital, who has recently separated from her husband: "I can't see hauling Robbie to someone else's home every day. It may cost more to have a sitter come to the house," Millie admits, "but it's worth it for what it saves in wear and tear on my own psyche and in the security it gives Robbie."

Most working mothers—nearly two out of three—with children under the age of six have their youngsters cared for at home. A number of advantages *do* come with this kind of setup: Keeping a child in his own environment can be less disruptive to him, especially when he's first getting used to your working. You won't have to agonize about what to do when your daughter has the sniffles or your son comes down with a stomach virus (although you may worry about the caregiver getting sick). Most important, your youngster will bask in the attention of someone whose major job is caring for her and her alone. She will have what child-development specialists consider the most important advantage: the chance to develop basic trust in a one-to-one relationship.

On the minus side: an at-home caregiver will cost you more than a day-care center, and she may offer less stimulation or companionship than your child would receive in a group situation. Says a bank teller who chooses a different solution—to have her four-year-old daughter cared for, along with three other children, in the home of a neighborhood woman: "I feel it's very important for her to be part of a family, since I'm divorced. They're a surrogate family, and an enormous help to me."

Another drawback of in-home care can be the lack of supervision. When you send a child to a reputable center, you're at least assured that the people in charge of him are not, as one woman complained from bitter experience, "talking endlessly on the phone, while the kids are eating potato chips and watching TV."

Despite these disadvantages, more than thirteen million of the sixteen million American children under the age of thirteen whose mothers are in the work force are cared for at home, either by a relative or a paid caregiver. If you decide on this route, you will no doubt have a lot of questions, among them:

- Will my child be lonely at home? Will she miss me?
- What exactly is a "surrogate mother"? How do I go about finding one?
- Will my child get too attached to the caregiver?
- What about values . . . discipline . . . daily routines?
- How can I be sure my own child-rearing style is maintained?
- How much will it cost? Can I afford it?

There are no easy answers to any of these questions. Like parenting itself, childcare arrangements are rarely perfect, and what works well for one family can be terrible for another. But experts and mothers agree on one vital point: *Consistency of care is the single most crucial factor for a child's well-being.* Noted child psychiatrist Stella Chess assures us that this does not mean you can never, never change caregivers once you've found one, or that you can't have a couple of people who alternate caring for your child. Warning against a "constantly changing array," Dr. Chess reminds us, however, that children are resilient and, in fact, that it is important for their growth to learn to deal with more than just a parent as caregiver. "Part of what children have to learn in this world," she says, "is that people are different and that you behave in one way in one situation and another way in another."

To provide predictable, consistent care, you will be looking for a caregiver who has a proven track record of reliability, who will be warm and friendly toward your children, and who will do her best to give them the kind of care you yourself give them.

WHAT ARE YOUR OPTIONS?

Depending on where you live and what your financial situation is, a number of choices are available to you—from the starched nanny dispatched by the big-city domestic agency, to the college drop-out who winds up mothering the children and you. Whatever the options in your own community, arm yourself with the following facts, based on what other working mothers have experienced, about what to look for and what to expect.

CARE BY RELATIVES

It seems like a perfect solution. Your mother hasn't got much to do; she'd love to take care of your son while you're at work. Or, your mother-in-law has been thinking of going to work herself but can't find an interesting job; what better opportunity for her than watching over her own granddaughter! You'll have lots of company if you choose this solution: nearly five out of six children under the age of thirteen are cared for by a relative. That special warm feeling that can exist between grandparent and grandchild, or between a child and any loving relative, is what draws so many parents to this type of childcare arrangement.

If your mother or aunt or sister-in-law agrees to take care of your child but refuses to accept anything for her services, override her generosity. *Insist on paying her.* Even a small sum (avoid paying in gifts) will put your relationship on a better basis. Paying your relative will repay you in two ways: She'll learn to appreciate your role as a working mother; and you'll feel less uneasy about sharing maternal responsibilities.

You can still run into trouble if you don't take the time to come to an agreement on the basic issue of your working. Laments the mother of an eighteen-month-old: "My mother is proud of my career, but she can't stand that her grandchild is not being cared for by his own mother." If your relative constantly makes you feel guilty—if she sees herself as the protector of your children, rather than as your helper—you may have more headaches than help. Seek out a different arrangement, no matter what hurt feelings result.

Sometimes the best relative to be in charge of your child is her own father. And many a graduate student, at-home worker, or house-husband (whose wife is taking her turn at supporting the family) has found caring for his children an enriching experience. But be prepared: your neighbors may be irritatingly inhospitable to a daddy who carries Pampers instead of a briefcase. "Nearly everyone looked at me suspiciously," says one young father who cared for his daughter for the first eight months of her life. "No mother or baby-sitter ever talked to me in the park, and I had trouble finding other men to be friendly with." This isolation undermines some men's confidence; but others ignore lifted eyebrows and manage to find enough companionship to help make the experience rewarding for themselves and their children.

If your children are of school age, you may have a childcare solution right under your own roof. Leaving a younger child in the care of his older brother or sister can work out fine, *if* the older child is reasonably responsible and mature. But be sure you take a few precautions. Watch out for resentment, which can quickly lead to problems. An eleven-year-old who's missed batting practice because he's had to mind his little sister can make life miserable for everyone around him.

Be realistic in your expectations; remember that not every child considers himself his brother's keeper. And don't forget that some youngsters are afraid to complain about helping out because they have an investment in pleasing their parents. Show your appreciation and respect by paying the older child, either in cash or extra privileges. Explain exactly what you want him to do—which days he's expected to cover, what the house rules are when he's in charge—and don't violate your agreements.

COMMUNAL LIVING

Group living is less common but certainly a viable way to deal with the problem of childcare. It can vary from two single parents sharing a home to a full-scale multifamily commune. Those who've found happiness in a group situation point out that, besides being economically practical, it gives children a chance to experience other adults as role models. Before you plunge into a communal arrangement, however, be sure that you and the others agree on such sticky matters as work and childcare hours, housekeeping responsibilities, financial arrangements— all the nitty-gritty details that can spell the difference between a cozy extended family and wall-to-wall bedlam.

LATCHKEY CHILDREN

Despite the need for quality care and supervision of the children of working mothers, the fact is that one out of every ten children under the age of thirteen is a "latchkey child," a youngster who has no adult supervision during the day.

You are not likely to feel comfortable leaving a child under six home alone for any length of time, but you may have enough confidence in your eight-year-old to let her stay alone at least for a few hours. And many an independent ten-year-old prefers his own company after school to that of a hired caregiver. How you handle this in your own family depends on how grown-up and responsible your child is, on the kind of neighborhood you live in, whether or not an older child will also have to be responsible for a younger sibling, and what time you or your husband expect to be home.

Some children can handle this situation for one or two days a week, but start to feel lonely if they come home to an empty house every day. One mother of ten-year-old twin boys got around this problem neatly by hiring a woman to come in two half-days, straighten the house and cook dinner, and supervise in case either of her boys had a friend over.

Here are some other tips to follow if your children come home to an empty house:

- Warn your children to come straight home, unless they've arranged in advance to visit somewhere. Some mothers insist that children check in with them by telephone as soon as they come home.
- Play it safe by insisting they not use the stove or other potentially dangerous appliances.
- Make sure your child carries his key in a safe place—on a string around his neck or inside his schoolbag. Leave extra keys with a neighbor.

- If you worry about how your child will spend her time alone at home, schedule some chores. But keep them simple. She needs to unwind after a busy day.
- Leave a friendly note and some prepared snacks in the refrigerator to help your child feel less lonely when he comes home.
- For children under ten or eleven—unless your child is unusually responsible, don't permit him to have friends over when no adults are around.

Mothers-in-law, older sisters, and group living are at one end of the childcare spectrum. At the other end are the paid housekeepers and baby-sitters that approximately one in six working mothers have in mind when they look for someone to take care of their children at home.

HOUSEKEEPERS

At the very top of the list, both in expense and service rendered, is the woman (or occasional man) who often becomes a "surrogate mother"—the housekeeper. This is the person whose role most closely approximates your own. The full-time housekeeper's tasks may vary from so-called light housekeeping (what one woman calls "everything I would do if I ever got around to it") to such heavy-duty chores as cooking for twenty-guest dinner parties, ironing shirts, and running the household while you and your husband are traveling in Europe. All this in addition to assuming full care of the children. Look behind any supermom career woman and you are likely to find this supersurrogate.

A housekeeper may live in or out, but either way you must be prepared to pay her more than you would a person who just takes care of children—a minimum of $75 a week in smaller cities or suburbs, up to $150 a week in large metropolitan areas. Salaries for live-in help are usually lower, since you are providing room and board.

Expect also to provide such benefits as two weeks' paid vacation, sick leaves, social security payments (many employers pay both their own and their employee's share), and regular salary review. Many housekeepers work a 5½-day week, which usually means they will work for you every other Saturday ("If she hesitates for a second on the telephone when I mention Saturdays," says one determined mother, "I don't even bother to set up an interview").

Who hires a full-time housekeeper? Money, of course, is the major consideration. Only a single mother or a married couple with a substantial salary can afford to part with a good portion of it in exchange for the peace of mind that comes with round-the-clock coverage. But don't assume that high-ticket help is necessarily a guarantee of security. A lot of mothers who employ competent housekeepers live in a perpetual state of terror that the housekeeper will quit. Many mothers have been known to make concessions that range from full summers off with pay to allowing the housekeeper to bring along her own children. And most have learned the hard way to maintain a list—the longer the better—of reliable backup help.

Families with very young children often find housekeepers a worthwhile investment. Kids under the age of six still need a lot of supervision; they can't yet be counted on to bathe, feed, or pick up after themselves. And riding herd on them and the household chaos that accumulates around them demands a lot of attention. The luxury of coming home to a house that is not strewn end to end with toys, to a roast in the oven and no dishes in the sink, has inspired many a working mother to sacrifice a hefty chunk of her salary to pay a housekeeper. "It's as if I hired a wife," one formerly married woman says with relief.

THE MOMMY MAFIA

When is a housekeeper more than a housekeeper? When she's an ally, that's when. Listen to a New England mother, the general manager of a trade magazine:

"For months I had been waging silent warfare in a no-win battle with the Mommy Mafia in our university town. These at-home women seemed to thrive on criticizing mothers who held paying jobs. As my daughters and I left our apartment house each morning, I could practically hear behind closed doors as bathrobed figures poured second cups of coffee and celebrated the scandal of my neglect of kids and kitchen.

"The cardinal sin was Having a Housekeeper. Laura, a wonderfully efficient and good-humored woman, cooked, cleaned, and kept a practiced eye on the children in an arrangement that suited both her and me perfectly. It was she who served up home-baked cookies and frothy chocolate shakes when neighborhood children came to visit.

"I was getting pretty sick of these children's mothers snooping around my house when they picked up their kids, searching for a fatal flaw in my setup. I was planning to confront one particularly irritating woman when Laura took matters into her own capable hands.

"This woman arrived at five o'clock one day and struck up a conversation with Laura, who was preparing dinner. 'Oh, do you do the cooking, too?' she asked nosily.

" 'Oh, no,' Laura answered quickly, 'Mrs. Gendel does all the cooking . . . I might make the salad, peel a potato . . .'

" 'Really?' said the woman disbelievingly. 'When does she get home from work?'

" 'She's home at five-thirty,' answered Laura briskly, 'and dinner's always on the table at six.'

"Still not satisfied, the woman glanced up at the weekly menu I always post on the kitchen wall and said, 'I see it says "Chinese food" on Wednesday. I guess they order it in from a restaurant.'

" 'Certainly not,' Laura answered firmly. 'Mrs. Gendel loves to cook Chinese food,' and with this she threw open the cabinet and said, 'See all the Chinese spices.'

"There was indeed an assortment of oriental ingredients left over from a brief fling I had had with wok cooking. And Laura, dear Laura, had remembered, and had used them to put this woman in her place and save my reputation as a homemaker."

BABY-SITTERS

Next in responsibility to a housekeeper is a baby-sitter, who might be defined as anyone from your neighbor's teenage son to the middle-aged woman down the block whose primary responsibility is caring for your child. Most people agree that the term "baby-sitter" is an unfortunate one. Whether she lives with you or comes in each day while you're at work, *a sitter should not just sit.*

Beyond the routines of childcare—diapering, feeding, playing with children, helping with homework, transporting kids to and from lessons —what can one reasonably expect of this kind of caregiver?

Sitters are paid less than housekeepers—anywhere from $1 an hour for a young teenager to $3 an hour or more for a mature person who lives in a large city—and thus are usually not expected to do major household chores. But just as you yourself would not simply sit with your children if you were at home, so you can ask a sitter to take on many time-consuming tasks that don't really fit into the category of housework (these can be done while her charge is napping or playing by himself). Consider how much time you would save if you asked your sitter to:

- cut up celery and cheese for after-school snacks
- pick up milk and bread
- mail a package (while out wheeling the baby carriage)
- take clothes to the cleaner
- empty the dishwasher
- fold laundry
- put a casserole (which you've prepared) into the oven
- sew on name tapes
- make the cupcakes you promised to bring to the school fair

You can easily double this list without abusing the working relationship. But be sure to define the job clearly at the beginning (be specific: don't just mention vague household chores).

Au pairs and mother's helpers are among the kinds of baby-sitters you might hire. Both of these terms refer to a person who usually lives in your home and helps care for your children in exchange for room and board and (sometimes) a modest salary (between $25 and $60 a week is customary).

A typical arrangement is twenty hours of light housekeeping and baby-sitting in exchange for full room and board.

The *au pair,* a term that originated from the custom of cultured young ladies of two different countries switching with one another as governesses, has now generally come to mean a foreign student or other young man or woman who exchanges domestic and childcare services for the chance to experience another style of life for a limited period, usually a year. In the last few years, the Department of Labor has cracked down on importing this kind of help and, except in rare instances, will not grant a prospective *au pair* the necessary work visa. Still, in those large metropolitan areas where there are domestic agencies and an abundance of foreign-language newspapers, it is sometimes possible to import an *au pair* (you must pay the fare both ways) or to hire one whom another family has sponsored. Sometimes having a family or other personal connection with officials in another country can help you locate and bring in an *au pair.*

A *mother's helper* can be a high school student who might welcome the chance to change his or her living situation or to earn a little extra money. A typical candidate is the oldest child from a large family whose experience with younger children and housekeeping skills will stand him or her in good stead in your home. College students are a natural for mother's-helper positions, particularly those who attend a school that offers no housing facilities. So are would-be actors, writers, musicians, artists—men and women who do the kind of low-remuneration work that lends itself well to a live-in childcare situation.

One problem with mother's helpers and *au pairs* is that young people who seek these jobs often tend to need a lot of mothering themselves. Many a busy woman has found herself acting as therapist-cum-mother-substitute to a youngster escaping from an unhappy family situation. (One woman nursed an eighteen-year-old through morning sickness and an abortion, only to find the mother's helper pregnant again three months later!) Avoid this type of relationship if you are not willing to cope with a certain amount of dependency. And if you're turned off by the prospect of sexy young things turning your husband on, stay as far away as possible from the long-blond-hair, twenty-inch-waist set, no matter how terrific they are with your kids.

THE RIGHT PERSON FOR YOU

There are, of course, as many varieties of caregivers as there are mothers, and beyond the basics of reliability, warmth, and good sense, no set rules exist about what makes a good one. Many women admit that they look for a friend, someone on their own wavelength whom they feel will then relate to their children the same way they do. Says one: "I figure if I like her, the kids'll like her, and we'll all get along better."

Are you seeking that certain someone "just like me"? Be more realistic: Find a person whose attitudes and style will mesh comfortably with your own. In fact, there is a virtue in hiring someone not at all like you. Your children may find a happy-go-lucky type a nice contrast to your own seriousness. And you may all flourish better with a keep-every-thing-tidy sort than your own once-a-week, tear-the-house-apart brand of housekeeping.

When choosing a caregiver, decide on your own priorities and then be prepared to compromise on what is less important to you. If you care more about developing your child's independence than maintaining a spotless house, forget about the woman who insists on spoon-feeding your three-year-old, even though your kitchen never looked cleaner. If you absolutely have to leave the house at eight o'clock, don't even interview someone who must travel an hour or more to your home (no matter how good her intentions, she's bound to disappoint you too often).

Trust your own instincts; they're more reliable than someone else's advice. Consider the unfortunate experience of Marcia, a young teaching assistant in an eastern college town who had always fared well with "a kind of flower child, hippie-type baby-sitter" for her son, Ethan. She allowed herself to be persuaded by an overcritical mother-in-law to hire instead Darlene, a kindly but "incredibly dull" housekeeper. For only slightly more money Darlene would take care of both child and house.

The results were disastrous. "Ethan was used to having college girls around him, people whose heads were in a place he understood. Along came Darlene, uneducated, not concentrating on him, actually more interested in the dishes, the laundry, and the cooking. One night Ethan came into my room in the middle of the night and just screamed at me, 'I hate Darlene!' "

Marcia admits that she, too, hated having Darlene in the house. She would certainly have done better sticking to her original priority of hiring people on her own wavelength.

Here are the choices you'll have to think out when you are looking for a caregiver:

Live-in or Live-out? If you have the room and are willing to sacrifice a certain amount of privacy, a caregiver who lives with you can be just the ticket. Her salary will be lower, she is available evenings and early mornings (an important plus for nurses, teachers, and other women whose jobs have irregular hours), and she may even be prevailed upon to work some weekends.

If you are a divorced mother with small children, a live-in person—especially someone who's willing to exchange her services for room and board and only a token salary—can really ease the stress of working and raising children alone. Having someone on the premises all the time will give both you and your children a sense of security and continuity. And it will let you go out in the evenings or work late in the office without the hassle of arranging for sitters in advance.

Because a live-in person is sharing your home, it's essential that you establish personal rules of conduct that are acceptable to you both. Is she to use the telephone? Is she free to invite friends to your home, and if so, at what hours? (You don't want to deprive a teenager of a normal social life, but you also don't want to wind up playing hostess to an ongoing party.) Will you all eat together or will you expect her to feed the children ahead of time? Will she join you on family vacations or weekend holidays?

Don't be afraid to set down firm rules such as no smoking, no boyfriends in the house, no drinking (again, these are your personal decisions to make). Be sure you both agree to these prohibitions right in the beginning. You can always relax them later on.

Male or Female? Young men can make wonderful caregivers for both boys and girls. As living examples of males in nurturing roles, they help break down the sex-role stereotyping that so many families are trying to combat. An added bonus: They are usually much more relaxed than young women about doing housework.

One of the most successful situations we came across involved a man. Sally, a busy lawyer who has two children in school and who describes herself as working "seventeen hours a day," has managed beautifully with the help of Robert, a "lovely out-of-work actor . . . and a marvelous cook." She comments that she deals much better with him than with the women she had hired, probably because "the women were overqualified (I wanted only creative, bright people around my kids) and resisted doing things."

It is sad but true that overqualified women may resent domestic duties. The question of what constitutes "overqualified" when it comes to childcare is a painful issue (can anyone really be "too capable" to care for our most valuable resource?); but the fact is that some women avoid this controversial subject entirely simply by hiring a man and not "exploiting their sisters."

Do children cared for by a male gain a different perspective on sex roles? Research on families in which the father is the primary parent is still too new to offer conclusive results, but informal observation suggests that the more contact boys and girls have with males in nurturing roles—as caregivers, primary-school teachers, homemakers—the broader and richer will be their concept of their own options in society.

Old or Young? Older women have traditionally worked as sitters; many a grandmother who has raised her own children will find caring for yours a perfect way to supplement her pension or social-security income.

And hiring a grandparent as a sitter can be a marvelous means of giving your children experience with another generation—especially if they have no grandparents of their own nearby.

Besides checking that the person you choose is healthy enough to chase after your active youngster, you'll want to make sure she can successfully bridge the generation gap. When you interview her or observe her with your child, watch out for telltale traces of a bygone age of child-rearing. These needn't be as extreme as the elderly lady who proudly reported that her one-year-old charge had stopped sucking his thumb after she tied his hands to the crib. Or the woman who left a two-year-old on the potty for an hour, telling him to "be a good boy and surprise Mommy." Or even the well-meaning grandmother who couldn't spend the morning in the park with the children because she had to put up baked potatoes for their lunch.

But if an older woman seems unable to adjust to today's more casual style of childcare—if she won't tolerate a little paint on an overall or she is afraid to let your nine-year-old ride his bike—you and she had better not sign on for any full-time commitment.

Another problem with older people is the feeling described by twenty-eight-year-old Nina: "I thought of her as my grandmother. But how do you tell your grandmother what to do each day? She's older; she's supposed to know more than you do." If you feel this way, better hire someone closer to your own age.

A Non–English-Speaking Caregiver? If you live in a large coastal city, a university community, or any area in which there is a substantial foreign community, you may want to hire a non–English-speaking person to care for your child. Recent immigrants (many of whom can find no other work here) may be well educated in their own country, come from middle-class backgrounds, have fewer master-servant hangups, and thus treat their jobs with a high degree of professionalism. Elizabeth, a California history professor who wanted a sitter comparable to herself in values and intellectual capacity, found this need well served by hiring the wives of foreign graduate students. Describing a woman caregiver who had been trained as a pharmacist in her native Chile, she comments, "Her English was not perfect, but I'd rather have someone whose English is not perfect because they speak a foreign tongue than someone who uses language that I wouldn't want used in my home."

Hiring someone who speaks virtually no English at all is another matter (we are still marveling at the New Jersey psychotherapist who engaged a Bulgarian woman to care for her newborn son, and then called home twice a day, "so that David can hear English spoken while he's up").

If you are thinking of hiring a caregiver who is not fluent in English, the age of the children is an important consideration. Dependability and a pleasant disposition may be all the person you hire needs to see that your nine-year-old and your seven-year-old don't get into trouble after school. But you would certainly think twice about leaving a toddler who is just beginning to express himself verbally with someone he can't talk to easily.

Making things work with a foreign-speaking person can simply be a matter of buying a dictionary and having a little patience. If the person possesses other desirable qualities, the inconvenience may be well worth it. One mother hired Maria, "a fat old lady, very motherly, who spoke hardly any English." She was supposed to do housework and start dinner, but "her idea of housework was washing the dolls' faces and giving the children lots of kisses. I overlooked a lot, though, because the kids loved her dearly." In fact, Maria's arrangement with the family worked out so well—and her English improved so speedily—that she continued working for them long after they no longer needed full-time help.

For Now or Always? Be prepared to make changes. Even after you've found the right person for you and your family, remember that what works now may not work forever. Children's needs change as they move through different developmental stages. The kindly grandmother who happily bounced your baby boy on her knee may not look so cheerful when at age two and a half he turns the house upside down. Your four-teen-month-old may be content to play alone in his playpen under the eye of a neighborhood teenager, but in another few months, he'll need a group situation part of the time.

Just because you are relieved to find any solution at all to the child-care problem does not mean you should cling to an arrangement after it's outlived its usefulness. This can happen when a second child is born and the sitter is unable or unwilling to care for a baby. Or when a child clearly needs the company of other children—true of all children beyond eighteen months—and the sitter is reluctant to play hostess to a handful of toddlers. This is often a problem with the kind of older caregiver who loves babies but lacks the imagination or playfulness to deal successfully with an older child. If your caregiver does not seem able to grow with your child, you may have to make new plans at some point. Don't wait for your son or daughter to become actively unhappy; keep a watchful eye on the situation, and take prompt action if you feel it's necessary.

FINDING A CAREGIVER

You've got before you your own private image of Mary Poppins, that near-perfect right arm who will help you perform the delicate balancing act of working motherhood. Now how do you go about making her (or him) materialize in your own home?

For starters, accept the fact that there is no surefire formula for success in this arena. Although it's possible that one phone call will miraculously produce an energetic grandmother whom your children adore, you are more likely to sweat it out for a few weeks on the phone with friends, neighbors, and assorted employment services before the right person comes along. The most important thing to remember is: *don't panic and, above all, don't settle for someone you don't really like.* Better to press your mother or other relative into temporary service while you explore all possibilities of finding permanent help.

We find that old standby, word of mouth, is still the best way to locate your baby-sitter or housekeeper. Asking around can mean making a pest of yourself on supermarket lines and at dinner parties, but it may also be the only way you'll ever hear of Mary Jane's sitter's sister who's moving here from Ohio and needs a job.

If you find yourself in the pediatrician's office or a playground or any other place where mothers and children gather, keep your ears open for possibilities (one woman latched onto a first-rate housekeeper by eavesdropping on a waiting-room conversation). And by all means ask the sitters of people you know if they have friends or relatives looking for work. Be persistent; take the initiative. Follow up with phone calls rather than waiting for someone to get in touch with you.

Tacking up notices on neighborhood bulletin boards is another way of finding help. Type or write your message clearly, and write your phone number vertically a number of times along the bottom of the notice so that interested applicants can tear it off.

Help Wanted

(a newspaper advertisement)

Responsible, warm person to care for 2-year-old girl and 7-year-old boy. Live in or out, 5½ days (every other Saturday). Light housekeeping. Recent references required. 999-6410 (days); 998-3345 (eves.).

Energetic Housekeeper Wanted

(a bulletin-board notice)

Pleasant, mature person needed by working couple to care for large house and 3 school-age children. 11 A.M. until after dinner, 5 days. Must have recent references and driver's license.

921-6410 | 921-6410 | 921-6410 | 921-6410 | 921-6410 | 921-6410 |

Encourage your pediatrician (or even your obstetrician) to serve as a clearinghouse for childcare information. Suggest that he or she hang up a bulletin board on which parents can post notices.

Placing an advertisement in a local newspaper involves a small investment, but it's usually worth it. Be as specific as possible. And be sure to say "References required." If you expect the person to work Saturdays or some evenings, say so; and indicate whether or not the job includes housework ("light housekeeping" and "plain cooking" are good, unambiguous terms).

It is usually best to specify the number and ages of the children: While it's true that "two preschoolers" or "four children" might scare off some applicants, you will be left with fewer but stronger candidates. Leave your options open by not specifying the salary in the ad.

HELP—AND WHERE TO FIND IT

- Employment offices of colleges and nursing schools (those without living quarters are especially good for live-in help, and most have good screening services)
- Foreign-language newspapers (especially if you speak the language or would like to learn it)
- Small-town newspapers (if you live in an urban area, ads here may help you uncover eager and capable helpers who want to try the big city)
- Notices in high schools (a good source of after-school help) and in the pediatrician's office
- Senior-citizen centers (an excellent source of part-time help)
- Employment agencies specializing in domestic help (note, too, that some locales have agencies for mother's helpers and other temporary help)
- Your state employment office (check here too about government-funded training programs, such as CETA, the Comprehensive Employment Training Act, which may supply well-trained household help at a fair price)
- Social welfare agencies, including Family Service Association, Catholic Charities, Federation of Protestant Welfare Agencies

When placing an ad, keep an eye on the readership of the paper in which it appears. If, for example, you don't want a hippie-type unemployed actress or a part-time sculptor, steer clear of a counterculture newspaper.

By all means, follow up any likely billboard notices or advertisements that appear under "Situations wanted." People who go to the trouble of advertising themselves can often be counted on to be responsible and mature.

INTERVIEWING A CAREGIVER

Judging a person in an interview calls for a combination of intuition and careful evaluation. Gut reactions are indeed important; how a person looks, talks, even the way he or she enters the room reveal a lot immediately. But a carefully structured face-to-face meeting can tell you both a good deal more about each other. Here are some guidelines that will help you make the most of each interview.

1. *Exchange basic information on the telephone before even scheduling an interview.* "I was amazed how many people you can weed out right away," one woman told us. "So many people just don't read ads carefully or maybe don't really know what they want themselves. My notice clearly said 'sleep-in' and three women called who only wanted sleep-out positions."

2. *Ask for recent references, and be sure to check them.* Many a mother, happy to find that the prospective employee has worked steadily for the last few years, neglects to actually talk to previous employers and to find out about the applicant's past performance. Information like "she's a marvelous cook and wonderful with kids, but you have to get after her about coming in on time," can be extremely helpful. Be sure, too, to find out why the applicant left her last job.

3. *Describe the job in detail, using as a general rule "the worst comes first."* If watering the plants and feeding the cat are included in the duties, this is the time to say so. Try not to fall into the gratitude trap ("As long as the kids are safe . . . I don't really care about anything else") and don't be ashamed if the list of duties is a long one, as long as you are paying fairly for the work.

   Be specific about the salary, raises, hours, holidays, sick leave, and any other details you haven't covered on the telephone. Enumerate any childcare responsibilities that you think might pose a problem (give some thought to these in advance; try writing them down).

4. *Have your children present for at least part of the interview.* As one woman put it, "If they stick around, chances are that person has something." Children are uncanny at sensing people's interest in them; watch them smell out the gushing "child lover" even as you're trying to convince yourself that her phoniness is just nervousness.

   The response of very small children can be particularly revealing. Says the mother of a two-and-a-half-year-old about her interview with a grandmotherly baby-sitter: "She sent out such loving signals that Rebecca simply walked over and climbed into her lap. I'm glad she stayed in the room. She really made the decision for me."

5. *Ask specific questions that will encourage the applicant to express herself honestly rather than to try to second-guess you.* For example, you will learn more from asking, "What would you do if David hit Martin while they're in the park?" than you will by inquiring, "What are your feelings about discipline?"

"WHAT WOULD YOU PLAY WITH A FOUR-YEAR-OLD?"

Some Interview Questions

- "Josh is about ready for toilet training. How would you go about that?" (Here's a chance to discover her attitude about a sensitive issue.)
- "How many days were you sick on your last job?" (*Not* "How is your health?")
- "What games would you play with a four-year-old?" Give her an A+ for proficiency in games like Candyland or Trouble; any skill whatsoever in arts and crafts, especially if you're weak in those areas; an honest answer like "I'm willing to play anything they want." Remember, too, that older children also need companionship. Says one anxious mother: "Every time it rains and I know the kids are home alone with Hilda, I worry they'll either be fighting with each other or watching TV. I'd give anything to have someone who'll drop everything and organize a game of checkers."
- "What would you do if one of the children had a nosebleed?" (Or cut himself? Or burned herself?) Once the person is hired, you will make clear rules for safety. At this point, you want to get some feeling for her ability to handle everyday mishaps.
- "What do you like to cook?" (A better question than "How is your cooking?") Again, give credit for honesty. If a responsible-seeming person confesses that she can't do much more than broil a hamburger, give her points for credibility and think about simplifying your meals.

---

6. *Give the applicant plenty of time to answer your questions and to ask ones of her own.* (If none are forthcoming, you can say, "Do you have any questions?" or "What would you like to ask me?") Be an active listener, and be encouraged if you and she feel comfortable talking to each other.

   Watch for direct eye contact, for enthusiasm that seems genuine and not likely to burn itself out in a few months. Look for a real appreciation of children, for a professional attitude toward working, for signs of enough flexibility and intelligence to adjust to the unpredictability of daily life around youngsters.

7. *Finally, remember that the purpose of the interview is not to see how many questions the applicant can answer successfully.* Rather, it's a chance for you and her to size each other up. Keep in mind that you are not looking for someone to bring up your children. That's your job. What you can expect from a good caregiver is the support that will help both you and your children grow as independent human beings.

Chapter Three
MANAGING CHILDCARE AT HOME

I wanted to work but I didn't want to have a servant. It went against my grain. I ended up calling the baby-sitter Mrs. Mullins and she called me Nina.

—A TWENTY-EIGHT-YEAR-OLD MAGAZINE EDITOR

Nina is not alone. Indeed, women who can successfully manage whole departments in an office are often thrown by the prospect of employing a person in their own home. Grown women have been tyrannized by teenagers; thirty-year-olds are intimidated by women twice their age.

Whether you have hired a grandmother or a teenager, *establish a businesslike relationship right from the start.*

SALARY AND BENEFITS

At present, few government guidelines about salary and benefits exist for domestic workers. Legally, domestic workers have been covered since 1974 by federal minimum-wage legislation (before that time, their median annual income was under $2500, and their benefits were strictly at the caprice of their employers). By law, any sitter who works more than twenty hours a week must be paid the minimum wage ($2.90 in 1979). In practice, however, wage and benefit standards for household workers are nearly impossible to enforce, and a great many workers continue to suffer from unconscionably low salaries and virtually nonexistent benefits (for example, it's not unheard of for a family to "lay off" a housekeeper in the summer when the children go to camp).

You can enjoy a dignified relationship with your caregiver by sharing the wisdom of experienced working mothers: *Don't exploit the situation.* Maintain the same standards of professionalism you would expect on your own job. Agree in advance on a set number of sick days and holidays (many women base this on the benefits given by their own employers). Set up a schedule of regular salary review. Outline the hours, duties, and privileges clearly at the outset (see below for a code of standards that covers all these issues). You may even want to establish these terms in writing.

If you are not sure what to pay, ask friends who have hired baby-sitters. Or be guided by the current federal minimum wage. And when in doubt, overpay.

If you only need help a few hours each day—say, from three o'clock, when the children come home from school, through the dinner hour—overpaying can be a fine way of assuring yourself the best possible people at what amounts to the least cost. Carol, a California mother of three school-age children, pays $4.50 an hour (three times the going rate in her community) to a twenty-five-year-old faculty wife to supervise the children's activities and generally manage the household during the after-school hours. The $60 a week she pays for this service is still less than she would have to pay for full-time help.

STANDARDS FOR HOUSEHOLD EMPLOYMENT *

Wages

- Salary should conform to local cost of living (at least minimum wage, higher in expensive areas) and wages should be increased at least once a year.
- Specialized skills—for example, gourmet cooking, tutoring children, altering clothing—should command a higher wage.
- Gifts of food, clothing, or household goods should not be considered part of the wages.
- Pay periods should be regular and means of payment should be agreed upon in advance.

Hours

- Live-in workers should earn one and a half times their hourly rate for work done in excess of forty hours a week; two times the rate after forty-eight hours.
- Full-time, live-out workers should earn one and a half times the hourly rate after forty-eight hours.

Benefits

- Employers must report earnings and make payments toward Social-Security insurance. They should also file quarterly statements with the IRS. Check your local Social Security office for further information.

Sick Leave and Holidays

- There should be a minimum of one day of paid sick leave a year for each day per week worked—in other words, a five-day-a-week person would be entitled to five days of paid sick leave a year.
- Live-in employees should have at least eight legal holidays a year. Full-time, live-out workers are entitled to six such holidays; day workers, at least one paid holiday a year.

Vacations

- Two weeks with pay is the rule for full-time employees (families who have longer vacations often elect to give their employees the same time off). Vacation time for part-time employees should equal at least two days a year for each day per week worked.

* Based on *Standards for Household Employment,* by the National Committee on Household Employment.

GOOD CHILDCARE CAN BE TAUGHT

Remember that it is up to you to see that the caregiver handles the children in a way that is acceptable to you. "What many women don't realize," says a psychologist who conducts parent-education groups, "is that baby-sitters can be *taught* to care for children in certain ways, just as mothers and fathers can be taught to be more effective parents."

Go over with the caregiver everything you can think of about your own and your children's likes and dislikes—their favorite games, lunch menus, when and where they should go outside, even what they should wear.

In the beginning, leave little to chance: Don't expect the caregiver to know intuitively that Debbie can't fall asleep unless the closet door is closed or that Jason is allowed to take his bear into the bathtub or that Nicky is the only child in the world who loathes French fries. Laying down a firm foundation of *your* values and preferences will help her use her own judgment as she gets more accustomed to the job. Unless you're an incurable optimist or your caregiver has signed a lifetime contract in blood, it pays to write down all these instructions; you never know when you may be breaking in someone new.

As the weeks go by, take a good look at how the person interacts with your children; listen carefully to the children's reports; ask direct questions. If you don't agree that your children should wash their hands five times a day, simply state what you expect along these lines. ("Please have the kids wash up before meals, or if they've played with mud and it looks like they're going to smear it on the walls.")

If your sitter or housekeeper is given to watching soap operas all afternoon, assign her specific chores that will occupy her during that time. If you worry that she will use the television as an instant sitter—a fear of many working parents—consider forbidding television entirely. Or lay down firm limits as to which programs the children can watch and for how long. If you like to see your children more actively involved, plan a trip to a museum or library and have the sitter accompany them. Watch your local newspaper for announcements of interesting events they might enjoy.

If you are committed to nonsexist child-rearing and you overhear your sitter telling your five-year-old son that "big boys don't cry," sit her down and explain carefully your own attitude about what boys do or don't do. If her feelings differ markedly from your own on important matters like this, consider replacing her with someone more sympathetic to your point of view.

Discipline is another sensitive issue. Make it clear to the caregiver and to the children that she is in authority when you are not there, but be sure that you and she see eye to eye on how that authority is to be enforced. Be as specific as possible. Saying "The next time Jeff throws a ball at his sister make him sit on his bed for half an hour," is more effective than the vague "You have my permission to punish him if he misbehaves." Be on guard against the caregiver who enforces no discipline at all to show you how kindly and loving she is. Or for the one who tries to impress you with her rules and regulations.

Watch out, too, for the unsociable caregiver. The parents of eight-year-old Mike, for example, were puzzled when he suddenly refused to stay with the sitter, insisting that she didn't like him. It turned out that Mike's budding sense of humor was being squelched because the sitter didn't laugh at his jokes or listen to his stories. "She never cares about anything I tell her," Mike complained. And he was right. This kind of unresponsiveness can be as harmful to a child's development as out-and-out unkindness.

Physical stimulation is also important. Cuddling and kissing a baby, giving a hug to a toddler, a friendly pat on the back to a ten-year-old—all the everyday expressions of affection—these are acts that you can expect and encourage in the caregiver.

THE TRIAL PERIOD

Some experts recommend an actual tryout period—say, a day or a weekend during which you try out a few sitters—but this can be time-consuming and impractical. Instead, hire carefully and make it clear that the first few weeks will be a trial period. Set a date for a meeting at the end of that time, when you can both air your beefs and renegotiate if necessary.

The trial period is also the time for your children to adjust to the new person in their lives—and for you to keep tabs on that adjustment. Try to take a few hours off to observe the caregiver in action. Make your leave-taking as casual as possible, and impress upon your child that the caregiver is in charge while you are away. It helps to remind your son or daughter of exactly when you will be home. If you express confidence that you are leaving your youngster in good hands, chances are he will be comfortable. Do not be overly concerned if your child cries or is otherwise upset when you leave; this is natural in the beginning, and should only become a source of real concern if the crying doesn't stop soon after you leave or if it persists for more than a week or so. (For a further discussion of children's adjustment, see pages 69–72.)

SPIES

No matter how trustworthy the sitter is, regardless of how happy your child seems, it is a good idea to get firsthand reports about the caregiver's conduct. A neighbor, your child's teacher, the parent of a child who visits yours, a relative—ask any of these people who see the sitter with your child to let you know how they appear to be getting along. Don't wait for volunteered reports; ask specific questions. Was she talking to the child? Did he seem occupied happily? Was she on time picking him up at school?

"EVERYTHING'S FINE . . ." AND OTHER DANGER SIGNS

No matter how carefully you choose a caregiver, there will be times you can't help worrying. You'll probably have no trouble spotting evidence of neglect, abuse, or indifference, but there are subtler danger signs you may not have thought of.

The "everything's fine" syndrome. Remember, the sitter has a stake in issuing only good reports to show she's doing a good job. If that's all you get, encourage her to share with you some of the day's events, including any problematical incidents, no matter how insignificant they seem to her. Remind her that you want to take an active interest in what goes on in your home and with your children. If she persists in painting only rosy pictures, you may have to replace her with someone more realistic.

A busy signal on the phone every time you call. One mother who tried to rationalize this as "just bad timing" paid a surprise visit to her house and found the housekeeper chatting merrily on the phone to a friend while her children were glued to the TV.

Your children seem consistently subdued when you arrive home. Most young children are excited and even boisterous at this time. The sitter may be exerting too much control. A serious talk with her can help ease the situation.

SAFETY

Make sure that anyone in charge of your children knows how to stop bleeding (applying direct pressure on the wound or cut will stop bleeding from all but the deepest lacerations, yet a surprising number of adults don't know this and will just keep mopping up the flow until they and the child panic) . . . what to do if a child is choking . . . how to handle a burn, and so on. Consult your local Red Cross chapter for information on first aid and home nursing courses. Also, keep a copy of the Red Cross *Standard First Aid and Personal Safety Manual* (Doubleday, 1973) on hand and encourage your caregiver (and yourself) to become familiar with it..

Paste a list of poisons and their antidotes on the inside of your medicine-cabinet door (you can photocopy this from a home medical guide, or write to your local board of health). Be sure to paste the phone number of the nearest Poison Control Center right next to your telephone; a Poison Control official will give emergency telephone instructions on how to deal with any harmful substance your child may have ingested. These and other numbers—pediatrician, internist, dentist, and so on—can be incorporated into a "Baby-sitter's Card" (see below).

Post your own card in a prominent place in your kitchen or in another room that has a telephone:

Baby-Sitter's Card

Mother's office:

Father's office:

Julia Brown (grandmother):

Leslie and James Stonier (neighbors, apt. 5C):

Sally's school:

Jerry's school:

After-school playgroup (Tuesdays and Thursdays):

POLICE:

FIRE DEPARTMENT:

TAXI SERVICE (call for emergency transportation):

Dr. Lipsett (children's doctor):

Mercy Hospital:

POISON CONTROL:

Martells Pharmacy (they will deliver):

Reliable Grocery (will deliver in an emergency):

Plumber:

Electrician:

Washer/Dryer Repair Service:

Have on hand an easy-to-read children's home medical guide. *A Sigh of Relief* (Bantam Books, 1977) is a good choice.

Tell your sitter exactly how she should handle an emergency that requires she go to a hospital. For example, you may want to be sure she calls you or your husband first so that you can meet her at the emergency room. Make sure always to leave enough money in the house for a taxi ride to a doctor or hospital.

If you travel or are otherwise inaccessible during the day, it is a good idea to leave a release letter authorizing the person in charge of your children to give permission for emergency surgical procedures (some hospitals will not even remove a splinter or set a broken bone without written permission from a parent). Check with your local emergency room for the exact wording they would prefer on a release letter.

To avoid unnecessary accidents, child-proof your home even more diligently than you would if you were there all the time. And be sure to stock your medicine chest with antiseptics, Band-Aids, aspirin, and other staples.

A CHECKLIST OF CAREGIVER CAUTIONS AND PRECAUTIONS

1. Are all important phone numbers posted clearly near the telephone? (Your office number and your husband's and any other key relatives'; the pediatrician, pharmacy; trusted friends' and neighbors' numbers; your children's school; Poison Control Center)
2. Is the sitter familiar with your home? (Does she know how to use the appliances? Where to find the children's rain boots? Where you keep the fuses—and how to change one?)
3. What are the ground rules for the caregiver? (Can she entertain guests? Use the telephone? Watch TV?)
4. What about the children? (Can they invite friends over without checking with you first? Are they permitted to call you at the office?)
5. Are rules for safety clearly spelled out? (Is your four-year-old allowed to plug in an appliance? Is your six-year-old allowed to stay alone for fifteen minutes?)

WHEN THE CAREGIVER IS ABSENT

The truth is *you* may drag yourself into the office with the world's worst migraine, but the person you hire to care for your children won't necessarily have the same blind devotion to her job. Baby-sitters get the flu. Housekeepers leave suddenly to nurse ailing relatives in far-off lands. *Au pairs* come down with the chicken pox and take to their beds in your house.

How can you best handle these unexpected absences? First of all, expect them. Keep a list of backup sitters or neighbors who will not flinch at an early-morning phone call. Don't be shy about asking a friend to pinch-hit for you; you can always repay the favor on the weekend. Second, make it clear to your caregiver right from the start that you expect her to give you as much early warning as possible if she's going

---

IN CASE OF ACCIDENT . . .

If your housekeeper breaks her leg putting away the groceries, if your cocker spaniel bites the baby-sitter, you may wind up losing more than just a trusted household employee. At-home accidents have been known to cost employers the equivalent of a year or more in salary, particularly if the injured person is unable to work for any length of time.

To be sure that you—and your employee—are protected, check your homeowner's insurance policy very carefully. Most liability clauses cover only a modest fixed payment, usually under $1000, although some insurance policies provide for much higher sums if the injured person should sue for negligence.

A recent development is the expansion in some states of workmen's compensation laws. Workmen's compensation, long a staple benefit for factory and office workers, provides payment to an injured party without that person having to prove negligence. Essentially a form of no-fault insurance, it varies in premiums and coverage from state to state. But in those states in which it operates, workmen's compensation will require that you reimburse an injured household employee for the full amount of her medical and support expenses. Ask your insurance agent if workmen's compensation applies in your state and make sure that you are fully covered should an accident occur in your home.

to be absent or late. You and she have agreed on a fair number of sick days; encourage her not to abuse this agreement. Finally, consider this novel idea: Have the sitter herself be responsible for backup—with the backup person subject to your approval, of course.

Your community may be a source of last-minute baby-sitting help. In Berkeley, California, for example, the Sick Child Care Program, financed by a combination of city, state, and federal monies, supplies trained caregivers for a sliding-scale fee. Although it is intended as a resource for parents whose children must stay home from school or day care on account of illness, this kind of program can also serve as a backup when the sitter is ill.

FIRING A CAREGIVER

She's tippling from your best Scotch . . . your children simply hate her . . . you and she have turned out to be worlds apart in child-rearing styles. So why does your heart go into your throat when you say tonight's the night to fire her? Remind yourself that if you hire for professional competence, on occasion you must fire for professional incompetence.

Don't Procrastinate. The experience will be worse for you, the children, and the sitter herself if you allow your displeasure to linger on. Simply summon up the same skills you practice all day on your job and tell her she will have to go, and why. Depending on the circumstances, you may want to give her two weeks' notice and/or severance pay to tide her over. Try to apply the same rules of fair play you would expect of your own employer.

If you do find yourself firing a caregiver, ask yourself how you might have avoided getting into that predicament. And try to learn from your own mistakes. Did you, for example, fall into the trap of being so grateful that someone was "doing your job" that you never made any demands at all? This kind of misguided guilt practically guarantees that you'll be disappointed.

Amy, a Chicago school librarian with two small boys, describes how when she first began working, she would say to the sitter, "I just want you to watch over the baby and love him." And that's what each sitter did—leaving Amy to be greeted each evening by unwashed lunch dishes, an obstacle course of Tinker Toys and building blocks in the front hall, and the unhappy prospect of dinner to prepare from scratch. Eventually she discovered that she could, for the same $2 an hour, find a sensitive, loving baby-sitter who would also take responsibility for certain basic housekeeping chores. "Now when I interview," declares Amy self-assuredly, "I say, 'This is a very hard job. I want dishes done, I want all the toys picked up, I want you to start dinner some days.' And I've had no trouble finding terrific people."

A WORD ABOUT JEALOUSY

The intimacy that develops when a child and the person who cares for him interact warmly is, we believe, a necessary and important quality to be nourished by parents and caregivers alike. But if you find yourself resenting the person who takes care of your son or daughter, if you start to get the feeling that your child actually prefers her company to yours, it's a good idea to take a hard look at your own relationship with your youngster.

Is your son preferring the caregiver because she is actually warmer and more loving to him? Does your daughter perhaps sense a tension in you about your own qualities as a mother? Sometimes just making an effort to spend more time with your child—without the distractions of your job, your marriage, your household responsibilities—will help ease feelings of competitiveness you may have with others who care for him.

What you call jealousy may really be regret at having missed out on some important event in your child's life. "My baby-sitter saw his first steps and I was heartbroken," says one woman. But she quickly adds that the feeling passed when she realized that there are few one-shot experiences in a child's development, and that she would have many chances to share in other events.

Jealousy and competitiveness can sometimes be tricky feelings to confront and work through. If you persistently resent your housekeeper or baby-sitter, don't give notice at the office; instead, consider seeking professional guidance to help you cope with these complicated emotions.

Chapter Four
CHILDCARE OUTSIDE YOUR HOME: DAY CARE, FAMILY DAY CARE, AND OTHER OPTIONS

If a baby-sitter or housekeeper is beyond your budget, or you've interviewed dozens and still feel uneasy, or if you simply feel your child will be lonely or bored alone at home with a baby-sitter, consider having her cared for outside your home.

What are your options if you make this decision? You can send your son or daughter to a public or privately funded *day-care center.* Or you can take him to the home of someone who cares for a small group of children, an informal arrangement known as *family day care.* Your school-age child can go to an *after-school* or *extended-day program.* Finally, like some 6 percent of all working mothers with children under thirteen, you can bring your child to the home of *your mother or other relative.* With the exception of the last option, each of these choices is a form of *group care,* as distinct from the one-on-one care your child receives in your own home.

WHAT SHOULD YOU LOOK FOR?

At a recent meeting in New York City, working mothers engaged in a lively discussion about what they considered "quality" group care. All the women spoke of "warm, nurturing, stimulating" environments. It should be "low-key, unpushy," remarked one, adding, "I don't want my kid to have to go outside if he doesn't feel like it. I think the care-givers should adapt to him, too, not just him to the adults." The women were unanimous in not wanting a television set on the premises and in insisting on a relaxed attitude about toilet training, eating, and napping.

How likely are you to find these qualities in the group situation you choose? Let's look at the pros and cons of the options available to you.

56

Can You Predict Your Child's Height?

By Robert B. McCall

We humans are curious, especially about the future; and the future height of our children is something parents have been trying to predict for generations.

Until recently, we have had some simple rules of thumb, but most are not very accurate. For example, parents often suppose that birth size tells them something about how tall their child will be as an adult. It doesn't. Nature adjusts the growth of the fetus partly to fit the prenatal environment, so birth length is not a very accurate forecaster of later size.

Another rule of thumb is to double the child's height at two years and add one inch. But this strategy ignores the fact that boys grow up to be taller than girls, so the method is not as precise as it might be.

An accurate predictor. Recently,

meters					
1Foot	2Feet	3Feet	4Feet	5Feet	6Feet

THE FORMULA

First, determine your child's height in inches at one year of age. Next, take your height and your spouse's height in inches and divide the sum by two. Then use your calculator:

FOR BOYS

Child's height × 1.07 =

Parents' height × .61 =

Total:

Subtract: 1.69

Predicted adult height:

FOR GIRLS

Child's height × 1.12 = 33.00

Parents' height × .57 = 40.64

Total: 77.5 — 46 3/4

Subtract: 4.43

64.5

A day in the small world of Gerber begins with a very special Nurser System.

Soon, all of your days will start with a very special time…the close and satisfying time spent nursing your baby with breast or bottle. That's why we'd like to take some time now to tell you about a very special nurser system… the Gerber Disposable Nurser.

As you may know, all disposable nursers allow your baby to nurse in a more natural way. The bag-type bottles collapse as baby nurses, so there's less swallowed air. And because each bottle is pre-sterilized and disposable, there's no need to scrub or sterilize as you would conventional bottles. But these are just the beginning of the advantages offered by the Gerber system.

GERBER DISPOSABLE NURSER SYSTEM.

Our disposable bottles slip out of the box one at a time, so there's no

Our twist-on nipple collar is easy to

Only Gerber prints ounce and milliliter markings right on the disposable bottles, so you can easily see through our clear holder to more accurately measure baby's formula. And when you compare our "more-bottles-to-the-box" price to a leading brand's price, you may find yet another Gerber advantage.

The small world of Gerber is more than baby food.

Gerber®

*Babies are our business...
and have been for over 50 years.*

Gerber Products Company, Fremont, MI 49412

We've designed our nipple hood to snap on and off easily for sanitary storage and convenient travel.

height. Unfortunately, as you might expect, it's a bit more complicated than these simple rules of thumb.

A team of scientists headed by Dr. Alexander F. Roche at the Fels Research Institute of Wright State University in Yellow Springs, Ohio, have developed a whole set of fancy equations that predict adult height by using the child's height and weight, the average of the heights of the child's biological parents, and the skeletal age of the child as determined from an X ray of the hand/wrist area.

Fortunately, the formulas can be made somewhat simpler without great loss of accuracy. To use them, you need your child's length at one year of age and the average height of you and your spouse (the child's biological parents) in inches.

Robert B. McCall, Ph.D., is a senior scientist at the Boys Town Center for the Study of Youth Development, near Omaha, Nebraska, and author of "Infants." (Harvard University Press).

sure your infant's length, place a table against a wall, lay the child faceup on the table with feet flat against the wall, and gently press the knees down to straighten the legs. Now slide some square object, such as a book or a carpenter's square, along the table until the upright edge touches your infant's head. Mark the table at this spot, pick up your child, and measure the length in inches along the table. Use decimal equivalents for fractions of an inch (i.e., 29¼ = 29.25).

To measure your own height, remove your shoes, stand erect against a door frame, and use that square object in the vertical dimension just as you used it along the table for your child. Then average the heights of both you and your mate, and follow the formula on this page.

How accurate are these estimates? Dr. Roche's research shows that for approximately half of you, the prediction will be within about an inch of your child's actual eighteen-year height. For roughly 90 percent of you, the prediction will be within approximately two inches, and in almost no case should it be off by more than four inches.

isfy the curiosity of parents. There is not much you can do about your child's height if you don't like the prediction. Even expensive medical therapies, which are used only in very extreme cases, do not typically increase or decrease height by more than an inch, except in the case of certain rare conditions, such as hypopituitarism.

Conditions affecting growth. The complicated formulas that Dr. Roche has worked out for children from one year through adolescence are primarily intended to be used by physicians for children who are extremely tall or short, or for those suffering from certain diseases that affect growth. For example, they can be used to judge the need for treatment and the long-term effects of certain medical therapies. In such cases, pediatricians must supply a complete set of information, including X rays, and the estimates are made by computer, not by the above simplified procedure.

But for most of us, this formula is for our own entertainment. If you are still concerned about the result, check your measurements and math before dialing your pediatrician. Otherwise, happy calculating.

BRUCE PLOTKIN

DAY CARE

Probably more controversy and misconceptions swirl around the issue of day care than any other child-related subject today. Day care, in fact, is many things—from the all-day prenursery that charges a hefty $2000 a year, to the federally funded center that caters to low-income families.

Any facility that accepts children beyond regular school hours can be called a day-care center. Although many are set up to accommodate preschool children on an all-day basis, most will not accept infants or even toddlers who are not yet toilet trained. Most nonprofit day-care centers service both families who can afford to pay a fee and those whose income level qualifies them for government subsidies. For-profit centers, particularly the chains of "learning centers," should be regarded with caution (see page 59).

If you do choose to send your child to a day-care center, you will be in the distinct minority of working mothers. In 1975 (the last year for which Bureau of Labor Statistics figures are available), less than 2 percent of working mothers' children (some 279,000) under the age of thirteen were enrolled in this kind of group care.

Group day care is also the most expensive out-of-home care: when student-teacher ratios are as low as three to one (which they must be if very young children are present), salaries and other expenses bring the cost per child up to as high as $80 a week. In a nonprofit center, much of this expense must be absorbed by government funding.

The Pluses. Day care offers some definite advantages:

1. Because centers must be licensed by the state, you can usually be assured that at least minimum requirements of safety and health are fulfilled.
2. Day-care centers are staffed by teachers trained in early childhood education. In the best centers, nonprofessional support staff are chosen for their special sensitivities to the needs of very small children. A special plus in some centers is the presence of male staff members.
3. Unlike a caregiver in your home, a day-care center can always be counted on to be there. And even if some of the staff is absent, you can still rely on adequate supervision.
4. Because a good day-care center is a professional institution devoted to improving childcare in general, many offer a great deal

of support in parenting to inexperienced mothers. Moreover, they offer you as a working parent a chance to meet others like yourself, which is in itself supportive.

5. Most day-care centers maintain long enough hours—typically staying open from 8 A.M. to 6 P.M.—to accommodate all sorts of parental working schedules.

6. Children in day-care centers enjoy the company of others their own age and don't suffer from the isolation that a child in his own home may experience. If you are divorced, the contact of your child with another "family" may help break up the tight dependency of single parent and child.

The Minuses. Those who see day care as less-than-ideal or even harmful point to a number of drawbacks:

1. Because staff members usually work in shifts, children are cared for by a number of different adults during the day. Critics point out that this diversity prevents children from developing close attachments to the people around them. However, the validity of this point of view is being challenged by investigators who feel that children can actually benefit from learning to deal with a variety of adults as caregivers.

2. A day-care center is an institution rather than a personalized system, and so it just may not deliver the kind of individualized care you would like your child to have. Even the most "liberal" centers must operate on fairly fixed schedules, which can present very real problems for the child who doesn't want to nap or go to the bathroom or drink juice at the same time as everyone else.

3. Good day care is a very expensive proposition. Government-supported centers are in constant danger of losing funding; private, for-profit centers run the risk of not filling up, and therefore are often prone to cutting back drastically on facilities and services.

HOW TO FIND A DAY-CARE CENTER

Look first to the grapevine, but don't rely on the reports of a friend, no matter how trustworthy. Be sure to check out any facility to which you send your child even for part of the day.

"KENTUCKY FRIED CHILDREN"

Some Words of Caution about For-Profit Daycare

Proprietary or *for-profit* day care has developed a terrible reputation for cashing in on the dreadful shortage of public funding to support quality childcare. The major cause for suspicion is that proprietary day-care centers manage to charge less than the federal guidelines for per-child expenses (approximately $25 to $35 a week per child, about half the government's estimated per-week cost). To maximize profits and to attract as many children as possible, they tend to put their money into fancy buildings and showy materials, rather than investing it in such less noticeable commodities as professional staffs and individualized environments. The prospect of a standardized day-care "kit"—curriculum, plant, materials—blanketing the country has prompted social critic Joseph Featherstone to wonder if we will then turn out "Kentucky Fried Children."

Nonetheless, if your community has no nonprofit centers, or if your hours do not mesh with those of the local center, proprietary day care may be your only option. Here are some precautions to keep in mind:

1. Because of strict financial corner-cutting, most proprietary centers have no social worker, nurse, or psychologist to service families.
2. Caregivers are often less well trained than those in nonprofit centers. Behavior problems or emotional difficulties may be handled less sensitively.
3. Teacher-child ratios may exceed optimum. It is unlikely that your child will get much adult attention with a ten-to-one ratio under the best of circumstances, and if much of the staff is nonprofessional and/or poorly paid, the situation becomes that much worse.
4. So-called sophisticated equipment and clean, new buildings may conceal a program that is sterile and unimaginative. An observer at one center noted that there was "the latest in word games, audiovisual equipment, and other devices. . . . But inside there were no shades to close out the light when the children napped; the paint in the easels had dried; and one of the teachers admitted that she rarely used the more sophisticated equipment."

Your community may have a nonprofit clearinghouse or resource center that supplies information via a newsletter and makes referrals to day-care and baby-sitting setups. San Francisco's Childcare Switchboard and the Preschool Association of the West Side in New York City are examples of such agencies. Check with your own board of health or department of social services for information about your own locale. But be warned. Day care U.S.A. is still a frustrating jumble of uncoordinated efforts from private and public sources. And you may find untangling them an exercise in futility. Sometimes your local Women's Resource Center or the office of N.O.W. or other women's advocacy organization may be more helpful. Another source of information is the office of your local school board.

Day-care centers sometimes advertise in community newspapers. Check off a few that sound likely and try to narrow your choices by finding someone who has sent a child to any of them. Preliminary phone calls should narrow the choices further.

Churches and Synagogues. These often operate excellent all-day nursery and prenursery programs. Usually well equipped and staffed, they may be surprisingly nonsectarian. Even when the walls are festooned with crosses or Stars of David, these symbols usually are ceremonial rather than indoctrinating. Remember, too, that children love the festivities that go along with religious holidays.

YWCAs sometimes operate drop-in day-care centers at modest cost. Since these are rarely publicized, call your local Y to check on what service is available.

Universities and Corporations. If you are in any way connected to a university, you may be able to take advantage of free or inexpensive day care under their auspices. Although typically they are in constant danger of losing funding, these facilities are usually well staffed and well operated (often under the supervision of departments of education or psychology).

A few—very few—corporations operate day-care centers for their employees. Notable among these is the Stride-Rite Company, the shoe manufacturer located in Roxbury, Massachusetts. Stride-Rite has attracted well-deserved praise for its enlightened childcare policy and, as a company brochure states, its commitment to "a sound program geared to young children's social, emotional, physical, and intellectual needs at various developmental stages." Those employees who don't qualify for welfare assistance pay approximately 10 percent of their salaries for full-day care; the remainder is paid by the company, with costs averaging about $54 a week per child.

University- and industry-operated day-care and other on-site programs run by hospitals and government agencies offer you the chance to visit your children during the day, which is a nice advantage, but they do have the drawback of requiring that you travel each day into commercial districts with children in tow.

CHOOSING A DAY-CARE CENTER

Complains a young mother: "I've read all the articles on day care, and I read about 'responsive caregivers' and 'parent involvement' and 'nonsexist programs,' but I still don't know how to really evaluate a center when I to go observe one. There's so much going on, and I'm trying to watch so many different things, that I come away with nothing but gut reactions."

Don't ever ignore gut reactions. But learn to bolster your impressions by zeroing in on specifics. After setting up an appointment to visit a center, make a careful list of key points to observe. Carry it with you and don't be self-conscious about making notes or referring to your list while you're at the center.

Try to spend about a half-hour with the director, ten to fifteen minutes with the teacher, and at least one hour observing in the classroom. During these periods, you will have a lot to find out about the center's philosophy and regulations, its facilities and the qualifications of the staff, the kinds of families that send their children there, and, most important, whether or not the center can provide a warm and stimulating environment for your child.

The Director. Ask him or her about costs, hours, schedule of payments (most centers will permit monthly payments), whether or not the center can accommodate your child when she is sick (many centers have sick bays for children who don't have serious or contagious illnesses). Question the director about his and his staff's professional qualifications. And ask about the caregiver-to-child ratio (most day-care centers observe the Federal Interagency Day Care Requirements of 1 to 5 for children three to four years old; 1 to 7 for four- to six-year-olds; 1 to 7 for children older than six). Ask the director how the center handles the children's adjustment period and how he or she would recommend you prepare your child for his day-care experience.

The Caregiver. You are looking for responsiveness to children, a sense of competence about their activities, and a relaxed attitude that will get the caregiver through a day that invariably is peppered with accidents and incidents. Does she look directly at a child and listen to him carefully, or is she glancing nervously around the room to see how the group is doing? Watch for the caregiver who gets on her knees to talk directly to a child at his level. This is a good sign.

A CHECKLIST FOR OBSERVING A DAY-CARE CENTER *

1. *Arrival/departure.* These two time periods will reveal a lot about parent-staff interaction and also about how children react to these crucial periods.
2. *Structured eating situation.* Are mealtime and snack time relaxed? Do teachers join the children, and are children free to sit where they like?
3. *Indoor activities.* How do teachers relate to children? What sort of activities are planned—quiet play, storytelling, games, puzzles, naps?
4. *Problem behavior.* How do teachers handle acting out, sharing toys, nonparticipant children, separation anxiety?
5. *Consoling/comforting.* Are the teachers fair in arguments between children? Do they pay attention to hurt feelings and fears?
6. *Active group play.* Can this take place both indoors and out? Is it encouraged for both boys and girls?
7. *Transitions.* Switching from one activity to another is a sensitive time in group situations. Do children move comfortably from one activity to another? Is consideration given to the pace of each, and are they allowed to finish one thing before starting the next?

   * Based on studies done at Boston Children's Hospital, as reported in "Directory of Child Care on the West Side," published by the Preschool Association of the West Side, Inc.

When she intercedes in an argument between two children, does she offer comfort to both the "wrongdoer" and the "injured party"? Is she sensitive to the needs of the loner or withdrawer?

Does the caregiver treat the children with respect? As an observer, you have an interesting opportunity to judge this. If she comes over to you at the expense of paying attention to the children, be suspicious. Watch, too, how she treats boys and girls or minority children. Can you detect any prejudice or any sign of sexism? (Does she, for example, make any comment when a little boy wheels a baby carriage or a girl plays with a gun or a truck?)

Is the caregiver basically accepting rather than judgmental? Do you hear her rewarding positive actions rather than issuing a lot of don'ts and no-no's?

In the course of your visit, she is likely to come up against at least one discipline problem. Focus your attention on this and ask yourself if you feel comfortable about the way she handled the situation.

Do the caregivers work well together? Nothing can upset a child more than conflict among the adults who care for him.

The Children. Do the children seem happy and relaxed? Do any of them cry when their parents leave? Do they settle down quickly? Do the children seem actively engaged with each other and with the activities of the center? Betty Van Wyck, director of the Biddeford, Maine, Children's Center (quoted in *The New Extended Family*), suggests that if several children turn their attention to a visitor, there is probably not enough going on for them in the classroom.

Focusing on one or two children for a half-hour or so is a good way to catch the general mood. Are the kids learning to experience self-control, to deal with their peers? Do they have a chance to rest and withdraw from social interaction? Are they learning to respect the equipment and materials in the room?

Activities. Is there a regular schedule of active play, quiet play, rest period, snacks, meals? Do children move from one activity to another smoothly? How is going out handled? Is there a workable system for having children put on coats, boots, and hats? Are they encouraged to handle this themselves? Are the activities absorbing and likely to foster growth and development? Do the children seem interested, or are they bored and restless? Are children given a choice of activities or is everything handled as a group? (Many youngsters will cry or misbehave when they find total group activity too demanding.) Are field trips to nearby places of interest planned?

Materials and Environment. Are materials accessible to even the smallest children, and are they arranged so that children can keep them neat? Is the equipment safe; is the room accident proof (watch for sharp edges on tables, exposed nails on shelving, no-slip surfaces on floors). Is the room well lit and cheerful? Are the materials plentiful and appropriate to the age of the children? If there are not enough, you will find children fighting over favorite items. Are they in good condition? (Check that puzzles are intact, that paints and clay are not dried out, that books are not missing pages or games missing pieces.) Are there little nooks or corners in the room where children can retreat for privacy, resting, or small-group play? (Even the most underfunded center can make imaginative use of limited space to provide these areas.) Is the children's artwork on display around the room?

After you have looked over a day-care center carefully, come back to your gut feelings. Betty Van Wyck, the Biddeford, Maine, day-care center director, suggests that you ask yourself if you would like to spend a day there. Or a week. Or a year. Your answers may surprise you.

Try, too, to be flexible in your requirements. As in choosing a baby-sitter, try to concentrate on those qualities most important to you and your own child. For example, most women would agree that plenty of fresh air is important for all growing children. Yet one intelligent and devoted mother was willing to trade that off for the comfort of an on-site day-care center located within the graduate school she attended. The school was located in a busy downtown section, so the children rarely went outdoors. But she was happy to sacrifice this because she knew her son was receiving high-quality care in a place that she could visit during the day.

FAMILY DAY CARE

It is eight o'clock in the morning. Two-year-old Mark Daniels is leaving his house with his mother, a secretary in a real estate office. He carries a favorite stuffed animal and a sandwich neatly wrapped in a school bag. . . . A fifteen-minute bus ride later, Mark and Mrs. Daniels arrive at the home of Esther Green. She greets Mark warmly and ushers him into her large, comfortable living room, which is fixed up as a playroom, complete with bright-colored toys and child-sized furniture. Two other children are already there and are having an early-morning snack. One, seven-year-old Amy, will leave shortly for a nearby school; she has been at Mrs. Green's house since 7 A.M., when her mother, a nurse, left for work. At the end of the school day, Amy will return to Mrs. Green's and be picked up by her mother at 3:30 P.M., when the day shift ends. Mark, however, will remain in Mrs. Green's care for the day, along with three other preschoolers. After 3 P.M., he will be joined by four children who range in age from six to ten. One of them is Mrs. Green's own nine-year-old son.

This is family day care, a childcare system that is overwhelmingly popular, accounting for approximately three out of four of the children cared for outside their homes. Family day-care advocates believe it offers a nurturing, homelike environment without the drawbacks of either large-scale, institutionalized day care or the isolation of an unsupervised baby-sitting arrangement at home. Critics point out that unless the family day-care program is administered by an organizing agency or is in some way committed to higher purposes, it can be nothing more than a child-minding service.

Certainly the worst image—of babies propped in front of television sets while a harassed and exploited day-care "mother" tries to manage her own and other people's children—is the reality in more cases than one wants to think about. And even a moderately well run day-care home may offer little stimulation to the children.

But, at its best, family day care can provide a warm, caring, and enriching experience for the children of working parents. And more and more parents, including those who can afford at-home care, are finding it a fine solution. Says the mother of an eight-month-old boy, who returned to her job as an industrial engineer when he was three months old: "I clung to the idea of his having his very own surrogate mother. But it wouldn't work for us financially, and actually I think he's much happier having a lot of action around and a lot of different people."

Family day care's intimacy and its ability to be responsive to the needs of children and parents make it a good choice for infant care—especially since babies are usually not accommodated at most large-scale day-care centers. Moreover, these homes can function as drop-in centers for before-school, after-school, and even overnight care. If you work odd hours, this flexibility can be a real lifesaver.

Licensing. In most states, caring for one or more unrelated children for more than ten hours a week requires that the caregiver be licensed by the state day-care licensing agency. Yet informal estimates suggest that at least half the family day-care homes operating throughout the country are, in fact, unlicensed. And many of these offer as high-quality care as the licensed ones.

When a family day-care program is licensed and supervised by a public agency, operators may be given courses in child development, nutrition, even music and art education. Some programs provide ongoing professional guidance from childcare experts. Others offer support from the community, including low-cost lunches and toy-lending services.

Costs. Costs for family day care vary according to locale, but you can figure on paying a minimum of about $25 a week (rarely more than $60) for full day care. You and the day-care mother can agree on how much you'll pay for lunches, diapers, and snacks.

What to Look For. Choosing the day-care home best suited to your child is a lot like selecting a baby-sitter. Here, however, you are looking not only at the day-care mother herself—judging whether her style of discipline, her manner with children, her own sense of poise and professionalism comfortably match yours—but you are also inspecting an ongoing environment, trying to judge whether it will suit your own child.

Keep in mind, too, that the day-care mother will also be interviewing you and your child to make sure he will fit into the mix she already has, and to see whether you and she will be able to cooperate together to give him the best care possible.

If possible, make two visits to a day-care home, once without your child, when you can observe the activity and talk to the day-care mother without distraction; and once with your child, so that you can see how he reacts to the adults and children. Because your time is probably limited, carry with you a list of specific questions and checklist items to look for during your visit. The criteria for observing a day-care center on page 62 apply to family day care as well. But because a family day-care home is a *home*, you'll want to consider the following:

1. *What is the place like?* Is there a safe outdoor area where children can play freely even in cold weather? Is the indoor area reasonably clean and spacious, and is it safely laid out for the

number of children the home accommodates? Are lunch or snacks nourishing and nicely prepared?

If the day-care home is licensed, these and other safety and health factors will have been checked out for you. But if you are observing them yourself, try not to be too rigid. For example, one popular day-care home in New York City repeatedly doesn't pass licensing inspection because the passageway to the outdoor area is slightly narrower than the law permits. And while you would certainly look with suspicion on candy and soda served at snack time, it may not be reasonable to expect the same granola cookies and hot lunches you would serve at home. Look for the family day-care center that is aware of parents' interest in nutrition and makes an effort to serve simple, healthy food like crackers instead of cookies, apple juice rather than soda, fruit instead of sweets.

2. *Is there some separation between the family's living quarters and the area the children will spend most of their time in?* One of the advantages of family day care is that it gives children the opportunity to participate in family life. However, the children need to feel that certain spaces are their own. Do they have a place to hang up their coats? Are there child-sized tables and chairs? Where can they nap or rest? That bed-making, cooking, cleaning go on is a plus—as long as they don't overshadow the children. If the house seems too clean and neat, be suspicious.

3. *Does the day-care mother seem healthy and vigorous enough to handle a group of children?* Watch her in action. Does she get harassed easily? How does she handle a crying child? A dispute over a toy? How does she react when children ask her questions or make demands on her? (If you spend even an hour observing the group, you will spot all these situations.) Does she seem to know the children as individuals, to be sensitive to their particular needs?

4. *If there are other people around—the day-care mother's children, husband, or other relatives—are they positive additions to the group?* The participation of older children, husbands (so many young children are unaccustomed to seeing men during the day), or grandmothers can be a strong advantage of family day care— provided it is not a distraction from the children. If the affairs of the day-care mother's own family take precedence over the

children, they will obviously start to feel like outsiders. This can be a real danger in very small groups.

5. *Are there toys and equipment for all the ages accommodated?* And what condition are they in? One woman was impressed by the shelves full of cheerful-looking toys until she realized that they were all for infants and that there would be nothing stimulating for her three-year-old. Toys need not be expensive; a good caregiver will be able to improvise with household objects and kitchen materials (it is a rare day-care mother who can't make her own low-cost play dough).

6. *What kind of activities does the day-care mother plan?* Remember, she is much more flexible than the director of a large center and can decide on her own routines. Does she take the children for walks in the neighborhood? Do they go to a park or on trips to nearby places of interest like the firehouse or library? In the house, does she read to the children? Do they listen to music? Can the older ones dress up or put on a play? Are there group activities like baking cookies or building a playhouse?

EXTENDED-DAY AND AFTER-SCHOOL PROGRAMS

If your children are in school all day and you only need coverage from three to five-thirty or six, an extended-day program is a good solution—if you can find one. The public schools themselves are the logical place for such programs, but financial problems, conflicts between day-care and custodial staffs, and union disputes make these a rarity. Where these programs do exist, however, parents are quick to praise the stability of the arrangement, the fact that the children remain with other children they know, and the enormous advantage of not having to transport them to other programs after school.

A typical public school extended-day program charges a modest $1 an hour per child and offers professional care from 7 A.M. until the opening of school, and then again from 3 to 6 P.M. Besides offering after-school care, these programs often operate as all-day centers during school vacations.

Churches, synagogues, community centers, and Ys are now reaching into the community to provide after-school care on a low-cost, nonsectarian basis. When no government funding is available, fees are often based on ability to pay, and, because these centers are not operated for profit, costs are usually within the range of most wage-earning families. Some such centers provide pickup and delivery services to local schools, and most offer after-school snacks and supervised activities.

In large metropolitan areas, there are many services that pick children up at schools, engage them in an afternoon of sports or other activities, and drop them off at home between five-thirty and six. With rare exceptions, these are profit-making enterprises, and the costs are high (as much as $50 a week). Because few maintain a central facility, relying instead on parks, ice-skating rinks, bowling alleys, and swimming pools for their activities, the afternoon can be exhausting and over-programmed for all but the hardiest youngsters.

A drawback of any after-school program is that your child rarely gets to spend time in his own home. For some children, going from one group situation to another, never getting a chance to be alone or to have a school friend visit at home, can be a strain. You can ease this problem by having your child skip the center on the one day a week you have cleaning help, or by actually hiring a sitter one day a week.

When you are choosing an after-school center, look for the same qualities you would seek out in any day-care center. Beyond these, however, make sure that the center is not simply an extension of school itself. Steer clear of structured, heavily scheduled programs. Be wary of any center that purports to offer "cognitive enrichment."

The director of a popular New York City center that accommodates up to fifty children in a church building says: "What we don't want is for the children to have a nine-hour school day instead of a six-hour one. It's a mistake to think that you can extend children's learning experience by giving them more school time in the afternoon." Like other well-run centers, this one offers a relaxed program of sports, free play, arts and crafts, and small-scale field trips. Two licensed teachers and two community volunteers help children with homework. And, because the children are in mixed-age groups, it works well for the older ones to help the younger ones with schoolwork.

GETTING THE MOST OUT OF GROUP CARE

Once you've selected a day-care center—whether it's a family setting, a large institution, or an after-school program—try to maintain contact with the facility, especially with the people directly responsible for your child's care. In those centers that make few demands on parents for active participation—this is typical of most—it's up to you to keep in touch and to monitor your child's progress.

Prepare your child. The first experience with day care is bound to produce some anxiety in nearly all children. You can keep this to a minimum by preparing yourself and your child thoroughly for the experience. Find out in advance exactly what will be expected of both you and your child. Small children can get very distressed if they feel unfamiliar with their environment. Where they hang their coats, park their belongings, go to the bathroom, where and when they will eat, where the parents pick them up—these are some of the things your child needs to know before she can feel comfortable in a new place.

Allow for an adjustment period. Psychiatrist Stella Chess urges us to remember that children can adapt much more easily than parents expect them to, and that they are neither more nor less vulnerable to anxiety about the new situation at any particular age. A crucial factor in helping your child adjust, Dr. Chess says, is understanding his basic temperament. For example, a "slow-to-warm-up" child may always have to take on new experiences slowly and hesitantly; acknowledging this, rather than forcing a quick adjustment, is the best course to follow. By the same token, it helps to understand that the shrieks and howls of the very intense child are simply his way of reacting to *any* new experience, from a skinned knee to a full day away from Mommy. On the other hand, comments Dr. Chess, a child who is "mild in intensity may not make enough of a commotion to make it clear that he needs a little attention to help him through the changes he's experiencing."

Most day-care centers will encourage you to stay on hand in the beginning, at least until the child shows that she can watch you leave without dissolving into tears. If you and the caregiver communicate your confidence that your child will be fine and can indeed handle the separation, his adjustment will be easier.

Don't make the mistake of lying to your child or sneaking out without telling her. A firm "Mommy is leaving now; I'll be back at five-thirty to pick you up," may call forth louder howls than a false promise to come back in a few minutes, but it's bound to smooth your child's adjustment in the long run.

If your child continues to cry at your leaving, ask at the end of the day exactly how long the crying persisted. If it lasts only a few minutes, or if it seems to be lessening each day, the chances are it will stop entirely within a few weeks. If, however, the crying persists for more than two weeks with no signs of abating, if your child shows signs of serious maladjustment, or is going backward in competence (reverting to baby talk, wetting his pants, refusing to dress himself), you should look at the situation more closely. Talk to the director. Try to evaluate the problem. Before you rush out to find another center or to quit your job, see if assigning your son or daughter to a different teacher or group of children will make a difference.

In fact, experienced day-care teachers report that children help each other work through their separation discomfort. Says Chris Parrot, director of the Magus Daycare Center in New York City: "I find that some of the children get nurturing from the other children, not only from the teachers. It doesn't have to be an adult."

Making extra time for your child at home, giving him a chance to chat with you about his new experiences away from the center itself, can also be a big help.

A key to helping children adjust is your own attitude. Sometimes your feelings will have to be bolstered by a little false bravado. But if you have made your choice conscientiously, you can put aside *your own* separation anxiety to help your child get used to his new environment. Says a woman who, with some trepidation, left her two-year-old at a small family day-care home: "I hung in there for a while to help him get adjusted. I wanted him to feel that the day-care mother was someone I knew and liked. So I'd talk to her and I'd give her a hug, letting him know that I thought she was okay. And then I'd grit my teeth and I'd walk out the door. And she'd pick him up and say, 'Go ahead, he'll be fine.' "

Make friends with the caregiver. When you deliver or pick up your child, stop and chat briefly with the caregiver. Try to establish a relationship with her that will help the two of you cooperate in nurturing and guiding your child's growth. Be sure to report important events and situations: Let her know if your son is cutting a tooth (which may explain his crankiness that day), if your daughter slept poorly the night before (she may need a nap), if there is illness or other disruption going on at home.

Encourage the day-care person to report back to you in the same fashion. Like some baby-sitters, day-care personnel may not want to burden you with the ups and downs of your child's day. If you make it clear right at the start that you very much want to hear about daily life at the center, you will be doing yourself and your child a favor.

GET INVOLVED

If the concept of day care in general is controversial, the issue of parent control surely calls forth the most intense disagreement. Ellen Galinsky and William Hooks observe in their comprehensive survey of childcare programs, *The New Extended Family:* "To many [parent control] connotes anarchy, a lack of structure, confusion, even abuse. They often feel that parents are trespassing in the territory of professionals, treading into areas that they neither understand nor are equipped to handle. On the other hand, many parents feel frustrated and helpless when they have no say in what happens to their young children for the long hours the children spend away from home."

It is often true that parent involvement does indeed go along with the highest quality care. But as a full-time working parent, you may simply not have the time—or energy—to participate actively.

Being the Thursday Lunch Hour Mommy or the Trip Day Parent are not the only ways you can get involved in your child's group-care program. Even if you work a grueling fifty-hour week, you can usually find time to go to day-care board meetings, which are blessedly not called too often and are almost always held in the evenings. It's here that you'll learn about the spirited debate raging between the financial committee, which wants to cut corners by cutting out hot lunches, and the education committee, which is fighting to keep the four-to-one student-teacher ratio *and* the hot lunches. You may even be able to give the board some tips on how to manage this without raising the tuition! Having this kind of say in policy-making is a fine way of sharing meaningfully in your child's day-care experience.

If you would rather participate more directly, why not volunteer to assist during your child's mealtime once in a while? With a little ingenuity, you can probably squeeze this into your own lunch period. Your child will be delighted to see you and show you off to her friends and teachers. The staff will surely appreciate the extra pair of hands. And you'll be rewarded by a valuable glimpse into your youngster's daily life.

TAX RELIEF FOR CHILDCARE

Childcare is expensive: according to a recent survey, working mothers spend a minimum of 20 percent of their paychecks for childcare, and some spend as much as 60 percent or even more! Until 1976, there was tax relief only for low-income women, who ironically could rarely afford to spend the amount required to qualify for the deductions. Happily, the Tax Reform Act of 1976 changed all that, bringing good news to all parents who must pay for the care of children under the age of fifteen.

The law allows you to deduct 20 percent of the first $2000 you spend for the care of one child, or 20 percent of the first $4000 for the care of two or more. The maximum, thus, is up to $400 for one, or up to $800 for two or more children.

The Preschool Association of the West Side, a New York City non-profit childcare information agency, gives the following highlights of the tax law. (For more information, read *Booklet 153,* available from any Internal Revenue Service office.)

1. A line about the childcare credit appears on the basic 1040 form. You can take the credit whether you take the standard deduction or itemize your deductions.
2. The credit applies no matter how high or low your income.
3. There is now no distinction between expenses paid for childcare inside or outside your home—day-care center, nursery school up through kindergarten; after-school program from grade one on.
4. Payments to a relative (for instance, your mother) entitle you to the credit even if this person lives with you. The exception is that the relative cannot be your dependent and you and the relative must pay the appropriate Social Security tax.
5. The credit applies even if one or both parents work part-time or if either of you is a student. (Under the old law, students and part-timers couldn't qualify.)
6. If you are divorced or separated and have custody of your child, you can qualify even if you don't claim the child as your dependent.
7. Add up what you spent for the entire year for childcare. (The old law required you to figure expenses month-by-month.)
8. The tax credit also applies to care of an incapacitated person of any age (someone physically or mentally unable to care for himself). Disability income of this person does not reduce your credit.

The Preschool Association also reminds you to save all proof of payments —canceled checks or written receipts—just in case your return is later challenged or audited.

Be sure to arrange these visits in advance (unscheduled drop-ins can be surprisingly disruptive, especially in a large, formally organized center). And if you cannot manage a daytime visit, talk to the staff about other ways you can involve yourself in center activities, such as contributing materials, helping with the annual bazaar, or perhaps even playing hostess in your office to a small group of child visitors.

A FINAL NOTE ABOUT GROUP CARE

Ask a middle-class mother of a day-care child where her son or daughter goes each day and you're likely to be barraged with a flood of apologies. Comments June, a bright young computer programmer from Illinois: "We actually could afford a housekeeper, but Maggie is so much happier at the center with the other children, and she's learning so much, and really it's not at all what you'd think a *day-care* center would be like . . . I mean it's cheerful, and the kids are so cute . . . and they have a nice room for naps. . . ." What June doesn't say is that she's fought each day with her own mother, who has even offered to help pay for a nursemaid; that her mother-in-law refers disdainfully to "that place that keeps Maggie while June's at her office"; and that one otherwise quite sensible aunt has been overheard saying to three-year-old Maggie, "I wish *I* could take care of you all day instead of those ladies at the center." June and her husband have managed to parry the objections and ignore the digs, but only because they truly believe they've made the best plan for their daughter.

In many circles, "day care" is still a dirty word. But while opponents condemn it as the enemy of children's individuality or their ability to love or think independently, a growing army of day-care advocates is opening our eyes to the value of this kind of childcare for all kinds of families.

As mother and educator Vicki Breitbart says in an outspoken plea for quality care: "Sharing the responsibility for children can challenge the ideological assumption of individualism and competition. Everyone sharing childcare can break down the feeling of possessiveness and the concept of ownership: *My* child is *my* problem and therefore *I* must conform to whatever demands the system makes of me so that I can care for my child. . . . Everyone sharing childcare will also demand new work routines in which all adults (male and female) have time to be part of child-rearing."

DAY-CARE RESOURCES

Association for Childhood International
3615 Wisconsin Avenue N.W.
Washington, D.C. 20016

Child Development Association Consortium
7315 Wisconsin Avenue
Washington, D.C. 20014

Child Study Association of America
50 Madison Avenue
New York, N.Y. 10016

Child Welfare League of America, Inc.
67 Irving Place
New York, N.Y. 10003

Day Care and Child Development Council of America, Inc.
1012 Fourteenth Street N.W.
Washington, D.C. 20005

Department of Labor
Women's Bureau
Constitution Avenue and Fourteenth Street N.W.
Washington, D.C. 20210

National Association for the Education of Young Children
1834 Connecticut Avenue N.W.
Washington, D.C. 20009

N.O.W. (National Organization for Women)
Task Force on Child Care
45 Newbury Street
Boston, Massachusetts 02116

It is not our intention to advocate any particular form of childcare. But we do feel that the more high-quality options there are, the better we will be as a society to support the kind of family life we claim to hold so dear. And we agree with Vicki Breitbart: "New forms of child-care that we create and control can help us begin to change our lives and change the way we feel about ourselves and each other. They can help make us all more human."

BOOKS THAT MAY HELP

The Day Care Book, Vicki Breitbart (Knopf, 1974). Subtitled "The Why, What, and How of Community Day Care," this is a no-nonsense survival manual for parents, community organizers, and the politically active or concerned citizen.

The New Extended Family: Day Care That Works, Ellen Galinsky and William H. Hooks (Houghton Mifflin, 1977). A fascinating and informative look at a variety of successful day-care programs all over the United States, from parent-controlled inner-city facilities to for-profit proprietary centers.

Day Care: How to Plan, Develop, and Operate a Day Care Center, E. Belle Evans, Beth Shub, and Marlene Weinstein (Beacon Press, 1971). A practical how-to that covers everything from theory of day care to shopping lists for materials. Less political than the Breitbart book, *Day Care* is an excellent guide to the nitty-gritty of group care.

Family Day Care: A Practical Guide for Parents, Caregivers and Professionals, Alice H. Collins and Eunice L. Watson (Beacon Press, 1976). Collins and Watson observed and participated in a variety of small-group situations, and report on them intelligently and thoroughly.

Day Care for Infants: The Case for Infant Day Care and a Practical Guide, E. Belle Evans and George E. Saia (Beacon Press, 1973). A well-documented plea for group care for infants and toddlers, plus a useful handbook on how to start and operate a quality infant center.

Chapter Five
ORGANIZING YOURSELF ON THE HOME FRONT

Successful working mothers learn the arts of the efficiency expert. "I've gotten to be a terrific organizer," says an accountant-mother. Another: "It would be bedlam if I hadn't learned to manage our household in one-third of the time I used to spend just thinking about the living-room color scheme."

Learning to get things done with the least fuss is not a gift but an acquired art. And in talking to women, we've discovered that there's no one system or secret that works for everybody. Instead, we've gathered a mixed bag of shortcuts, stratagems, and basic caveats that can make your busy life free of unnecessary strains.

THE BASICS

Making some crucial decisions right at the start can spell the difference between success and failure on the job and at home.

Should You Commute? With a full day at the office and a full set of responsibilities waiting for you at home, you simply cannot spend a great deal of time getting from one place to another. Even if you put travel time to good use catching up on paperwork or reading, commuting can take a lot out of you. Most working mothers feel that a trip of more than forty minutes puts a terrible strain on both family and work life. "I began to forget what my children looked like in daylight," says Marsha, a Connecticut urban planner, who used to travel more than an hour each way to her office in New York City. "I left the house at seven, came home at seven, and by that time the kids were bathed and fed. I was becoming a stranger to my own family." After much agonizing, Marsha and her husband decided to move closer to the city.

The Right Community for You. Living in a community where children can develop independence is a plus for any working mother. When children can play safely outside, ride to the dentist themselves on bicycles, walk to school or supermarkets or swmming pools, you will find life goes much more smoothly. Cluster-house communities, with their centrally located schools and carefully planned recreational facilities, are ideal. And although urban apartment-house living can be high on price and low on space, it does eliminate the problem of car-pooling, which can plague the suburban parent.

One Chicago mother, faced with the choice between staying in a five-room apartment and moving to a spacious ranch house within an easy commute to her and her husband's jobs, chose to stay in the city after considering all the options. "The building we live in has loads of children my kids' ages and lots of other mothers who work. It's almost like a small town. I never have to worry about transportation, since the kids can walk or take a bus to most places." Small towns and communal-type apartment houses have in common the opportunity for trading off baby-sitting and sharing in childcare and even housework.

Your Life-style. Not only should you decide *where* you live, but you also must make basic decisions about *how* you live. Take a good look at your priorities. Are you wasting precious time with your children screaming at them to stay off your velvet sofa? Are you spending evenings preparing elaborate meals that leave you exhausted before the last dish is washed? Do you socialize with other adults on weekends and then feel guilty about neglecting your kids?

When you choose to work and raise a family, you have to make other choices as well. This may mean covering that sofa in sturdy brown corduroy or limiting dinner menus to hamburgers and broiled chicken or paring down your social life to one or two close friends. It also means getting a clear fix on what is really important to you and your family right now . . . and then closing your eyes to everything else. As one especially relaxed mother says, "When I can leave the beds unmade, the dishes unwashed, the living room a mess, and go to the beach with the kids on a sunny Saturday . . . then I know I'm doing something right."

Accepting Help. Another basic prerequisite for successful working motherhood is accepting—even expecting—help from others. Although many of us have graduated from the I-must-do-everything-myself syndrome and have gotten our husbands and children involved in household management, far too few of us are willing to look for help outside our own front doors.

Learning that paid and unpaid help is just around the corner can be a valuable lesson. For example, press your mother-in-law into service as family cook when she comes to stay with you. Take advantage of your mother's weekly visits to get your mending done. Your retired uncle, the one who just adores children, may be delighted to fill in when your sitter is sick.

Don't overlook low-cost help in your community. A neighbor's eleven-year-old will be thrilled to earn a few dollars giving you a hand with dinner and baths for two toddlers. Local teenagers can be hired at low cost to help with cleaning attics, doing yard work, even painting and repairing.

Professional cleaning services are not cheap (they average around $50 for a full day of heavy cleaning), but many families swear by them for a twice-a-year complete overhaul.

Transportation problems, the bugaboo of so many suburban mothers, can be solved by making a modest investment in outside help. Dancing lessons, math tutoring, and Little League practice won't overwhelm you if the teenager you hire to supervise your kids and start dinner can double as a chauffeur. Make sure he or she has a valid driver's license, and go along for a practice ride to establish clear car-decorum and safety rules.

Consider the possibility of transportation tradeoffs: Mobilize any available parent for the Monday-to-Friday shift, while you handle weekend mornings. If you think she's getting the short end of the stick, hauling around a carful of kids in the afternoons, think of how grateful she'll be when you're behind the wheel for Saturday baseball practice and Sunday School and she can sleep until noon.

Taxi services are prohibitively expensive if your child rides alone. But when you combine forces with a few other working mothers, they are a quite affordable and dependable way of handling school transportation, doctor and dentist visits, and after-school activities.

KEEPING TRACK

There may be such a thing as being overorganized (a free-lance writer remarks that she was once so organized that she delivered her children to school a day early!), but we have yet to discover a working mother who hasn't benefited from careful planning. Here are some suggestions that will help you make your life run smoothly.

Write everything down. Efficient working mothers remember a thousand and one details because they're inveterate list-makers. Getting it down in black and white won't add hours to your day, but it will give you the feeling of control so many women complain they miss.

Don't jot down your appointments and "do" lists on little slips of paper that can be easily mislaid. Instead, find a notebook big enough to accommodate a working calendar. (One of the best all-purpose notebooks we've come across is the Star System, available in some large stationery stores or by mail from P.O. Box 15551, Santa Ana, California 92705. It's a pocket-size loose-leaf folder that contains refillable sections of blank paper, an address and phone section, daily and monthly diaries, expense records.)

Pin up a large wall calendar at home, the kind with big boxes for notations. Follow the example of one enterprising woman who sits down with her husband every Sunday night and uses the calendar to plan out the entire week: meals and shopping for the next seven days, play dates and after-school activities for her children, birthday parties (with a reminder to buy a present a few days before), social plans for herself and her husband. Taped to the refrigerator door, this plan lets everyone in the family keep track of activities at a glance.

Set up a communications center in your home. Station a bulletin board and pad of notepaper near the telephone. Your teenage daughter can leave word where she's going and with whom; you can post a shopping list for your sitter, along with a note telling her about your son's cold. This is also a good place to keep a running shopping list. For added efficiency, tie a string to a pen or pencil and hang it near the telephone.

Use a telephone-answering service to stay in touch when your youngsters are old enough to be in and out on their own. A real estate agent reports: "I check with the service between house showings in the afternoon. Before, my sons and I were always missing each other, and my small office staff resented taking messages for me. Now, with the service, the boys can always let me know where they are."

SETTING UP YOUR HOUSEHOLD

Neatness Counts—or Does It? Tell yourself that no one but you is keeping score. Nowhere is it recorded that your hall closet is a disaster area, that there are thirteen unmatched socks in your son's bureau drawer, that at least two cap guns and one headless doll are lurking behind the couch cushions. Although we don't suggest that you blithely breeze off to the office letting the dishes and toys fall where they may, clinging to rigid standards of tidiness can only be self-destructive.

With a little imagination and some common-sense strategies, you can have an efficiently run household without sacrificing your sanity. Here are some practical hints that will help you get started on the right path:

1. *Own as many appliances as you can possibly afford.* If you think a washer and dryer are beyond your means, add up what you spend at the Laundromat (be sure to include the dollar value of your own time) and compare costs. A dishwasher is a must, especially if you expect children to help with cleanups (even a 6-year-old can load and empty a dishwasher). Buy a slow cooker or food processer and watch meal-preparation time shrink. A lightweight electric broom is easier to use than your vacuum cleaner and is ideal for quick cleanups (kids can handle these, too). A no-frost refrigerator and self-cleaning oven are labor-saving investments that will pay you back in short order.

2. *Streamline your home to cut down on housecleaning time.* Replace lamps with attractive ceiling track lights (a lot safer, too, if you have a toddler or active youngster). Get rid of those cumbersome venetian blinds or draperies; install bamboo roll-ups or vinyl shades—or try hanging plants in the windows. Store tabletop ornaments—ashtrays, bowls, empty vases—in a closet. Set out your favorites when company comes.

   Next time you paint, try semigloss instead of flat paint throughout the house—dirt and finger marks will wipe off easily, and the glossy surface will give your walls a cheerful, modern glow. You can also paint floors; three coats of brightly colored deck paint will give any room an easy-to-care-for new look. Try coating tabletops and desk surfaces with polyurethane finish (the same durable finish used on wood floors). Or spruce up an old piece with two coats of Varathane paint, a flexible plastic liquid available in an assortment of colors, which dries to a glossy, dirt-resistant hardness. When selecting wallpaper, stick to vinyls or one of the newer scrubbable coated papers.

Coat wood floors with stain-resistant, high-gloss polyurethane (for best results, use three coats). Or use no-wax vinyl floors in kids' rooms and kitchen, easy-care industrial-grade carpeting in the rest of the house.

3. *Part with possessions that don't earn their keep.* Remember, the less you own, the less you have to clean, repair, and store. Have you worn that skirt in the last year? When was the last time your daughter played with that doll? Does anyone fit into those ice skates? Go through your cabinets and closets at least twice a year; give away anything you don't use regularly. Or have a garage sale that the kids can run. (If you donate to a thrift shop or charity, be sure to ask for a tax-deduction statement.)

4. *Make the most of storage facilities.* You can get control of creeping clutter by finding new ways to store your possessions.

Some suggestions: children's closets will hold twice as much if you use two rods, one hung above the other. Replace old box springs and mattresses with wooden storage beds (roomy drawers hold blankets, pillows, out-of-season clothing; practical on-the-floor design eliminates underbed dusting). Cooking utensils, cleaning equipment, even clothing will stay tidy hanging from pegboard on walls or inside closets. A full-length medicine cabinet attached to the inside of the door will make quick order out of the messiest bathroom. For last-minute cleanups, a pretty covered basket is a handy place to toss toys left on the living room floor.

5. *Reorganize your children's rooms for easier cleanups.* Don't spoil the time you spend with your children by forever nagging them to straighten up their quarters. Here are some ways to put an end to kids' room chaos: get rid of that oversized toy chest with its tangled jumble of odds and ends. Replace it with plastic shoe boxes, rubberized dishpans, old coffee cans (let the kids label and decorate them)—any convenient container that will store the hundreds of small items children love to collect.

Try baskets for marbles, crayons, stuffed animals; tuck yo-yos, puppets, penknives into the pockets of a hanging shoe bag. Keep puzzles intact with the kind of rack schools use (order from the Childcraft Company, 4 Kilmer Road, Edison, N.J.). Most kids hate using hangers. A row of hooks on the back of the bedroom door will keep your son's pajamas off the floor, your daughter's winter coat off the living room couch.

Are your kids too rushed to make their beds? Replace their top sheets and blankets with inexpensive indoor sleeping bags, which are lightweight, machine-washable, and available in cheerful patterns (including the most popular cartoon and sports motifs). Just zip them up in the morning for instantly neat beds. (Carry the principle into the master bedroom by topping your own bed with a down-filled quilt that doubles as a bedspread. A couple of quick shakes is all it needs to look plump and neat, shaving minutes off your morning routine.)

HOUSEWORK AND OTHER NECESSARY EVILS

Once you've simplified your home for easier maintenance, you'll find time spent on day-to-day care shrinking dramatically. The hours you used to spend laundering those frilly curtains or vacuuming that great expanse of light-beige carpeting can now be spent playing with your children or enjoying the company of your husband. Chances are you've already learned to save time and energy in keeping your home presentable: Studies show that unlike unemployed housewives, who still spend as much time doing housework as they did forty years ago, working women have substantially reduced their housekeeping time—and to good advantage!

But even the most well organized house does not run itself. Here are some tips for keeping things going with a minimum of fuss:

Clean as you go.   Throw out that broken toy instead of putting it back on the shelf. Empty the dishwasher after dinner, so that tomorrow's dirty dishes don't pile up. Insist that children straighten their rooms before they go to sleep or before dinner (the most painless method: sweep everything into the center of the room; pick out toys and clothing and put away; scoop dirt into dustpan). Have all family members pick up after themselves so that little cleaning jobs don't turn into big ones.

Schedule an all-family, all-weekend major housecleaning every few months.   As you do with your regular family schedules, assign tasks on the basis of preference. Draw lots for the ones nobody wants. Don't let yourself get trapped into always being the boss of the cleanup squad: Take turns with your husband or older children.

Little kids hate tidying up but they love a real cleaning assignment. Let under-sixes shine mirrors, wash everyone's comb and brush, polish silver, strip beds. Older children can divide among themselves the remaining tasks—washing and waxing floors, polishing furniture, cleaning finger marks off walls, straightening out closets.

Take the drudgery out of doing laundry by following a few simple rules.   Unless you find ironing relaxing, buy only permanent press and resist the impulse to "touch up" anything with a cool iron (touch-ups take as much time as the real thing). Solve the sock-sorting trauma by buying all one color for one child, another color for his brother. Finally, invest in large quantities of inexpensive children's underwear (try the dime-store variety), so that you can miss a week of laundry from time to time.

PUTTING A PRICE TAG ON YOUR TIME

Anything that buys you time—your most scarce luxury—is well worth the price. Splurge on ordering a full-course meal on a night you have to work late (check your Yellow Pages under "Catering"). Take a taxi home from the office on a day you're most tired; you'll be delighted at how pampered you'll feel. Here are some other timesavers:

The telephone.   Use it to order groceries (without impulse buying, you'll actually spend less), buy gifts, or even make big purchases such as bicycles or baby carriages (no problem if you stick to name-brand items).

Postcards.   These are indispensable for keeping in touch with family and friends when you can't find time for telephone conversations. Follow up with a phone call or visit at your leisure. Try preaddressing cards to the people you want most to stay in contact with, even if they live in the same city.

Shop by mail.   There's a lot more out there besides Sears. Department stores and specialty shops issue seasonal catalogues, usually with good buys on housewares, linens, even children's things. Watch your daily newspaper for sales and special offers. Many mothers of children up to age ten swear by England's Mothercare Catalogue, which features clothing, toys, and accessories of exceptionally high quality at reasonable cost. To order the catalogue, write to Mothercare Limited, P.O. Box 145, Cherry Tree Road, Watford, Herts. WD2 5SH, England.

For more adventurous mail-order shopping, look into the catalogue guides. A sampling: *The New Catalogue of Catalogues* (Random House, 1975), *The Whole House Catalogue* (Simon and Schuster, 1976), *The Complete Food Catalogue* (Holt, Rinehart, 1977).

Learn to shop efficiently. Don't waste time searching for sales and bargains in clothing. Ask yourself how much money you really save and then calculate your own hourly worth. Chances are you'll come out ahead by sticking to reliable stores and salespeople who help you get in and out quickly (with good planning, you can buy a child's entire wardrobe in a lunch hour).

Buying Christmas or Hanukkah presents will be no trouble at all if you remember to do it all year long. Take along your gift list the next time you vacation in a place that has attractive shops. Put your store-browsing time to good use purchasing some of those pretty scarves or good-looking ceramics you admire.

School-age children are bombarded with birthday-party invitations, each one demanding a gift. Kids are the best judge of what to buy, so encourage them to take over this responsibility if they are old enough to get to a store themselves. For younger children, the task falls on you and your husband. You'll never get caught again running out on your lunch hour to buy a last-minute Star Wars game if you make one trip to buy a stockpile of gifts suitable for girls or boys. Games, puzzles, and construction toys are all reliable standards. If you run out of parties, you can always give the gifts to your own children.

As soon as your kids are old enough to make reasonably sound decisions about their own clothing and other possessions, let them take over the shopping (an older sibling can accompany a younger one). If you worry about their handling money, open charge accounts with local merchants. Explain to the storekeepers that your children will be buying things from time to time and that you would appreciate their helping them out and also grant you return privileges.

Make every minute count by doubling up on duties. A dentist's waiting room is the perfect place to balance your checkbook. Learn to gulp coffee while applying makeup, read the morning paper in the bath (or save it for the evening when you have more time to relax), condition your hair while playing checkers with your daughter. Use commuting time to sew on a button, catch up on your sleep, write a letter.

Find professional and service people geared to your needs. Are you sick of cooling your heels in doctors' or dentists' waiting rooms? If you can't convince the doctor or his staff that your time is money, too, switch to someone more understanding. Or try what one determined free-lance writer did. When she paid her pediatrician, she enclosed a note explaining that she was deducting $30, her fee for the two hours' wait she'd had in his office.

Don't be tyrannized by the nine-to-five dentist. Encourage him or her to open the doors at 7:30 two or three mornings a week (one California dentist tripled his practice this way). If your garage mechanic won't stay open at night, find another. If you can't locate a beauty salon whose hours mesh with yours, hire a hairdresser who comes to your home in the evening and cuts the whole family's hair in one session. Or learn to cut your kids' hair yourself: All you need is a good barber's scissors and some clear instructions (an easy-to-follow guide is *How to Cut Children's Hair,* Simon and Schuster, 1976).

Your time is money; give yourself a bonus by getting up an hour earlier a few days a week. It's truly amazing, insist hundreds of working mothers, how much better that one hour can make you feel. Having the time to enjoy a leisurely breakfast with your family, a relaxed time to get dressed and put on makeup, can make the difference between a frenzied day ahead and a calm one.

FOOD

"The first few weeks we ate nothing but Chicken Delight," cheerfully announces Phyllis, a thirty-five-year-old Los Angeles store manager who returned to the work force after a ten-year absence. She is addressing herself to six other working mothers at a group meeting, and from the looks of amusement that greet her offhanded announcement, nobody believes her.

The fear of failing as a woman, of not being able to put a home-cooked meal on the table each evening, looms as a real dread for many of us considering full-time employment. "At first, I used to cook all weekend," confesses Leonore, a superefficient medical copywriter who has been working full-time since her youngest child was two and a half.

"I'd make casseroles, roasts, a chicken, and I'd freeze everything; my freezer looked like an aluminum mine."

After a while, Leonore realized that bending over a hot stove was not fostering warm family feelings. She learned that the way to her children's hearts was certainly not through their stomachs. Her family was more than happy to eat simply prepared meals in exchange for seeing more of her.

Leonore is one extreme. At the other end is Carol, divorced, somewhat disorganized, but basically coping. Her three small children wander in and out of the kitchen snacking on whatever happens to be available in the refrigerator. Fortunately, Carol keeps only nourishing food in the house. And although she's occasionally felt conscience-stricken enough to set before her kids a soup-to-nuts dinner, she insists they prefer the informality of taking what they want when they want it.

Somewhere in the middle of these two lies a more sensible approach to the care and feeding of your family. Keeping everyone healthily fed does not mean doing tricky things with tuna fish. In the time it would take you to devise six clever uses for cream of mushroom soup (none of them very appetizing), you can teach yourself the rules of really *good* advance planning, find new ways to use your freezer, learn to make delicious meals in less than half an hour.

Here is a potpourri of nutritionally sound and easy-to-manage food-preparation ideas that will start you on your way to carefree meals for the whole family.

BASIC PRINCIPLES

Before you begin loading up on TV dinners and frozen steaks, take time to survey your equipment. Are your pots and pans in good condition? Do you have a variety of sizes? Consult a basic cookbook, such as *The Joy of Cooking* or *From Julia Child's Kitchen,* for sound advice on what you should own. Are your knives sharp? If you've been sawing away at lemons with a dull blade or trying to quarter a chicken with a blunt cleaver, march to your hardware store and have all your knives sharpened professionally. Buy a hand sharpener for daily touch-ups.

Don't waste time searching for your 2-quart casserole or the slotted spoon. Hang pots and utensils on pegboards. Or consider open-shelf cabinets—they force you to keep things neat and make all equipment easily accessible.

Look into labor-saving equipment that can save you time and wear and tear on your nerves. Here is just a sample of what's available:

- Pressure cooker—These timesavers are enjoying a new popularity now, and, happily, today's models have foolproof safety features. If you buy one, be sure to purchase a good pressure-cooking cookbook (see pages 101–102).
- Slow cooker—Plunk meat, potatoes, vegetables, liquid into a slow cooker in the morning, and you'll have a delicious and nourishing hot stew for dinner. *Crockery Cookery* is an excellent guide to this type of cooking.
- Food processor—for under $60 (much more for the most prestigious brand, but the lesser-known ones are nearly as good), this is the closest thing to a robot you can own. Marvelous for both plain and fancy food preparation, and indispensable if you aspire to any kind of gourmet cooking.
- Seal-a-Meal—This clever device is ideal for the working mother. With this special heat-sealing gadget and a roll of plastic pouches, you can freeze extra portions of everything you cook. Reheat them by immersing pouch in boiling water. You don't even have to wash the pot!
- Microwave oven—This innovation has come in for some bad press (the high-frequency waves that permit food to be cooked so quickly are said to be dangerous in some models). If you decide you simply must own an oven that will bake a potato in three minutes, be prepared to spend about $500.
- And a bunch of small helpers like an electric can opener, toaster oven (great for reheating small portions), blender (handy if you don't own a processor), electric coffee pot (set it up the night before to save time in the morning), salad spinner (dries greens in 4 seconds), wok or electric frying pan (for quick stir-frying).

Once you've satisfied yourself that your equipment is in good order, turn to the human factor in your kitchen. If blood runs down the kitchen counter every time you cut a tomato, if your husband can't prepare a steak without setting fire to the broiler, and if your twelve-year-old doesn't know how to scramble an egg, it's time to upgrade the skills in your house. You and your family will do yourselves a real favor by learning the quickest and most efficient ways of getting the food from market to fridge to stove to table.

You'll be amazed at how much time you can save by mastering the easiest and neatest ways to slice an onion or sauté chicken breasts or chop vegetables. The introductory chapters of any good general cookbook (see pages 101–102) feature helpful instructions on these and other cooking basics. So do the many excellent articles in the women's service magazines. A cooking course at your local Y or adult education class can take you one step further, giving you a foundation of everyday techniques plus a repertoire of menu and meal ideas. If your husband and children enroll in these, too, you'll be well on your way to becoming a truly sharing family.

Take time to analyze your motions in the kitchen. Get in the habit of handling two or three tasks at once—put the spaghetti water on to boil while you greet the kids; make the salad while your nine-year-old tells you about his day at school (or better, have him tear up the lettuce while you slice the cucumbers and keep an eye on the meat sauce simmering). Clean up as you go; nothing's more disheartening than a sinkful of pots and pans before dinner's even on the table.

Underlying all these efforts are four basic principles:

1. *Plan in advance.* It is appalling but probably true that many children would be perfectly happy (and healthy) existing on a rotating schedule of pizza, hamburgers, fried chicken, and spaghetti. And unless you feel too guilty—or bored—with a rotating menu, you can actually eliminate the problem of menu planning entirely by making up a seven-day schedule of meals and simply starting over again each week (Ethel Kennedy is reputed to do this on a fourteen-day schedule).

   Whether you serve the same meals week after week or try to vary them, it certainly helps to plan menus in advance and to coordinate your marketing with them. If you post the menu next to the refrigerator, you will be reminded of what last-minute ingredients have to be bought or what must be defrosted each morning.

   When you plan the week's menus, try to include at least one two-night supper—say, a stew for Wednesday that can be reheated on Friday; or Sunday's roast chicken, which can re-emerge as fricassee on Tuesday. Whatever you do, avoid start-

TWO QUICKIE MAIN COURSES YOU WON'T BE ASHAMED TO SERVE YOUR MOTHER-IN-LAW

Jo Ann's Marinated Flank Steak

Before you leave for work in the morning, place in a bowl flank steak and 1 cup of chopped or sliced onions. Pour over them ½ cup of prepared Teriyaki Sauce (enough to barely cover the meat). Cover with foil and refrigerate. When you get home, broil the meat quickly, about 5 minutes on each side, basting with the sauce. While the meat is cooking, let the onions simmer in about 4 tablespoons of the sauce they soaked in. For a special touch, add sautéed fresh or canned mushrooms.

Note: Leftover flank steak makes a marvelous cold meat salad. Cube the meat and toss with a mixture of 1 part mayonnaise, 1 part mustard. Add some scallions if you happen to have them.

Helen Barer's Fish Fillets

Place any kind of fish fillets on a lightly greased baking pan. On each one, put 1 tablespoon of the following mixture (which you've kept in your freezer for just this occasion): butter, grated parmesan cheese, parsley. If you've got a bag of frozen shrimps in the freezer, boil a few for one minute, chop, and add to mixture. Roll fillets up, fasten with a toothpick, drizzle melted butter and/or lemon juice on them, and bake in a 400-degree oven for about 10 minutes or until fish flakes easily with a fork.

---

from-scratch cooking every night, even if you are reduced to serving grilled-cheese sandwiches or pizza from time to time.

Doing chores in advance gives you a well-earned sense of control. One superorganized computer programmer never leaves the house in the morning without setting the table for dinner. Other women make a point of preparing one aspect of dinner in the morning.

2. *Simplify.* Only one word, but loaded with meaning when it comes to working mothers and hungry families. Limit your first course to no-frill foods like melon or tomato juice; forget about fancy desserts unless you or the children enjoy making them. Forget about words like "garnish" (unless it's a sprig of parsley or a

lemon wedge), or "fold in slowly" or "stir constantly" (you can't afford to tie up two hands for more than three minutes). Tell yourself that those gorgeous platters in the women's magazines are the product of the retoucher's art, and stick to simply served one-dish or quick-cooking meals.

You can still have the niceties of gracious living, incidentally, by adding touches of your own. Pretty no-iron cloth napkins instead of paper ones spruce up the plainest dinner. Let the children take turns making centerpieces, or splurge on fresh flowers once in a while. Invest in attractive wicker trays with handles, one for each member of the family: you can eat from them and carry your plates and silverware back and forth to the kitchen in one trip.

3. *Stay stocked.* A basic cupboard of such foods as tuna fish, canned soups, tomato sauce, and noodles lets you put together a last-minute meal anytime. Make it an unbreakable rule always to keep onions, lemons, and parsley in the fridge—they're terrific flavor enhancers. Don't trust memory in keeping your kitchen well stocked: store extra bread and butter and other staples in the freezer. Not running out of necessities is harder than it seems; remarks one woman, "We always have bread or milk, but seldom at the same time." Use a list such as the one on pages 94–95 to keep on top of your grocery needs.

4. *Share the work.* Rid yourself of the notion that all bodily nourishment must come from you. Encourage your husband and children to develop cooking specialties; each one can be responsible for one evening's meal, from marketing to cleanup. Be generous with praise—even if the results are not up to your usual standards. Mobilize your baby-sitter to chop vegetables, season and start a roast, set the table for dinner. Try sharing the marketing or cooking with another family. A few logistics—and a lot of goodwill—are required, but you'll be rewarded when you come home to a boeuf bourgignon that you didn't make!

MAKE YOUR FREEZER WORK FOR YOU

If you're still making do with one of those top-of-the-fridge models, it may be time to consider buying a separate unit or a new refrigerator that has a really generous freezing compartment.

For maximum efficiency, keep your freezer three-quarters full (this helps maintain the proper degree of coldness). In general, freeze quickly. Cool hot food in the refrigerator or in ice water, wrap in moisture- and vapor-proof package, label with contents and date of freezing.

The freezer is indispensable, of course, for stockpiling staples like meats, vegetables, bread, butter, and orange juice. Here are a few freezable items you may not have thought of:

- chopped nuts
- grated cheese (a money-saving way of using up ends of any hard cheese)
- chopped onions, grated lemon, grated hard-cooked egg yolks (next time you grate or chop make a double or triple supply)
- cooking stocks and sauces (keep in small containers, defrost as needed)
- pastry and cookie dough
- herb butters (small portions of butter mixed with fresh or dried herbs)
- milk and heavy cream

Some things you cannot freeze:

- aspics or gelatins (they get rubbery)
- hard-cooked egg whites
- raw salad ingredients
- mayonnaise
- stuffings
- cooked potatoes (remember this when freezing a stew; it's easy enough to add the potatoes later)
- juicy fruits and vegetables (they turn soggy)

Stockpiling staples is only part of your freezer's work. Its special value for you in your constant battle against time is as a storehouse for half of every casserole, stew, and soup you prepare. Simply double or triple your best spaghetti sauce recipe and freeze it in two meal-size containers; with one hour's work, you've made three meals. For added time-saving (at only a slight cost to flavor), try freezing the spaghetti along with the sauce (undercook the pasta when you do this); defrost in the fridge, reheat in the oven.

Apply this three-meal rule to family meals like tuna-fish casserole or chicken a la king, company main courses like lasagna or coq au vin (you can have the same dinner party a month later), full-scale family suppers like pot roast or veal stew.

Never throw out the foil or plastic containers prepared foods come in; they're perfect for freezing dishes like these. Small items like grated lemon rind freeze well in individual ice cube trays. Corning Ware or other freezer-to-table containers are fine to freeze foods in, but they can be put to better use. Instead, line the casserole with aluminum foil, pour what you want to freeze into it, let it freeze, and then lift out the foil-wrapped portion and store in the freezer. To reheat, just empty the contents into the original casserole.

A great assortment of complete frozen dinners is on the market today, and although these are nearly always less economical and less nutritionally satisfying than your own concoctions, there are times when a chicken pot pie or a complete turkey dinner are the answer to a busy mother's prayer. If you do want to stock a few of these for emergencies, experiment with brands; you'll find that they differ widely in both price and quality.

MARKETING

For many families, getting the provisions into the house in the first place is winning half the battle. Again, advance planning is the key to success. And at the heart of the plan is the Master Shopping List, arranged by category and mimeographed or photocopied so you can check off your needs from your personal memory-jogger each week.

You won't dismiss this giant all-time catalogue as an exercise in compulsiveness when you realize that you're no longer forgetting to buy tomato juice and toilet paper, that you're halving the time spent in the supermarket, thanks to the by-category arrangement of your list, and that you're saving money by cutting down on impulse buying. Here are some other marketing shortcuts:

- *Never do major shopping right after work.* You're most tired and hungry at this time, least likely to make good choices, most likely to forget something important. If you've got a cranky youngster in tow, the job becomes nearly impossible.

GIANT ALL-TIME SHOPPING LIST

This list will help you devise one of your own. If someone else occasionally shops for you, be sure to include brand names and can sizes.

Dairy

___whole milk
___skim milk
___yogurt
___butter
___sour cream
___cream cheese
___American cheese
___Swiss cheese
___grated cheese
___cottage cheese
___other cheese
___eggs

Produce

___tomatoes
___cucumbers
___lettuce
___scallions
___radishes
___carrots
___celery
___string beans
___corn
___spinach
___lemons
___limes
___onions
___parsley
___herbs
___mushrooms
___potatoes
___oranges
___apples
___plums
___peaches
___grapes
___bananas

___pineapple
___melon
___berries
___pears
___grapefruit
___cherries

Meat and Fish

___fish fillets
___shrimp
___lamb chops
___flank steak
___frankfurters
___chopped chuck
___leg of lamb
___London broil
___veal scallops
___pork chops
___pot roast
___roast beef
___chicken

Drinks

___apple juice
___orange juice
___diet soda
___cola
___tomato juice
___beer
___tonic water
___ginger ale
___grapefruit juice
___punch

Frozen Foods

___French fries
___orange juice
___pie crust

___waffles
___lima beans

Drugs

___toothpaste
___baby shampoo
___Band-aids
___aspirin
___deodorant
___tissues
___Kleenex
___talcum powder

Breads, Crackers, Cereals

___rye bread
___pancake mix
___puffed rice
___bran cereal
___crackers
___graham crackers
___cookies

Staples

___tuna fish
___salmon
___sardines
___olive oil
___vegetable oil
___wine vinegar
___flour
___coffee
___instant coffee
___tea bags
___cornstarch
___sugar
___salt
___tomato sauce

___tomato paste
___whole tomatoes
___horseradish
___soy sauce
___teriyaki sauce
___salad dressing
___mustard
___rice
___macaroni
___spaghetti
___applesauce
___beef consommé
___chicken broth
___ketchup
___mayonnaise
___raisins
___Worcestershire sauce
___herbs and spices (jars)
___peanut butter
___jelly
___olives
___canned mushrooms
___pet food

Cleaning and Paper Supplies

___dishwasher detergent
___detergent
___cleaner
___liquid cleaner
___paper towels
___paper napkins
___toilet paper
___furniture polish
___soap
___bulbs (100, 75, 60, 3-way)
___trash bags
___wax paper
___aluminum foil
___plastic bags

- *Schedule large-scale shopping trips once or twice a month,* and buy in as huge quantities as your kitchen will accommodate. When you make up your weekly menus, take care that all ingredients are either on hand or can be purchased in one trip. If Wednesday's meal calls for broccoli and Friday's for string beans, buy them both on the weekend (or early Monday morning) and don't go back to the store unless you run out of milk in the middle of the night.

- *Keep a running shopping list* by posting your Master List or a blank roll of paper in the kitchen where everyone can write down what's missing as soon as he notices it.

DINNERS

These, of course, are your biggest challenge. But if you approach supper time with the same managerial attitude that you apply to your work life or the other aspects of housekeeping, you'll cope.

Evening meals fall into three basic categories: *make-aheads* (frozen extra casseroles, a crock-pot stew, a meat-and-vegetable dish assembled early in the morning), *quickies* (broiled and sautéed meats and fish, sandwiches, cold cuts, eggs), and *leftovers* (Monday's stew on Wednesday or Sunday's roast beef refurbished as Wednesday's Chinese dinner). There's also a fourth category—*order-ins* (as in, "I'm exhausted, let's get a pizza") —and if your budget can afford it, you owe it to yourself to take advantage of these once in a while.

Since *make-aheads* are your secret weapon—they yield the most amount of food for the least amount of work—it's worth taking time to perfect a limited number of standbys. A really rich meat sauce that can go into two lasagnas, on top of three plates of pasta, or be the base for a scrumptious chili dinner deserves a few hours of your effort. So does a first-rate chicken-and-wine casserole or a chopmeat and noodle dish.

Quickies, on the other hand, should not be labored over. If you want to perk up plain broiled fish or sautéed chicken breasts, make and freeze a few *food enhancers,* which can be stored in quantity and used as needed. *Tomato butter,* for example, is especially good tasting and versatile. Here's how you make it: Cream together ¼-pound unsalted butter, 1 teaspoon tomato paste, ½-teaspoon salt, ¼-teaspoon sugar. When the mixture is smooth, roll it in wax paper to make a 1-inch-wide cylinder, and freeze. *Onion butter* and *herb butter* are made along the same principles. You can add grated cheese or bread crumbs to any of these.

If you have a housekeeper or sitter who's willing to cut and chop vegetables and meats and have them ready when you get home, you can serve truly delicious Chinese-style wok-cooked meals. Stir-frying takes only minutes and is a most nutritious way of keeping the freshness in foods.

THREE THINGS TO COOK ON A WINTER SUNDAY AND EAT ALL WEEK

A Turkey Dinner

. . . Because you'll never have time to make this meal during the week, and because turkey is the quintessential leftover (remember to clip recipes around Thanksgiving time). Be sure to save a few slices plus gravy for small-portion freezing.

A Meat Loaf

. . . Because it freezes well, and because it's wonderful the next day at room temperature and can go to school in a lunch box or to the office in a brown bag tucked into your briefcase. The best meat loaves use a combination of ground beef, pork, veal, and lamb. A hard-cooked egg in the middle is a nice touch, but check with your children first. Kids tend to have funny ideas about what goes inside what.

A Stew

. . . Because you can put the whole family to work chopping vegetables. And because there's almost no end to the combinations you can concoct. Don't be afraid to make up your own recipes—and let the children add their flourishes. Keep in mind a few general principles: Brown the meat before adding liquid for a tastier dish; remove the part you're going to freeze a little before it's done, to allow for reheating time; make sure you're cooking enough for at least three meals (preferably more)—there's no point in doing all that work for one dinner.

The trick with *leftovers* is to change the form of the original meal without adding on substantial preparation time. Leftover meats can go into a wok-cooked dinner (along with such odds and ends as wilted lettuce, chopped onions, even tomatoes). You can add the remains of a roast beef or broiled chicken to a pot of yesterday's boiled rice and fry it in a little oil and soy sauce. Put pieces of last night's ham between layers of a macaroni-and-cheese casserole—you can even freeze half of it for another meal.

Easy and inexpensive meal ideas are the mainstay of the women's service magazines and the family pages of daily newspapers. Take the time to look these over; make a file of the ones that suit your taste and style. The cookbooks listed on pages 101–102 have been carefully selected by cookbook editor Helen Barer for well-tested, easy-to-follow, make-ahead and quick-cooking recipes.

BREAKFAST

Morning meals tend to be catch-as-catch-can affairs in most working mothers' homes, and when you're under the pressure of getting the kids off to school and yourself to work, it's all too easy to forget that eating can be fun.

The standard organizing principle, "Never leave anything for the last minute," can help restore order to chaos. If you set the table, prepare the coffee, section the grapefruit, and mix the juice the night before, you'll have a fighting chance to be ahead of the game in the morning. Some parents set out bowls of dry cereal the night before (if you want to be extravagant, use those individual-serving cereal boxes and let the kids pour the milk right into them).

Another way to ease the problem of rushed breakfasts: let your children invent new menus. For example, grilled-cheese sandwiches on English muffins are fine in the morning and kids can even eat them on the run. Make a double batch of supernourishing pancakes on Sunday (try including protein supplement, wheat germ, apple sauce, or yogurt); freeze half of them in small foil packets. Warmed in the oven, these make passable weekday breakfasts. You can do the same thing with waffles, French toast, even bacon. Try starting the day with yogurt mixed with honey, fresh fruit, or your kids' favorite jam.

For the most nutrition in the least amount of time, nothing beats a do-it-yourself breakfast drink. Make it ahead of time in the blender and keep in a closed-tight container in the fridge. Here's one recipe, which you can vary by adding berries or other fruits or by eliminating some of the ingredients:

To 2 cups of milk add 1 banana, 2 eggs, 1 tablespoon lecithin, 1 tablespoon vegetable oil, ¼-cup plain yogurt, ¼-cup soy flour, ¼-cup wheat germ, ½-cup frozen undiluted orange juice, 1 teaspoon vanilla. This pep-up drink is also good as an afternoon snack.

LUNCH

The most important thing to remember about this meal is that *you* should not be making it. If your children are home for lunch, make sure you are well stocked with leftovers and standards like peanut butter and jelly—and let the sitter take responsibility for seeing that the kids are well fed. Filling the lunch boxes should be the work of any child over six. Some variations on the sandwich-and-fruit routine: chunks of cheese, celery, carrots; tuna or chicken salad in a plastic container; ravioli, stew, or soup in a wide-necked Thermos (when using one of these for hot food, be sure to rinse it with hot water before filling).

SNACKS

After-school and after-dinner snacks are an important part of a child's eating pattern. Your kids won't munch on junk food if you lay in a good supply of raw vegetables, fruits, nuts, whole-grain crackers. Even a $1.50-an-hour baby-sitter can usually be persuaded to cut up carrots, carve cheddar-cheese cubes, and set out bowls of raisins and nuts. One mother's ingenious idea: wrap individual slices of pizza in foil, freeze, let kids reheat in the oven.

Other snack possibilities: melon balls, sesame sticks, granola bars, a bowl of yogurt as a dunk for cut-up apples and peaches, celery stalks stuffed with cottage cheese or cream cheese. Keep everything within easy reach in store-and-serve plastic containers. For other healthy snack ideas, see *The Taming of the C.A.N.D.Y. Monster,* by Vicki Lansky.

ENTERTAINING

Being a working mother does not have to mean saying good-bye forever to gracious living. Although Beef Wellington and strawberry soufflé

TWO DURING-THE-WEEK FESTIVE DINNERS
FOR KIDS OR GROWN-UPS

Taco Dinner

If you've got on hand kidney beans, some tomato sauce, and ground meat (or if you've cleverly remembered to defrost your homemade meat sauce), you can throw together a delicious chili con carne in about ten minutes. Serve this with tacos (you'll find these boxed in most markets), bowls of shredded lettuce, shredded cheddar cheese, chopped onions (the freezer again). Let each person assemble his own dinner-in-a-taco. For added gaiety, set the table with bright-colored napkins, a different color for each person.

Lasagna

The perfect freezer-to-table one-dish supper. Making a really superb lasagna is not the easiest task, but it's definitely worth learning how—and then preparing two at a time, one to freeze. With a loaf of herb-and-garlic bread, from your own or your grocer's freezer, and a big tossed salad, you've got a splendid dinner.

---

may be reserved for only the most special occasions, there's no reason your life-style can't include a new kind of informal entertainment for friends and for your own family.

Don't exhaust yourself making an entire holiday dinner. You can have a delicious Thanksgiving feast by sharing the work with other families. Making your favorite sweet-potato pie is a lot more fun if you don't have to truss the turkey and boil the onions. The principle works beautifully for dinner parties, too. Let each person bring a favorite gourmet dish.

A little ingenuity can raise these dinners many notches above those pot-luck suppers where everyone manages to bring forth the same noodle casserole. One group of four New York City couples has for years staged a memorably elegant Thanksgiving dinner, changing the menu each year. Everyone participates, including the children, and the competition is keen to see who can produce the most mouth-watering dish. Families like these have learned that asking a dinner guest to contribute a salad or a dessert is a compliment, not an insult, and they're able to enjoy the company of friends all year long without wearing themselves out in the kitchen.

Cocktails and hors d'oeuvres before an evening out with friends is another painless way to entertain. You can serve one lavish dish, such as a glass bowl heaped with cold shrimp in the shell (boil these the night before) or a salmon mousse (a cinch to make in the blender and very impressive looking).

Entertaining can also be a family affair. Let everyone help plan and prepare a big feast—a summer barbecue, a hearty cold-weather dinner, or maybe a small brunch—and invite another family as guests. Make sure the children participate, so that it's their party, too.

BOOKS THAT MAY HELP

Life Management

Double Duties, Cynthia Sterling Pincus (Chatham Square Press, 1978). A professional counselor offers an "Action Plan for the Working Wife," with sound practical and psychological guidance.

Getting Organized, Stephanie Winston (Norton, 1978). Ms. Winston, who owns a firm that helps people organize their lives, tells you how to get control of your home, your budget, your job, and your family.

Superwoman, Shirley Conran (Crown, 1978). Breezy, useful information on saving time, money, and energy around the house.

Cookbooks

A Mostly French Food Processor Cookbook, Colette Rossant and Jill Harris Herman (NAL, 1977). Time-saving, imaginative use of food processors.

Michael Field's Culinary Classics and Improvisations, Michael Field (Knopf, 1967). Don't be put off by the fancy title. This is an invaluable guide to using leftovers, by a master chef.

From Julia Child's Kitchen, Julia Child (Knopf, 1977). Everyday as well as company recipes, with wonderful advice on equipment and techniques.

The Joy of Cooking, Revised Edition, Irma S. Rombauer and Marion R. Becker (Bobbs-Merrill, 1975). Still the best basic cookbook.

The Night Before Cookbook, Paul Rubinstein and Leslie Rubinstein (Macmillan, 1967). Sound make-ahead party recipes.

Dinner Against the Clock, Madeleine Kamman (Atheneum, 1973). Shortcuts and solid recipes from a first-rate author.

Great Dinners from Life, Eleanor Graves (Time-Life Books, 1974). Exciting menus, broken down into time sequences and plan-ahead advice.

Jane Butel's Freezer Cookbook, Jane Butel (Coward, McCann, 1977). How to use your freezer to the best advantage.

Pressure Cookery Perfected, Roy Andries de Groot (Simon and Schuster, 1978). A must if you own a pressure cooker.

Crockery Cookery, Mabel Hoffman (Bantam Books, 1975). One of the popular slow-cooker recipe books.

The Taming of the C.A.N.D.Y. Monster, Vicki Lansky (Meadowbrook Press, 1978). Sensible and inventive suggestions for feeding your kids foods other than Continuously Advertised Nutritionally Deficient Yummies.

Chapter Six
THE SHARING FAMILY

One of the major decisions you will be making when you decide to be a working mother is how you will engage your family in the business of daily life.

Unfortunately, even in the most liberated households, the daily drudgery of keeping things running is no one's idea of fun. As sociologist Mary Jo Bane puts it: "Everyone's in favor of equal pay, but no one is in favor of doing the dishes." Yet dishes have to somehow be done, sheets and towels wear out and must be replaced, children have to be fed and clothed, their homework supervised, their report cards signed. Will you be the one to see that all these activities get carried out, taking on a job at home and outside? Or will you and your husband and children co-operate to create a sharing family?

One of the quickest ways to wreck your mental health is to insist on doing it all yourself. And great benefits to family life can result when other members of your family assume more home responsibility. No less an expert than the venerable Dr. Spock believes the business of raising a family should not be our responsibility alone. Fathers, he assures us, are quite able to "give bottles . . . change diapers . . . help with questions about homework . . . explain rules and assign duties." And when parenting is shared, children benefit from a larger emotional reservoir that helps them function independently and confidently. In the past, with fathers spending long hours at work and mothers assigned to watch over the home front alone, we in effect had one-parent families—"mother families." But when both parents are involved, you *double* the emotional reservoir from which your children can draw.

As you and other wives depart for offices, shops, and factories, more and more husbands are taking over where the women leave off. In California, a guidance counselor arranges to have the school bus drop her son at his father's newspaper office on the days she has to work late. A Denver service-station operator keeps his infant daughter at the station in a portable crib until his wife, a nurse's aide, returns from her early-morning shift. In New Jersey, a police officer rearranges his work schedule so that he can care for his son, while his wife is at school.

Prompted by necessity, men and women are discovering that very good things follow when the hand that's pumping gas also rocks the cradle. Not only is mother relieved of the burden of sole parenting, but father and child discover each other in ways that would never have happened had the father remained uninvolved in child care. Says a typical mother, Wendy, whose husband, a service-station owner, was forced to fill in for her in the mornings when she had an early nursing shift: "I found he's a very nurturing person. He's learned not only to diaper, but to bandage cuts and soothe and sing lullabies." Her husband, a burly man not accustomed to showing his feelings, speaks with rare emotion about his young son: "I've watched him grow from day to day, week to week. Seeing him learn so many things, some of them overnight, amazed

DR. SPOCK ON FATHERS

It will be a great day when fathers:

Consider the care of their children to be as important to them as their jobs and careers.

Seek out jobs and work schedules that will allow them ample time to be with their wives and children.

Give first consideration, when discussing with their wives where to live, to what favors family life.

Will resist their companies' attempts to move them frequently.

Will let it be known at their work places that they take their parental responsibilities very seriously and may have to take time off when their children need them—just as working mothers have always done.

Will try to get other fathers at their work places to take the same stands.

—from *Baby and Child Care,* Revised Edition, by Benjamin Spock (Pocket Books, 1977)

me. I keep thinking I would have missed all this if I hadn't been keeping him from six to eight in the morning."

Men are cooking and washing dishes, and, more important, they're also handling many of the niggling chores that can keep a working mother in a constant state of anxiety. Replacing shoelaces, buying toilet paper, remembering to defrost the chops for dinner are the necessary evils of household management.

Children, too, are contributing their share. When kids make their beds, sweep floors, or tidy up the living room, they know their efforts are important and valued. And as childcare expert Eda LeShan tells us, "Children need opportunities to feel they are helping and giving to others. When they have none of these experiences, they cannot discover their own strengths and durability; they cannot have the self-respect that comes with knowing you are a good person helping others."

SHARING—A LEARNED PROCESS

Enviable as these goals are, the path to sharing is rarely paved with enlightened family conferences shot through with insight, selfless performance of chores, and undivided desire to cooperate.

No family works through to new sharing arrangements without a lot of trial, error, and tears. Don't overlook your own attitude as an ingredient in the pot. Women, taught from childhood that domestic duties are their responsibility, often have to realize that giving up the role of serving all the family food does not mean giving up their womanhood. Men, including those who would be abashed to think themselves macho, are still used to measuring their success by what they achieve outside the home and may be slow to value the rewards of fathering and sharing in home responsibilities. Yet learning to take an active part at home is showing many men another kind of success—that which comes from the pleasure of participatory parenthood and a marriage deepened by mutual sharing.

Here's how three different couples each came to a system of sharing that suits them. Each arrangement is different, but matches the needs of the couple.

Joan and Larry Martin: "Something clicked in my head . . ." When Joan and Larry Martin married fresh out of college, in the late 1950s, the notion of husband and wife sharing equally in housework and childcare was as alien as the idea of women participating equally in the labor market. Joan, an honors graduate in English from a prestigious eastern women's college, put in an obligatory stint as an editorial assistant in a New York City publishing house, while Larry, with a master's degree in the burgeoning field of computer science, began a promising career as a systems programmer. When their first child, Laura, was born two years after their marriage, Joan retired to devote herself to child-rearing. "In those days, to continue working even part-time was considered the eighth deadly sin," she recalls.

Sitting in her large, sunny dining room on Manhattan's Upper West Side, which now doubles as an at-home office, Joan, a tall, attractive woman in her late thirties, reminisces about those early days as a full-time mother. "The only break in the daily routine was when I'd go to have my hair straightened," she remembers, laughing and running her hands through her now-fashionable "natural" hairdo.

Although they had tacitly agreed that Joan would not work until some vague time when the children "no longer needed her so much," Joan began to take on free-lance editorial assignments at home when Laura was three and their second child, Amy, was one. "I'd hire a baby-sitter for $1.50 an hour and go into the dining room and try to earn enough money to pay her." She soon found herself with not enough hours to handle the editorial work, the housework, and still have relaxed time to spend with the children. Larry, a lanky, serious-looking man, would help out if he was asked—"He'd buy the milk or toothpaste, but I had to notice we needed them, or he'd do the dishes but leave the pots and pans for me." And Joan felt she had no right to ask for more support. Like many couples, they were both still locked into economic determinism. "He earned more—at that time about eighteen thousand dollars to my six or seven thousand—and therefore I was expected to do more," says Joan tersely.

Although she did not admit it to herself, Joan was becoming more and more angry. "One night I was sitting at my typewriter," she recalls, "and I had this hideous deadline . . . I was getting ready to stay up half the night. The baby had diarrhea . . . I had been changing diapers all day, and Larry had done me the favor of changing her once after dinner, while I was doing the dishes. Around seven o'clock, Larry yelled, 'Hey, the baby needs to be changed!' And something clicked in my head. I thought to myself, imagine if I called him at the office and said, 'Please stop what you're doing now, and come right in here, and change the baby . . . it's your turn.' I was absolutely furious."

If Joan was surprised at her own rage, Larry was astonished at her feelings. "Over the next year, we spent hours fighting about the problem," she says, "discussing it calmly, sometimes ignoring it, pretending it would go away." Larry could not see himself taking energy away from his career to plug into the domestic front, even though he was sympathetic. Joan, sick of planning meals and worrying about baby-sitters, was determined not to have to "fall on my knees in gratitude just because Larry occasionally swept the kitchen floor or put on the baby's shoes."

A clue to a solution unexpectedly came from Joan's mother, a perceptive woman who pointed out that the bickering and rancor between Joan and Larry would be lessened if they respected each other's own problem-solving styles. Joan sought a complete philosophical overhaul; Larry turned his attention more to specifics: how to divide his time sensibly between home and career. In the end, the Martins put to use Larry's managerial skill by approaching the problems systematically. On the home front, Larry agreed to do all the laundry (saying, "Please help me with the laundry," didn't help; he had to take over the chore entirely, so he wouldn't feel like Joan's assistant), to handle most of the marketing (he has it down to such a science that he shops only once a week, on Saturdays), and to share with Joan the expense of a once-a-week cleaning service.

Larry also changed his schedule so that he could come home earlier three evenings a week and share the dinner hours with the family. And he began walking their older daughter, who was in first grade, to school each morning. Now *he* was the one who saw Laura's teacher each day, who reminded her about her lunch and milk money. The world began to see Larry as a father who really cared for his child, and both Larry and Laura took pleasure from that. Joan smiles over an incident from that first year. As Larry was leaving the classroom one morning, Laura's teacher called after him, "Don't forget the parents' meeting on Wednesday, Mr. Martin; and tell Mrs. Martin she's welcome to come, too."

Joan and Larry's new style of marriage is far from perfect, and it did not simply burst into bloom after a few nights of "intense confrontation." "It took a long time," Joan remembers, "before I could feel right about Larry cleaning a toilet when he had worked hard in an office all day. And it was a while before Larry was able to see that his marriage and his fatherhood are as important as his professional life. But it happened, and our sharing now reaches into most aspects of our lives and has nothing to do with how much either of us earns."

Barbara and David: "No one feels put upon . . ." Barbara and David Dongier, on the other hand, have learned that sharing can mean an equal commitment to raising children but a decidedly unequal division of labor. "David came to this marriage believing a man's household responsibilities consisted of taking out the garbage and changing the light bulbs," says Barbara Dongier, a lively twenty-six-year-old secretary in a San Francisco advertising agency and the mother of five-year-old Jed. "And he managed to be so incompetent around the house that I stopped asking him to do more than the basic minimum. . . . I think it took him a year to learn how to load the dishwasher properly and to remember to put the soap in and push the button," she adds.

David, a serious, hard-working litigation lawyer in his early thirties, is deeply involved in his career and works far longer hours than does Barbara. He also makes a good deal more money, $37,000 as opposed to Barbara's $8200, but both David and Barbara insist that this is not the reason that they do not share equally in household responsibilities. "David's job is much, much more demanding than mine," says Barbara simply, "and we both feel it would be unfair for him to assume half the work at home, too."

With the aid of a part-time housekeeper and David mobilized as an efficient helper, Barbara manages the household without strain or resentment. When it comes to the care of Jed, however, David considers himself an equal partner, even though he spends less time with his son than Barbara does. But, as Barbara points out, "Raising a child is not a matter of minutes and hours." David participates in all decisions about Jed's life—from what he will do in the summer to whether he should be allowed to go on a camping trip with another family to what to do about his poor grades in math. Says Barbara: "I know that David is there for me, that he'll figure out a way to be supportive, even if he doesn't do the work himself. Like last year when Jed was sick and I stayed home the first day and David just couldn't be home the next, he arranged for his aunt to come. He took care of everything."

Unlike the Martins, the Dongiers do not have a marriage in which sharing reaches into every aspect of their life together. But, for the moment, they are satisfied with a way of life that works well for the three of them. "The important thing," says Barbara, "is that no one feels put upon. David and Jed and I all feel we're pulling our own weight in our own way."

If Barbara's job were a more demanding one, the Dongiers might have had to deal with some of the problems faced by Howard and Fran, partners in an increasingly common arrangement, the so-called dual-career marriage.

Howard and Fran: a dual-career marriage. Howard and Fran Johnson-Carmichael (the hyphenated surname reveals their commitment to equality in their marriage) regard themselves as sharing fully in both managing their household and raising their two children—Tina, seven, and Peter, nine. And unlike Joan, Fran did not wait until she exploded with rage before she and Howard worked out a system of sharing.

A dynamic woman in her mid-thirties, Fran is much admired for her vibrant good looks and her warm sense of humor. A graduate of a two-year business school, she recently turned an administrative assistant job into a $20,000-year-a-year position as executive director of a non-profit professional organization. Her husband, Howard, more reserved and less casual than his wife, earns slightly less than Fran as research director of a small pharmaceutical firm.

For the Johnson-Carmichaels, sharing begins with the basics. They shared the childbirth experience. ("He was so involved," says Fran, "that if he could have figured out a way to take over part of the breast-feeding, he would have.") The decision for Fran to resume working was made jointly, after serious discussion of all the pros and cons. And both Howard and Fran participated in hiring Mrs. Davison, the grandmotherly woman who lives with them in their rambling suburban Philadelphia house. ("We interviewed four women together. Howard asked most of the questions and I formed the gut impressions. After each interview, we'd compare notes.")

Together they turn over as much as possible of the housework to Mrs. Davison, but what remains—planning meals, arranging children's activities, shopping, handling doctor and dentist appointments—they share in a surprisingly easy and relaxed manner. They both make "mountains of lists" and both try to keep track of what needs to be done. "We used to have a weekly plan. You know, he would plan the meals one week, I'd do them the next; he'd do the staple shopping, I'd do the impulse; he'd be responsible for any emergencies half the month, I the other half.

But it got ridiculous . . . it was too rigid. Like once the dog had to be rushed to the vet on my week for emergencies, and I wasn't available, and Mrs. Davison was afraid to call Howard because it wasn't his week."

The Johnson-Carmichaels decided that there was enough goodwill between them to work out their sharing as they went along. "Mostly we just wing it," says Fran, "which means that we sometimes have to talk to each other on the phone a few times a day, and that once in a while, everything gets fouled up and Mrs. Davison, Howard, and I all go to the store for the same container of milk."

Howard has not needed Fran's urging to carry his weight in the family. If anything, in fact, he is the more involved of the two. Relates Fran: "He picked up a copy of *Sisterhood Is Powerful* in an airport once, read Pat Mainardi's "The Politics of Housework," and he came home all fired up to do more around the house than before." Howard also expects to be involved in the community and in the children's schooling as much as his wife. "Once the class mother called to find out if we would contribute to the class raffle," Fran recalls, "and she asked to speak to me. Howard was offended. He said, 'Yes, *I* can contribute.' I think he was hurt."

The Johnson-Carmichaels' enthusiastic and energetic approach to their life-style seemed to us almost too good to be true. Were there any problems, we asked them directly, fully expecting an adamant denial. In fact, Fran admits, she's sometimes concerned about the amount of energy they devote to "keeping the ship running." Because of the intensity with which they imbue their family life, both Howard and Fran tend to talk themselves out, engage in endless discussions, soul searchings, and reappraisals, which she feels can consume too much of their time.

Fran also feels that the children sense a rivalry between them, a competition as to who is more successful at home and professionally. These concerns seem to be mostly Fran's, and vague discomfort about them is a source of irritation in the marriage. Fran wonders if Howard's fierce dedication to equality in the marriage is perhaps his way of avoiding some of the problems in his own professional life. She confides that if these issues continue to bother her, she may suggest talking to a marriage or family counselor. In the meantime, however, she's concentrating on her professional life and trying to stay tuned in to the state of her marriage and family life.

Each of these couples has worked through to a sharing arrangement that far transcends anything they expected when they first married. Their experiences and those of other women point to the fact that before you move toward a sharing family, everyone needs to do some soul searching —starting with you.

DON'T SABOTAGE YOURSELF

A curious phenomenon is the wife who sabotages herself. She can be the guilty, driven mother who's so uncertain about her right to work that she spends her evenings doing all the things that she'd do if she hadn't put in eight hours of work. She, however, is a dying breed. A more common species of the self-saboteur is a woman who insists on maintaining control even when her husband and children do a good share of the housework, who "can't get them to do anything right," and who insists, "I do it better so it's easier to do it myself."

Even those women who value their husband's and children's cooperation can be victims of their own stubborn preconceptions. For them, the image of themselves as nurturer-homemaker is so important to their female identity that they feel threatened when Dad takes over the laundry or the kids whip up Friday-night supper. Interestingly, too, some women find it hard even to recognize that Dad *has* taken over the laundry. Rona, a guidance counselor and an exceptionally thoughtful and intelligent woman, revealed this plight humorously when we interviewed her.

On the evening we met with Rona in the spacious, sparsely furnished New York City loft apartment she shares with her husband, Charles, and two young sons, she spoke plaintively of the difficulty of her life. "Everything's on my list," she said with weary resignation, "the cooking, the social life, paying bills, shopping, everything." We nodded sympathetically, as she explained that Charles, a talented painter, could not be persuaded to take part in the menial work of running a household.

Just then, Charles, a slim, sensitive-looking man, entered the bedroom in which we'd been talking and proceeded to scoop up a week's worth of laundry from a large wicker clothes hamper at the foot of the bed. "The boys have nothing to wear tomorrow," he matter-of-factly announced to Rona. Assuming that he knew the subject of our conversation, we commented at the irony of the moment. But Charles looked puzzled and went on adeptly sorting the clothes for the wash, a job he had obviously done many times before. Within moments, it became clear that, yes, indeed, this dedicated artist found time to perform "menial tasks," and, Rona admitted, to perform them well.

Rona, like many of us, was a victim of her own prejudices and presumptions, so much so that she had refused to see things as they really were.

If Rona and Charles's story strikes a chord of recognition—if you suspect that you, too, have been unwilling to let go of old patterns—take some time to consider your own concept of marital roles. Start by asking yourself a few crucial questions.

Do you always see yourself in the role of administrator-perfectionist? If you are going to insist on having the cleanest house on the block or the kind of dinners you used to serve when you had four and a half hours at your disposal, you are bound to be disappointed when your son concocts a Pasta Surprise or your husband gives the bathroom a once-over-lightly. Try exchanging perfectionism for the pleasure of letting someone else be the boss some of the time. And don't fall into the trap with your husband of Ms. Competent, Mr. Incompetent. As long as you criticize his efforts as inferior, he has a perfect excuse for not doing household chores, since "you won't be pleased with the way I do it anyway."

Are you willing to demand help from other family members? Letting go of perfectionism should not mean dropping your standards altogether. Says one woman: "I've gotten as far as being able to say, 'The hell with it, so I'll live with a messy house.' What I'm beginning to learn now is that I have a right to a clean house, but that it doesn't have to be me who makes it clean."

Do you have the patience to stick it out while everyone learns you mean business? One woman shut her eyes to the growing pile of unfolded laundry on the living room couch until her husband finally realized it wasn't going to disappear magically. Experiences like this can go a long way toward shifting the power base within a family.

HUSBANDS CAN LEARN

As we talked to husbands and wives, we were impressed by the spirit of sharing that is burgeoning in so many families. Of course, there are also some holdouts. There was Harold, whose idea of sharing is to order in a pizza on the nights his wife works late—and then to leave the dishes, the garbage, and two cranky, unwashed children for her to handle at ten o'clock at night. Many a single mother was once married to a Harold.

We also found Richard, whose sole contribution consisted of paying the housekeeper while his wife juggled a dizzying array of appointments, arrangements, and assignments. Men like Richard are amazed when their wives announce one day that they are fed up.

Some of the men practiced an expert brand of sabotage: While seeming to approve of their wives working, they also manage to undermine their ability to cope—"If you were home all day," their line goes, "the house would be cleaner . . . but I know how much your job means to you. . . ."

Even Richard and Harold might learn if their wives instituted some of these steps:

Don't let your husband fall into the I'll-help-you-when-it's-convenient-for-me trap. Men who view their domestic contributions as gifts are giving nothing to anyone. As Joan Martin comments, "When I stopped feeling grateful for the help Larry gave me and started realizing that for him to be a real support, he'd have to make real sacrifices, that's when we began to have the kind of relationship we have now."

Encourage your husband to take over certain responsibilities—and then let him handle them his way. Joan Martin: "Larry is the breakfast person in our house, and although sometimes I want to scream, 'Cheerios again?!' I don't, because I'm really delighted that he's in charge." Remember, too, that kids like to see a parent willingly at the helm, rather than one parent bossing the other around.

Agree on backup plans for emergencies, and be sure you're both prepared to put them into effect. You can't expect your husband to hire a last-minute baby-sitter, for example, if he has to phone you for her number. Leave word where either of you can be reached during the day, and make it clear to other people (including parents of your children's friends, who are often hesitant to deal with fathers) that either of you can handle arrangements or emergencies.

Try to share tasks according to preference and convenience. Don't make assumptions about "man's work" and "woman's work." Says Fran Johnson-Carmichael, "Howard and I just assumed that I'd buy the children's clothing, and I'd rush around on my lunch hour or on weekends doing that. Then we discovered a terrific discount kids' store near Howard's office, and now he does at least half the shopping. Last year he completely outfitted our son for camp."

Be willing to compromise. That old standby is particularly important when it comes to husband-wife sharing. Cooperation requires communication, and communication tends to fall down when everyone is busy keeping score.

CAN FATHERS MOTHER?

If a man is to share fully in the raising of his children, he and his wife must certainly be convinced that he can do as good a job of "mothering" as she can. If we were to ask one of the nearly 900,000 children under the age of eighteen who are cared for by their fathers alone, they would probably say that fathers make as good parents as mothers. One little boy put it well. When his teacher told him to bring his mother to school, he replied, "My father is my mother."

It was once believed that the mother-child bond constituted a unique relationship, and that fathers were indeed ill suited to nurturing the young, a view expressed succinctly by Bruno Bettelheim: "The male physiology and that part of his psychology based on it are not geared to infant care." However, current thinking tends to favor the notion that, as pediatrician Mary Howell remarks, "The childcare usually performed by mothers might just as well be carried out by fathers."

Do fathers have a readily identifiable style of parenting distinct from that of mothers? We don't really know. From the cases of fathers who function as the primary parent, we learn that men can be as nurturing and as sensitive to the needs of children as women can. Fathers seem to wipe tears and mop up spills in much the same way as mothers do. James Levine, who explores these issues in *Who Will Raise the Children?* has found that rather than men and women differing from one another, "the differences between two men or between two women . . . are likely to be far greater than the differences between any two groups. The fact is that the differences among homemaker-fathers are great, as are the styles of interacting with their children."

Perhaps a better question than "Can fathers mother?" is "Can fathers parent?" Says Levine: "Taking as a premise that woman means 'nurturer' and man means 'breadwinner,' social scientists have hardly been able to entertain the idea—until recently—that both mother and father mean 'parent.' "

Children need both mothers and fathers. Not so that they can go fishing with Dad and bake cookies with Mom, but so that they can experience tenderness and strength, guidance and affection, from two people who love them. The sharing of household management and childcare will lead, we hope, not to more fathers who "mother" but to more actively involved male and female parents.

GET THE KIDS INTO THE ACT

Having children take on tasks and develop the responsibility for carrying through on them is not only an old American tradition, it's also a centuries-old method for building character and confidence in a child.

Even very young children feel important when they are given chores to do at home, whether it's taking care of a younger brother or peeling potatoes for dinner. If they are assigned responsibilities from the time they are old enough to toddle around dusting the baseboards, they will grow up knowing that the work they do is meaningful.

Be sure to let the children themselves participate in any planning of shared household tasks. When children help decide how chores are to be parceled out, they are far less likely to balk at fulfilling their obligations. Here is how to go about getting the kids into the act:

1. *Plan to have regular family meetings at which everyone helps set up household routines.* Make a list of all the necessary tasks and have each family member choose what he or she likes to do best; then plan to rotate the jobs no one wants. Be sure to make no assumptions about preferences—your ten-year-old son may actually prefer ironing to taking out the garbage, your daughter may find washing floors more satisfying than clearing the table. Schedule regular follow-up meetings, at which everyone can air beefs, renegotiate if necessary, or suggest improvements.

   Schedules work best when each member cares for his or her own personal belongings. Says one woman: "I'm the laundry person in our house, but I'm sure not going to be the one to fish my kids' underpants out from behind the beds; they've learned that if they don't put them in the hamper on laundry day, they'll just have to go to school with bathing suits under their jeans!"

2. *Once work assignments have been made, write them on a schedule.* Post the schedule where everyone can see it (taped to the side of the refrigerator is a good place).

   Seeing that his or her chores are done should be up to each person, but some families allow switching around. One dismayed mother described how her three children, ages nine, eleven, and fourteen, had elevated the trading of household tasks to such a high art that much of the dinner-table conversation consisted of negotiating and bargaining. Amazingly, however, everything got done, and she admitted that these strategy sessions probably helped keep the kids' enthusiasm from flagging.

3. *Consider carefully each child's ability when tasks are being distributed.* Your four-year-old may be quite sincere when he offers to cook dinner while you clean his hamster cage. It takes tactful guidance to engage children in work they can handle themselves, but assigning chores that are appropriate to their ages will help them take the plan seriously and to sustain interest in it.

    If a small child insists on doing something you think she's too young to handle, why not try helping her along? One eight-year-old became quite expert at removing wax from the kitchen floor (a chore no one else wanted) after a session of instructions from her father. And many an adolescent has graduated from sloppy joes to steak au poivre after a few cooking lessons.

    Most youngsters can be remarkably efficient and creative when it comes to housework and cooking. Let them take over as much as they are willing to do, and remember to offer generous praise and encouragement. Even very small children can take charge of keeping their own things neat, especially if you teach them from the beginning the basics like making beds and sorting out clothes and toys. ("Those little green pieces all go with the Monopoly set . . . see, that's where you keep shoes . . . here's the place for papers and crayons. . . .")

    Children over the age of six can be expected to do such things as sort and fold laundry, set and clear the table, and empty and load the dishwasher. There are even ten-year-olds who can cook a credible Sunday dinner, eight-year-olds who can prepare breakfast for the family every morning, and at least one five-year-old we encountered who did a splendid job of vacuuming the family room rug.

4. *Be realistic in your expectations.* If your husband's job requires that he look perfectly groomed all the time, it may be best to send his shirts to the laundry rather than have your eleven-year-old iron them. But if you're willing to put up with an occasional burned pan or socks that sometimes turn up in the wrong dresser or a table that never got set because football practice ran a little late, you'll be rewarded many times over not only by the reduction in your own work load, but by the spirit of cooperation and

caring that invariably comes when a whole family works together. As psychologist Lee Salk has said: "It's not the speed of setting the table that's important, but the joint participation, what you communicate in the interaction, that's crucially important."

Should you pay children for the work they do? There is great difference of opinion on this question. Some parents are adamant that children should be expected to help out at home without money changing hands; others feel that in a society that tends to reward work with money, children will perform better and feel more appreciated if they are paid for their efforts.

Most parents do agree, though, on the wisdom of giving a weekly allowance. A child's allowance should be scaled to his needs. As children get older and take on more of their own financial responsibilities—paying for movies, buying school supplies, purchasing hobby equipment—they are entitled to receive a larger weekly stipend. A good way of handling the payment problem is to supplement this allowance with additional money for chores beyond the routine ones. Older children or teenagers, for example, might receive money for work they would be paid for doing outside the home, such as baby-sitting, yard cleaning, and window washing.

Paying with added privileges or with tokens like gold stars is a good way of rewarding children for work especially well done. To some parents, letting a youngster stay up past her bedtime for a special TV program or allowing her to accumulate enough stars to purchase a new bike seems less like the bribery of cash payments.

If you do decide to pay your children for their chores, set up a strict schedule of values, and do not let yourself be persuaded to stray from it. If you and your five-year-old have agreed that folding laundry is worth a quarter, it is not fair of him to demand fifty cents two weeks later, just because his older sister explained inflation to him. Varying the dollar value of children's work capriciously can only undermine the seriousness of their efforts.

For sensible guidance on how to reward children for work, see *Children and Money: A Guide for Parents,* by Grace W. Weinstein (Schocken, 1976).

Kids sometimes need a little help. Children are not miniature adults: Even the most responsible among them sometimes dawdle infuriatingly over a job, forget their notebooks, or lose their rubbers. Be patient. Children have a natural drive toward competence, and they'll get there if you give them your love and support—and an occasional helping hand. Here are a few tips passed on to us by working mothers:

- If your children dawdle in the morning or linger too long over some household chore, make them a present of an inexpensive kitchen timer and watch them try to "beat the clock."

- A note pasted on the inside of the front door won't win you any awards for interior decoration, but the simple message— "Do you have your keys, bus pass, lunch?"—will save you and your kids a lot of aggravation.

- From Eleanor Berman, the author of *The Cooperating Family*, comes wise advice on handling the child who refuses to do his chores: "If tasks are continually neglected . . . let him see the consequences." If the person who's supposed to do the dishes lets them pile up in the sink, the rest of the family can go out to dinner without him until he comes around.

A commitment to a job should not mean a pledge of servitude. Getting up at six to iron your daughter's school dress, or dashing home again at five-thirty to pop a perfectly seasoned casserole into the oven you scrubbed clean the night before may win you a ticket in the Supermom sweepstakes, but it will not gain you the affection and respect that flourish when family responsibilities are shared.

Chapter Seven
SUCCEEDING WITH YOUR CHILDREN

You've found new ways of organizing your household to accommodate a family and a career. You've hired the best baby-sitter you can find; the kids seem to like her, and you no longer turn pale every time the phone rings in the office. With these basics behind you, it's time to turn your attention to your relationship with your children.

Whether you're returning to work after years of full-time child-rearing or heading back to the office at the end of a six-week maternity leave, you and your children will have fewer conflicts if you yourself are clear about your reasons for working. Notes a feminist psychotherapist: "The most crucial thing is for a mother to figure out what is important to her, and especially *why* it's important that she work, and then to deal with her relationship with her children."

TIMING YOUR RETURN TO WORK

In a pleasant switch to unanimity, developmental psychologists generally agree on the timetable of a child's evolving psychological needs. Here are checkpoints in your child's development that may help you time a return to work.

Early infancy (up to 7 months). If you definitely plan to work, working straight through without taking time off does have its advantages. Since the baby never knows any other arrangement, he doesn't have to deal with loss or change. And his ease of adjustment helps you adjust. If you wait, the child's later, more specialized needs for Mother may make it more difficult for him to come to terms with your absence.

Seven months to three years. During this period, a child struggles to differentiate himself from his mother, but is still very dependent on her. It is now that he forms his attachments to the important adults in his life (see page 121). The child used to having Mother around all the time may experience great stress if he is suddenly separated from her. Psychologically, he can differentiate "Mother" (whether that figure is a biological mother, father, or nanny) from other caregivers, and that awareness can lead to separation anxiety, manifested by crying and perhaps depression. If you do begin working during this time, be especially tuned in to your child's feelings and behavior.

Three to six years. It's no accident that nursery schools begin taking youngsters at age three, for children at this stage of development need socialization with others. With your three- to six-year old in gainful activity away from you during part of the day, she will usually be able to adjust to your working.

Six to eleven years. Now your child has a "job" of his own—school—and you may be dismayed to find him so embroiled in his own activities and friends that you see less and less of him. Contact with Mother may decline to touching base from time to time. Both from the child's viewpoint and a time-management angle, most mothers find these are the best years to return to work. And returning now, when you've not been out of the work force too long, will make reentry much easier than if you wait until you're in your forties or an "empty nester."

Eleven to fourteen years. This might seem like an ideal time to you, with your adolescent becoming more and more self-sufficient, but beware. Like the seven-month-old baby, adolescents are plunged into a critical period, experiencing spurts of physical growth and emotional turmoil as they struggle toward adult identities. Your twelve-year-old daughter can be expected to burst into tears at least once a day without discernible cause, while your adolescent son may retreat, moody and incommunicado, for hours in his room. Although your teenager may appear mature enough to tolerate your absence, the sudden change in family life can throw her into a tizzy. If you return to work at this time, be extra vigilant for trouble signs (see page 121).

GETTING OFF ON THE RIGHT FOOT

"Never apologize to your kids for the fact that you're working," cautions a successful film producer. "Let them know that they are important to you, but that your job is important, too." Regardless of your child's developmental stage, if he realizes that your going to work is a non-negotiable reality, he will be much better able to accept it.

When you first start working, however, smooth the transition with a few precautions:

Get your child used to the childcare arrangement you've chosen gradually.   Hiring and trying out a sitter or enrolling your child in a day-care center two months before you start your job may seem like unnecessary expense and trouble. But you'll be well repaid by less friction—and less worry on your part—when you do start. Both you and the child will gain from a dress rehearsal.

Minimize disruption of usual home routines.   If your family has always eaten dinner together at six, try to keep to this schedule, at least in the beginning. Keep reading bedtime stories, if that's what you've always done. But watch out for overcompensation. If you've never allowed TV treats after dinner, don't start now. Remember, you don't want to give the message "I'm doing something that's hurting you and so I'll make it up."

Don't let your new enthusiasm for your work life take over your home life.   Talking about your exciting new life and new friends may only rub salt into the wounds of a resentful youngster. There'll be plenty of time later to share your experiences with the children. If you must bring work home, handle it after the children are in bed.

Anticipate and encourage questions.   Not only the easy ones like "What do you do at your office?" or "How much do you get paid?" but also the hard ones like "Do you like the kids you teach better than you like me?" or "Will you ever be here when I get home from school?" Dealing openly with a child's apprehensions, if she has them, is the best reassurance you can offer.

ATTACHMENT AND SEPARATION—THE THEORIES

Many of our fears about the effects of separation on an infant stem from early, exceedingly limited studies of childhood attachment carried out two decades ago by John Bowlby in England and René Spitz in America. They direly concluded that children who do not "attach," that is, form an intimate, caring relationship with one specific person, preferably the biological mother, will almost inevitably develop gross pathology, growing up as "affectionless characters" unable to give or receive love, since they have never known the delicate reciprocity of a constant loving relationship. Investigators then declared that in order for this warm relationship to develop, the child must have the benefit of unbroken mothering during the first two and a half to three years of life.

But the flaw in this argument is that the studies were performed on hospitalized infants separated traumatically from their families, an environment far removed from that of babies whose mothers go off to work and return home each evening. Unfortunately, many professionals and lay people have been generalizing from these investigations and making grim predictions for the children of mothers who work during their children's early years.

The fact is that *few systematic studies support the contention that unbroken mother-presence is necessary for the development of later relationships.* Researcher Barbara Tizard, who studied children reared in institutions before being adopted, found no appreciable ill effects of their early lack of one-on-one mothering. In fact, Bowlby himself was unable to locate any inability to form deep relationships in adolescents who suffered hospitalization during their early years. Moreover, today, experts are questioning the *exclusiveness* of the mother-infant bond.

Jerome Kagan, the distinguished professor of developmental psychology at Harvard University, has concluded on the basis of extensive study that children can be attached both to their caregivers *and* to their mothers. Citing the importance of quality rather than quantity of time spent with the child, he contends that attachments can be formed between parent and child even if they see each other only a short time each day.

Pediatrician T. Berry Brazelton echoes this view. If the parent is basically loving, even an hour in the morning and an hour in the evening may be sufficient for attachment to take place.

Rudolph Schaffer, professor of psychology at the University of Strathclyde, Glasgow, has found that children can make *multiple attachments* (29 percent of the infants he studied formed several attachments at the same time; 87 percent had formed multiple attachments by the age of eighteen months).

The conclusion being drawn today is that if the baby can indeed successfully become attached to a number of people, he can receive comfort from them, too. Thus, if there is consistency of care—if there is a small core of constant caregivers, including the parents—the child will develop a number of emotional investments and will be able to build the trust necessary for healthy emotional growth. Or, as one young mother said, "I've discovered there's no limit to a baby's love. The more people he has to love, the better."

WHY WE WORK—A CHILD'S-EYE VIEW

How your child reacts to you working is strongly colored by his conception of *why* you're going off to a job. You'll want to give careful thought to explaining it to him—but don't make the mistake of getting overly involved in explanations beyond his grasp. The eleven-year-old has little trouble understanding "We need a second income to help pay for your brother's college education and for your summer camp." She may even be able to sympathize with her mother's need for a life separate from that of the family.

But let a mother who is the sole support of her three-year-old son tell him that she's working because she needs the money and he might make her a present of $100 in play money as an inducement to stay home (one inventive youngster did just that, and gift-wrapped the package, too!). Instead, the preschooler will accept the entire concept better if you present it matter-of-factly and with as little explanation as possible: "Mommy goes to work, Johnny stays home and plays with the baby-sitter. . . ."

The school-age child isn't swayed by lengthy explanations, either, but will respond easily to the fruits of her mother's labors. Says one woman, a long-time victim of guilt despite her financial need to work: "I only started to feel better when Joanie was old enough to understand that the $35 ice skates, the skiing trips—all the extras that she was enjoying—were coming from my salary."

Fortunately, older children can understand our need for fulfilling work, and some can even identify with it. Belinda, a talented commercial artist, confided her discouragement over a difficult project one bleak day to her twelve-year-old daughter and was gratified to hear her say, "But Mom, you know you love your work . . . it's so creative." A few years earlier, the same complaint would probably have only confused this youngster, who was still grappling with the reality of her mother's absence.

SOME GUT ISSUES

Career-Family Conflicts. No matter what contortions you go through to avoid these dilemmas, you are sure at some point to come up against the school play that coincides with your annual sales conference, the stomachache that befalls your son on the first day of an important busi-

BOOKS FOR CHILDREN

Introduce young children, through these words and pictures, to the idea that women can hold satisfying and useful jobs, and be mothers and wives as well. In these books, youngsters will meet women in diverse fields, from letter carriers and riveters to orchestra conductors and eye surgeons.

Mothers Can Do Anything, Joe Lasker (Whitman, 1972).

Mommies at Work, Eve Merriam (Knopf, 1973).

Girls Can Be Anything, Norma Klein (Dutton, 1973).

Women at Their Work, Betty Lou English (Dial, 1977).

---

ness trip. These kinds of career-family conflicts are a fact of life for every working mother. But if you handle them sensibly and honestly, they'll be a lot less troublesome to you and your children.

If you must leave your child at a time when both of you would prefer to be together, sharing your own feelings about the conflict is often the best course of action. You can say: "I know how you feel. I wish I could stay home with you. But this is one day I can't do that. And I understand you feel bad about this. But I think you will feel better by tomorrow." Assuring your son or daughter that this will not happen all the time will also help. So may a promise of spending some extra time alone with your children. You might add: "How about if, on Saturday, you and I go downtown and go shopping, just the two of us, and have lunch in a restaurant?" If this plan is made out of your own real desire to be with your child, rather than from guilt or obligation, you will usually find that he will harbor little resentment.

Bringing a present from the office is another way of telling a child you care about him. (Don't make the mistake of thinking a goody from Mommy is an admission of guilt. No one suggests that your son is guilt-ridden when he brings home his latest collection of finger paintings.) Keep the gifts simple—a puzzle, a comic book, some colored pens; but don't fall into the pattern of bringing something home every day, or you'll wind up like the poor woman whose children's outstretched hands and cries of "What did you bring me?" greeted her before she could even pull her car into the garage.

If you are afraid that your child will be frustrated or resentful because you work, remind yourself that children whose every need is always met never have the opportunity to find their own solutions to problems. If, for example, you take a day off from work every time your daughter seems to miss you, she will never learn to deal with these uncomfortable emotions. Nor will she learn how to use her own resources to make herself feel better. Children grow from experiencing stress, and they are reassured by learning that they can deal with it well.

Mothers who worry a great deal about the effects their working may have on their children may actually be worrying about their own basic competence as parents. Participating in an interactive parents' workshop can be a valuable confidence builder. So can the more programmed courses in parenting effectiveness, particularly for parents of older children. For more information on these write to: Parent Effectiveness Training Information, 531 Stevens Avenue, Solana Beach, California 92075.

Fostering Independence.   There is no doubt that, whether out of conviction or necessity, most women find themselves being less overprotective and more encouraging of their children's independence once they start working. This development is usually all to the good in a society where the trend has been to make full-time mothers their children's full-time servants—and children often grow up to be overly dependent young people, clinging to mothers who are reluctant to let go. A thirty-six-year-old social worker remarks: "Now that I have more control over my life, I've stopped needing to control my kids. I tended to be a dominating, over-organized force in their lives; there was too much input from me. Working's really forced me to let go."

Some women say that their working encourages the children to seek out other adults in their lives—to good effect. Learning to depend on neighbors, sitters, or other children's parents helps youngsters cope successfully with the world about them, not just with their own families.

The fact that working mothers are usually happy to see their kids' growing independence contributes to the children's confidence. Say researchers Lois Hoffman and Ivan Nye in *Working Mothers:* "To the non-working mother the move from protector and nurturer to independence trainer is often difficult. For the working mother, however, the child's growing independence eases her role strain."

With a little thought, you can help your child get used to his new independence. Following in a second bus when your daughter takes her first bus ride alone . . . making a few phone calls to the child who stays home alone . . . entrusting a child with a long supermarket list (and being tolerant about mistakes)—show your child that you trust and can depend on him while at the same time giving him your support and love.

Independence, of course, is a relative matter. As Dr. Lee Salk and other experts caution us, children must be allowed to be dependent before they can learn to be independent. Mothers who have given their children a firm base of security—whether by staying home for the first years, by establishing a pattern of consistent, attentive care from other adults, or by making every effort to be available to their children on a regular basis—report that the move to increasing independence comes with very little difficulty.

Don't be too quick to force independence on your child. Be realistic about his capabilities. Allowing a four-year-old to walk a mile to school alone is foolhardy, no matter how much time it saves you and how willing he is to do it. On the other hand, you can say to an eight-year-old: "You are old enough now to go to the dentist by yourself." And you can help him by adding, "I will show you exactly how to get there and how to get home." The first time your youngster goes to the dentist alone, you may both feel uneasy. The second time, he'll probably regard it as routine. And by the third time, he'll turn his nose up at his friends who are still escorted by mothers.

Consult a basic book on child development (see page 146) if you have any doubt about when you can expect your child to handle certain tasks, but remember that children differ enormously, and the experts give you only broad guidelines about ranges of social, cognitive, and physical growth. Discuss individual issues with your pediatrician for professional feedback. And trust your own children to tell you when they are ready for the next step.

Emotional Problems.   Most of us would agree that our children's growing independence is a positive element in their lives. But what about the other side of the coin? Does a loosening of the apron strings lead to emotional problems? Will your son or daughter's need for your attention lead to trouble at school and at home?

In fact, no studies support psychologist Lee Salk's contention that children of working mothers will "use physical complaints to get [their] busy parents' recognition." Moreover, there is no evidence at all that "being destructive" or "getting into trouble at school" is any more prevalent among children whose mothers work than among those whose mothers are home all day.

However, if your child does misbehave or seems unhappy, it may well be his way of telling you he wants more attention from you. And remember that kids deliver their emotional messages in all sorts of ways.

There was no mistaking the meaning of two-and-a-half-year-old David's howls of "Me! Me! Me!" as he grabbed the telephone out of his mother's hand. Or of seven-year-old Lisa's simple request: "Why can't you take me to school? I want to be a walking child, not a busing child." Sulking, misbehaving, and acting out can be subtler indications that a young child needs more attention from his mother. Nightmares, toilet-training difficulties, and eating problems should also be a warning to you that something is amiss. Here are some general danger signs to watch out for:

- any persistent change in eating or sleeping habits
- aggressive or destructive behavior
- excessively obedient behavior
- listlessness or a tendency to withdraw
- excessive fearfulness or timidity

Children require more than attention, though; they also need limits. And here is where many working mothers fall down on the job. Eager to compensate to their children for the time not spent with them, they sometimes fail to make clear what they can and cannot do—with unfortunate results. Children to whom "I said no, and that's final" is a foreign language, eight-year-olds who stretch "five more minutes" to a two-hour sprawl in front of the television set—in short, children who have turned their mothers' guilt into a powerful weapon of their own—make life difficult for themselves and everyone around them.

Don't wait for problems to become full-blown before you take action. If your daughter keeps saying, "I wish you could stay home with me today," take a good look at your childcare arrangement. Maybe a change is in order. If your son keeps complaining about school, don't wait for him to start cutting classes. Have a talk with the teacher. Right now.

Be on guard for what your kids *don't* say, too. The school child who withdraws and the baby who never cries (but rarely smiles, either) may be telling you a lot more than the screamers and complainers. If you set aside time just to play or talk with an uncommunicative child, you will most likely find out what's bothering him.

Women who are not defensive about working report that they have few unusual problems with their children's behavior. Part of the reason is that priorities shift slightly when both parents work. As one mother says, "I'm more able to tolerate my children's little behavior problems because I'm not with them all day."

NEW WAYS TO BE TOGETHER

For the children of nonworking mothers, daily life means Life with Mother—an accepted and taken-for-granted reality. Children of job-holding mothers have a different reality. And how well they adapt to it depends a lot on how willing everyone in the family is to devise new ways of relating to one another.

You can make your working a positive experience for the entire family, but only if you are willing to restructure schedules, rethink priorities, let go of old prejudices. This may mean allowing young children to stay up till ten in the evening, substituting a giant Monopoly game and a living-room-floor picnic for a traditional Sunday dinner, or taking a week's vacation with your daughter, while your husband stays home with your son.

Pay careful attention to your child to discover what his needs are. Don't make any assumptions based on someone else's experience. Try to find out what your own children care about.

"It's funny," remarks Alice, a Dallas bank clerk whose two-year-old son shares his mother's shy smile and expressive eyes, "I'd expected Ben to cry for me as I left the house. But he'd cry *after* I was gone. So I figured out that he missed our cozy breakfasts together. And, to be honest, I missed them, too. Gulping a cup of coffee and tossing him a bottle left me feeling sort of empty."

Alice mentioned the problem to her pediatrician, who came up with a simple solution. "It was so simple, I don't know why I didn't think of it myself," Alice confesses with embarrassment. "He told me to get up an hour earlier so that I could have breakfast with Ben." That extra hour gives Alice a chance to socialize with Ben without pressure, and even to catch up on household chores.

If you aren't sure how your children would like you to spend time with them, try asking them directly. "Don't ask the experts," cautions a family counselor. "They don't know *your* kids. Ask the kids themselves. They'll tell you more than anyone else can. If you really listen to what your children have to say, you'll be able to learn what's bothering them and what they need."

KEEPING IN TOUCH

How do you keep in touch with your children when you are gone for up to ten hours each day? Most women answer with two words: "the telephone." "I call it my ten-cent umbilical," says Jennifer, a West Coast legal secretary who emphasizes the importance of calling at a time the child is likely to have something he wants to talk about. "I try to call when he's bubbling over with all the news. You know, like in the old housewife scenario. Hubby calls from the office. 'How are you doing? What's going on?' It makes the wife feel terrific. It's the same thing with the kids."

Mothers of toddlers often wonder whether they should call home every day. Although some children under three may be reassured by a call, many will find their mother's disembodied voice anxiety-produc-

---

CAN A WORKING MOTHER NURSE HER BABY?

Is it possible to breast-feed while you're working? The answer is most emphatically *yes*. In fact, while it may call for careful logistics, nursing can actually make your return to work easier for both yourself and your child. The warmth and intimacy of the nursing relationship helps the baby tolerate your absence, and usually makes him more content and less demanding when you are home.

When you nurse your baby, you and he quickly establish the deep psychological and physical bond so important for both of you. "When I come home," says Shirley, a midwestern teacher who's nursed her daughter for the first year of her life, "I immediately nurse her and we're in touch again instantly." Another benefit for the working mother: the relaxation and serenity that come after a hard day at work. "I sink into a comfortable chair, with her in my arms," says Shirley, "and we feel at one with each other after not seeing each other for six hours."

Here are some pointers for successful breast-feeding:

As soon as possible after the baby's birth, learn how to express milk from your breasts and to store it in the refrigerator or freezer (a nurse in the hospital or another nursing mother can show you how). Accustom your baby to a relief bottle as soon as possible after birth. This may be a formula feeding (prefilled bottles that don't require refrigeration are now widely available) or a bottle of breast milk.

If possible, rearrange your schedule to accommodate the nursing relationship. One woman leaves her baby with a sitter only five minutes away from the factory at which she works. She's arranged with her employer to combine her lunch hour and two fifteen-minute breaks into two forty-five-minute breaks during the day. With five minutes to the sitter's house and five minutes back, she has thirty-five minutes to nurse her baby twice a day.

Take especially good care of your own health during the nursing period. Try to get as much rest as possible (avoid social engagements and other obligations during this time). Make sure your diet is well balanced, and for extra energy, try a supernutritious drink of fruit juice and brewer's yeast.

La Leche League, a worldwide organization dedicated to helping nursing mothers and their families, offers support and reassurance in the form of educational pamphlets, workshops, lectures, and personal counseling. If you live in a large metropolitan area, you can find the address of your local La Leche representative in the phone book. Or contact La Leche International, Inc., 961 Minneapolis Avenue, Franklin Park, Illinois 60131.

For more information on nursing, read *Nursing Your Baby* (Pocket Books, 1976) or *The Womanly Art of Breast Feeding,* available by mail from La Leche International ($3).

---

ing. Lorraine, an executive secretary, had always made sure to call her ten-month-old son each day. "He was too young to answer back then," she recalled. But he certainly wasn't too young to cry. And that's what he did. "The sitter said he'd whimper and look sad after I called," says Lorraine. "Finally I decided that this need to call him was really my own ego trip. I think I was afraid he'd forget who I was."

Lorraine wisely took her own realizations seriously and stopped telephoning home until her son was old enough to talk to her comfortably. But other women are compelled, either by feelings of guilt or by their own needs, to maintain telephone contact regardless of whether it makes them and their children feel good.

One woman described a common reaction: "Every time I called, Josh would say the same thing—'When are you coming home?' He never seemed glad to hear from me, and I'd hang up feeling guilty and miserable." A good solution is to have your child call you, so that the contact is based on his need rather than yours. If possible, share this task with your husband: Your child calls him on certain days, you on the others.

NIGHTS AND WEEKENDS

Mothers who are home all day are always available for their children's questions, for shared confidences that tell a child he is loved and cared about. When you are out of the house all day, you have only the weekends and evenings in which to establish this kind of open communication. But this is no reason you and your children can't build strong and enduring relationships with each other. Just remember that, like all relationships, these take work—and a bit of planning.

The Reentry Frenzies. MOMMY'S HOME—EVERYBODY CRY, announced a headline in a recent issue of *Family Circle*. And thousands of readers grimaced in recognition. For some women, the hardest thing about going to work is coming home.

Jacqueline, a Memphis personnel director and the mother of two boys, eight and nine, and a five-year-old girl, describes an all-too-familiar scene: "Everything would be quiet and calm, and I'd come home and suddenly everything would go crazy. Kids whining, screaming, hitting me. Once I literally took my coat and walked out."

Jacqueline used to feel as if her children were saying "Who needs you? Why did you come home? All was settled until you came home." But she's come to understand the phenomenon better. Children need to let out all their feelings, to air their grievances and their triumphs many times during the day, but they learn to keep some of this emotion under control when they're with teachers and baby-sitters. A parent gives unconditional love. Your children know that no matter what they do, you will not reject them. And when Mommy walks in that front door, it is a signal to them to release the energy and passion they have been holding back.

Once you understand what the end-of-the-day frenzies are all about, it becomes easier to deal with them. As three pairs of sticky hands grab at your purse for the presents you promised to bring home, as your oldest asks you if he can sleep at his friend's house next Friday, your youngest tries to tell you how the plumber had to come because the toilet water came up over the seat and flooded the whole nursery school, and your sitter reminds you that she's taking tomorrow off, you try to sort out the voices from the cacophony and keep telling yourself that since you can't fight it, you might as well join it. Mothers who devote the first half-hour or so to their children—answering questions, running in to see what they built with their blocks, even getting down on the floor for a quick game—find the rest of the evening goes much more smoothly.

Other parents try to defer focusing their complete attention on their children until they can make a civilized reentry. Generally, the older—and fewer—the children, the easier this is. Still, one must admire the willpower of the divorced mother of three school-age girls who says: "I made an agreement with them that they'll leave me alone for the first hour. We say hello and then they go to their homework and I start dinner. By the time they're into the homework, the dinner's cooking and I'm ready to help or hear about their day." She adds that because she is so much more cheerful, they have learned to accept this "Mommy's hour."

Here are some tried-and-true strategies to help you make the most of your time with your children:

Use travel time to be companionable with your child. When you take a child to school or day care or pick him up at the end of the day (even if he's old enough to make the trip himself), you have a chance to talk more comfortably than at home, where there are all those household distractions.

Be flexible about schedules. Nothing traps a working mother more than a rigid attachment to set routines. Margaret, an advertising copywriter, was able to rearrange her nine-month-old son's nap and feeding times so that he would be awake during her at-home hours. If she had let the baby nap early in the day, he would have gone to sleep at seven-thirty, just as Margaret and her husband were gearing up to be with him.

Pediatrician T. Berry Brazelton agrees with this practice. In *Who Cares for the Baby?* he says: "When I see a mother who is working I tell her to tell her sitter or her day-care operator to give the baby a good two-to-three hour nap and then the child will stay up to 9 o'clock at night so that they have the time together . . . there's no reason to be so rigid and so fixed in our ideas about what can and can't be done, if you have priorities . . . and you value the quality of family interaction."

Reserve at least part of the evening just to be with your children. For the working mother, evening activities such as helping with the homework, giving a bath, and telling a bedtime story take on added significance. Don't rush through the evenings. Be available to your children—for your sake as well as theirs. "Bath time in our house used to sound like a speeded-up movie," admits Nina, the mother of a five-year-old boy. "I had so much to do at night, and I was frantic that I wouldn't get it finished, so I rushed and screamed at Andrew when he dawdled. When I read a story, it sounded like a *Reader's Digest* condensed book. I managed to reduce *Dumbo* to four minutes."

Nina, like many women juggling two roles, was obsessed about time—or the lack of it. But even as she was finding time for her chores, she was losing her child. "I may have suffered during that period more than he did," Nina told us. "He kind of adjusted; it was I who missed the bedtime stories, the friendly bath times. One day Andrew said casually, reminding me of a game we used to play with the boats in his bath, 'That was when you were my Mommy; now you're my Nina.' That did it. I decided then and there to give myself back to my son . . . and him to me. I've just stopped worrying about the wash or dinners. No one ever cared about all that stuff but me anyway."

Avoid phone calls or guests during the time you've set aside to be with your child. Sounds easy? Not always. The women we interviewed were nearly unanimous in their intention to do just this . . . and in their frequent lapses.

Children's jealousy of the phone, especially when it's pressed to the ear of a parent they haven't seen all day, is nearly universal, and retribution is usually quick. "My three-year-old calmly flooded the kitchen floor while I was talking on the phone," recalls Deena, a good-humored midwesterner who works as a receptionist in a large manufacturing firm. "I was furious, but I understood . . . he hadn't seen me all day and he felt entitled to my attention. And he was right."

It helps to tell friends not to call during the hours you've reserved for your children, and to dismiss other callers with a polite "I'll call you back later or in the morning." If you are still plagued by interruptions, try taking the phone off the hook. Or use a telephone-answering service or recording machine.

Make some evening and weekend activities a shared experience.

This again calls for flexibility. If you insist on eating promptly at six, you and the children may miss out on the fun of a predinner jog through the park.

Realistically, it's not always possible for the whole family to sit down to dinner together. Children are notorious for being ravenously hungry as you walk in the door and demanding food before you can manage to plunk a hamburger on the table. If you force them to wait until seven o'clock, you may find yourself eating with small people who have already consumed half a loaf of bread and several hunks of raw chopmeat. Encouraging the children to eat nutritious snacks after school may solve this problem. So may letting your sitter feed them before you get home. They can then join you for dessert when you and your husband eat dinner later on.

Don't worry if the time you spend together is hectic, as long as you are satisfied that each child gets at least some time alone with a parent. "Some of our best evenings have been the wildest," says a mother whose family sometimes picnics in a nearby park on pleasant evenings. "All of us in the kitchen making sandwiches together, the kids all trying to talk to us at once; but there's an awful lot of love and warmth flying around during those times."

Be available to your children in a way that's comfortable for you. You may not choose to include your children in adult activities; this kind of togetherness is certainly not everyone's cup of tea. Nor may you be able to tolerate long stretches of time when everyone in the family is together. Most of the mothers we met tried to make Saturday and Sunday family time, but several admitted to suffering from overdoses of togetherness if they tried to spend every waking hour with their children.

Fiona, the mother of three active youngsters, had a whole list of "shoulds" for the weekend hours. "I was convinced," she told us, "that if I didn't make a big Sunday dinner—a roast with all the trimmings—to make up for not cooking all week, I wasn't really a mother. That I was cheating my family. And so every Sunday I'd slave in the kitchen, and we'd all sit down to dinner, like a Norman Rockwell painting. And then my son would start fighting with my daughter. And my husband would scream at my son because he was talking with food in his mouth. None of the feelings I wanted to be at the table were there."

Fiona found a solution by varying the Sunday activities. There was much less tension when the whole family went to a movie or an ice show and then stopped for a quick bite at a Burger King or a Chinese restaurant. Fiona was able to preserve her dream of togetherness without assuming the control herself and thus putting strain on the entire family. And she found that their time spent together was now more likely to be "quality time."

WHAT IS QUALITY TIME?

What do we mean when we say "quality time," a phrase working mothers seem to use a great deal? Quality time is best defined by what it is not. The quality in time has nothing to do with ballet lessons or fancy summer camps or lavish parties. It may well be the two hours spent sitting next to your daughter at the hottest play in town, but it can just as easily be the twenty minutes you spend perched on the edge of the bathtub while your four-year-old is taking a bath.

Spending quality time with a child means simply *being with him, showing him that you care about him, that you are interested in what he is doing, in what he has to say.* It hardly matters what you are doing with the child, as long as your attention is given over to the relationship between you.

Don't make the mistake of thinking that because your children are involved in their own activities, you are not needed. This is a particular pitfall with school-age kids, who sometimes seems to need no more contact with their mothers than a passing "Hi, Mom, what's for dinner?"

Actually, nothing could be further from the truth. Warns a family counselor who deals with many children of working parents: "Mothers and fathers who see their children so absorbed in activities with their friends should remember that parental attention serves a different purpose. . . . Parents are needed to give children the adult guidance and affection they need to negotiate the difficult task of growing up.

Successful families in which both parents work have devised new ways to spend quality time with their children.

One-on-One. Quality time can mean simply one parent, one child, and no distractions. A family dinner, no matter how tasty or how long you've labored to prepare it, will be a lot less appealing to your nine-year-old than a date in a restaurant with just you and no other siblings. A three-year-old will delight in a trip with his father to a nearby ice-cream parlor.

One mother has devised an ingenious night of Christmas shopping—in June, when the stores are not crowded and she and her daughter can browse happily while checking off their holiday purchases. Another mother makes a point of taking a taxi from her office to meet her daughter for a school-day lunch date. Other possibilities: check your local museum for a night in the week they stay open; let your husband take one child to a basketball game while you escort the other to a movie. Resist the impulse to combine forces; remember, the point is to enjoy the intimacy of a night alone with one child.

Times That Matter. Every child gets special pleasure from sharing certain activities with a parent. Your son may learn to ice skate more efficiently if he takes professional lessons, but you and he will always cherish the memory of staggering around the ice together that winter you taught him to skate. And your daughter will surely never forget her father running after that precariously balanced first two-wheeler. Learning to skate or ride a bike or swim are milestones in a youngster's life. Find the time on weekends or evenings to participate in these events with your children.

Children also care about holidays. Making a jack-o-lantern, buying and decorating a Christmas tree, filling up an Easter basket are activities that even the busiest parent can squeeze into a crowded schedule.

Fun and Games. Many of us are so busy we forget that playing games with our children is a valuable family experience. When you and your kids play games together, remember, once again, to be flexible. You'll never enjoy an all-family poker game if you try to convince your seven-year-old son not to pull to an inside straight!

Sara Friedman, author of *How Was School Today, Dear? (Fine, What's for Dinner)*, in which she details new ways of enriching the lives of both children and their parents, has this to say about the benefits of game playing:

"We play a lot of games in our family, in two's, three's, and all together. We argue a lot; some of us cheat; some of us are terrible losers. But we also find the experience a valuable means of communicating when we don't feel like talking. Playing games with our kids helps them channel their competitive and aggressive drives toward the world in general, toward each other, toward us in particular—not to mention ours toward them. Family games also help our kids work out growing pains and develop intellectual skills. They give our kids the chance to be on equal footing with us. And most important, they seem to give us all a chance to explore and work out naturally many of the complex family dynamics—both stressful and affectionate—that seem to smolder unheeded in so many families."

Kids' Time, Parents' Time. In our eagerness to spend as much time as possible with our children, some of us are tempted to let them join in all activities. Baking an apple pie together is quality time spent with your eleven-year-old. Allowing a five-year-old to fold the eggs into a soufflé is not. If you absolutely must get that porch railing fixed today, don't try to combine it with a pleasant visit with your toddler. Wait till she naps to do your hammering, and let her keep you company while you sort laundry instead.

KEEPING IN TOUCH WITH SCHOOL

Many a confident working mother is turned into a sniveling wreck by none other than her child's teacher. ("I'm so sorry you won't be able to stay, Mrs. Green; Jennifer would so like you to watch her in the spelling bee.") Or by that formidable adversary, the school nurse. ("Jennifer's throat sounds a little scratchy, Mrs. Green, perhaps you'd better come and get her.") There are women who admit to shedding tears at the very sight of a note that begins with the familiar "Dear Parents: Tomorrow is the fourth-grade play. We very much hope. . . ."

"All the Mommies Were There But You." Writer Linda Bird Francke has said, "There is only one face that the school child who is the third violet from the left on stage, or has four alto recorder notes to blow in the recital is looking for in the audience. And that face belongs to the mother."

Not necessarily. In a truly modern family, those small eyes might just as well search out Daddy's face. Or Grandma's. Or even a favorite baby-sitter's. But certainly you want to be present for school events, not only because they are important to your child, but also because missing them is missing out on the joy of sharing in your child's life.

In the beginning of the school year, *inform the teacher that you are eager to attend all functions, but that you must have ample notice so that you can make arrangements.* Insist that you be notified about meetings, plays, and recitals with both a note and a reminder note (don't count on your child to tell you about these events). Giving the same information to the class mother will also help.

Encourage your husband or other relatives and friends to stand in for you on those occasions when you cannot be in attendance. Knowing that the grown-ups in his life care about him in this way will help your child feel secure and loved, and will add an unexpected pleasure to the visiting adults' life as well.

Get involved in school affairs. If your time is very limited, leave the cake sales to less busy parents, but try to attend Parents' Association meetings or any other community events that affect school policy. Not only will this give you a needed say in what happens in your children's school, but it also reassures your children that you care deeply about an important aspect of their lives. "My kids always seem pleased when I tell them I'm going to a meeting at their school," comments one mother. "I think they see my going as a kind of involvement in their lives."

If you can't manage to bake the brownies or sell the raffles, support the parents who do. Offer your home for a special event; agree to chauffeur parents who don't have cars; donate money in lieu of your services.

Keep in touch with the teacher. Make sure he or she knows that you are a working mother who happens to be concerned about your child. Explain that you want to be kept informed about both progress and problems (if you're lucky, you'll then hear about Johnnie's star performance in the math test, not just about his abominable behavior in gym). Give the teacher your phone number, ask her for hers, and suggest that you and she confer on a regular basis.

If you want to participate in classroom activities and are not sure what's important to your child, enlist the teacher's help in finding out what's likely to be most meaningful. One mother simply said to the teacher, "Look, I want to do as much as I can. What do you think is most important? Tell me, and I'll do it." That way she found out about the most interesting class trips and can sometimes manage to take a few hours off to accompany the class. "I also found out," she told us, "that my son was intensely interested in the Rocky Mountains and in mountaineering, which the class was studying that term. And I sent along some slides we had taken on a trip last summer."

Share with the teacher information about changes in your home life that might affect your child's performance in the classroom. A new baby, a divorce, moving to a new home, even a change in your husband's or your own job situation can have an impact on your child.

KIDS NEED A SOCIAL LIFE, TOO

Young children need their parents to participate in their social lives. And even teenagers will appreciate friendly advice on party-giving or dating.

Joan, a Florida physical therapist whose private practice and hospital affiliation keep her busy more than nine hours most days, still manages to get involved in the social lives of her two boys, ages six and nine. "I find time for birthday parties," she says, "no matter how hard it is to get the whole act together. But you know they expect birthday parties; every kid does. It's other kinds of social things that they really get a kick out of."

Joan not only manages a full-scale birthday celebration for each boy, but she, her husband, and the kids plan and enjoy a Halloween party ("We put in a red light bulb and my husband tells scary stories . . . the kids love it"), a Christmas-tree-trimming get-together for children and adults, and even an occasional sleep-over for a handful of boys.

Is Joan a "supermom"? Definitely not. "My closets are a mess. The fanciest meal I've cooked in three years was veal scallops with mushrooms, which my kids hated. And there are days I cry a lot because I'm exhausted and there's so much to get done. . . ."

But Joan made a decision some time ago to turn her back on clean closets and lavish meals—things her children cared little about—and to funnel some of that energy into helping her children have fun.

FIVE SURE-FIRE HINTS FOR A SUCCESSFUL CHILDREN'S PARTY

1. *Observe the Golden Rule of Number.* The number of children invited should equal the age of your child. Thus, if you are celebrating your son's fifth birthday, there should be a total of six children; at your ten-year-old's party there will be eleven children. The rule is not inviolate (that ten-year-old may prefer three close friends and a trip to a hockey game), but it's a useful standard to remember the next time you are tempted to stage a large bash for a small child.

2. *Send out written invitations.* Kids get a kick out of buying or making these. And you will find that addressing them actually takes less time than making phone calls.
3. *Decorate with balloons.* Balloons make for an instant festive look, and children of all ages seem to enjoy playing with them. Festoon the table and the walls with brightly colored balloons (they'll stick to the walls simply by rubbing them gently against them) and let the children take them home as favors.
4. *Hire a teenager to help with games and cleanup.* Even five four-year-olds can be a handful to entertain. Your neighbor's twelve-year-old may be delighted to help out for a small fee, and you will find yourself enjoying the party more if you have an extra pair of hands to tie on blindfolds or dish out ice cream.
5. *Limit the menu.* Pizza, hot dogs, and peanut-butter-and-jelly sandwiches satisfy as readily as fried chicken or hamburgers, and are a lot easier to prepare and serve. And if you serve ice cream cake instead of ice cream and cake, you'll be guaranteed no leftovers.

HARD TIMES—
AND HOW TO COPE WITH THEM

"My life is like a delicate well-built house of cards. One thing goes wrong and it all collapses."

"I get so frantic when somebody gets sick that I've stopped taking temperatures."

"Right after Thanksgiving I start worrying about Christmas vacation . . . the closer it gets the more desperate I feel."

Sound familiar? Juggling roles is difficult enough when everything is going well; when we are struck by circumstances beyond our control, the best of us have been known to falter. Even supermoms push the panic button when a child is sick. And there's hardly a working mother who has not agonized through the day-by-day planning of a school vacation. But the wisest working mothers have learned to cope with these hard times by constantly reminding themselves that: (1) their nonworking sisters are probably not managing any better than they are; they're just worrying about it less; and (2) mobilizing resources and tackling problems immediately is the best antidote to panic.

When a Child Is Ill. The glazed eyes of a feverish five-year-old, the croupy cough of an infant's bronchitis, hold special terror for the working mother. Says one: "Even as I'm shaking down the thermometer, all I can think of is which of us—my husband or me—will stay home tomorrow."

Not all of us can be as enterprising as the Baltimore judge whose daughter recovered from the chicken pox in her mother's chambers ("I granted every request for a recess for three days"). Or as lucky as the New York account executive whose boss thinks so much of her he pays for a sitter when her children are sick. But most working mothers do cope when their children are ill. Many feel perfectly comfortable leaving a child with the regular sitter, or with someone called upon for the occasion (experienced working mothers have long lists of emergency backup help). Many day-care centers have sick bays that can take care of children who don't have a serious or contagious illness. Some mothers even let a child who's feeling under the weather accompany them to the office for the day (see pages 170–174 for advice on bringing kids to work).

Many of us cherish memories of our own mothers sitting at our bedsides, faithfully spooning out medicines and helping us with our coloring books. But many children actually prefer to be left alone with a good book or a rare chance to watch TV for a whole day.

Children under the age of eight or so usually cannot stay at home alone. And even if you have a trusted person fill in for you, you may want to give your child some extra emotional support when she is sick. A good way to manage this is to stay home for a few hours: Your child gets the clear message that you care about him and are there to keep him company while he is feeling so miserable, and you are still able to fulfill your obligations at the office. If your child must be home for a few days, try to take turns caring for her with your husband.

If you do leave a child home alone in bed, be sure to call home periodically ("I let him stay in my bed, which is next to the phone, so he won't have to get up to answer it," says one mother) and have the foresight to leave a prepared lunch. Try to arrange for a neighbor to look in on him, and remember to leave plenty of reading material and other in-bed diversions.

Many a parent has found that not coddling the child with a cold or other minor ailment has actually helped him get better faster. Sensible advice along these lines comes from a New York City politician: "I handle it exactly the way my mother did. I remember it was extremely

STAYING IN TOUCH WITH TEENAGERS

We all expect an attack of guilt when we go off to work and leave a whimpering two-year-old behind. Or when our nine-year-old daughter reproaches us for never having time to help with her homework. But the truth is that nothing chills the working mother's blood quite as quickly as the sullen glances of a hostile fourteen-year-old girl. Or the look of disdain on the face of a teenage boy when we ask whom he's seeing tonight!

To many of us struggling to raise our children while satisfying our own career needs, it seems as if our adolescent offspring are pushing us away and embracing us at the very same time. Which is exactly what's happening.

Teenagers are engaged in their own struggle to establish their identities separate from ours, yet based on our role models. Even as your daughter dismisses your job as "gross and boring," she may really be planning to follow right along in your footsteps (studies show that adolescent daughters of working mothers are more likely than those of nonworking women to name mother as the person they most admire). Your son's offhanded "Yeah, my mother runs a travel agency" probably barely conceals his pride that you are not "just a housewife."

Dealing with teenagers is no picnic for any parent. For the wage-earning mother, it presents special problems. Here are a few guidelines:

- If you have only recently returned to work, you and your youngster may find yourselves clashing in the identity-seeking arena. Two people "searching for themselves" in the same household is potentially explosive. In the beginning, *be especially sensitive to this conflict by putting your child's needs before your own.* Don't talk too much about your job; be available to hear about your son's or daughter's plans and aspirations.
- *Don't make the mistake of assuming your teenager wants you out of his hair all the time.* In fact, his fear of freedom can be as fierce as his demand for it. And while he may appreciate the privacy of an empty house, he very much needs to know you haven't forgotten him entirely. Leave him a note or call him from the office— not to check up but to check in and enjoy a friendly moment.
- *Keep the lines of communication open.* You may be surprised at how interested your teenage children are in what you do and whom you do it with. When you share with them the meaningful and daily events of your life, they are more comfortable about confiding in you. Try inviting a teenager to your office for the afternoon, and follow this by dinner in town for just the two of you.
- Drugs and sex are serious concerns for all parents of adolescents, not just those who are absent during the day. It is a fact that more

and more teenagers are experimenting with alcohol, marijuana, and sexual activity, but whether or not this becomes a problem in your family has a lot more to do with the values you impart and the standards you set than with how many hours you spend at home.

If you *present the real dangers of drug and alcohol abuse to your teenager in a nonjudgmental, matter-of-fact way,* you'll have more of an impact than if you nag or try to spy on him. Similarly, acknowledging turbulent sexual feelings, while at the same time setting down rules about curfews, dating, and partying, will demonstrate both your respect and your concern.

---

disappointing, but I also remember surviving it. The general message is, 'You're sick, but I'm not and I'm going to work, and you stay home and I will call you twice during the day, and you can have ice cream for your throat. And you'll be much happier and much less bored when you're back in school.' " She reports that, like herself as a child, her children tend to have few illnesses and to recover from them very quickly.

School Vacations.   Try trading off with a nonworking mother (you take her children on Saturday or Sunday) or teaming up with another working parent to hire a high-school student who can entertain your children for the day. If your children attend an after-school center, check their schedule; many centers offer a full-day program on days that schools are closed.

Keeping children happily occupied during the Christmas and Easter vacations presents more of a problem than do one-day holidays. An obvious solution, of course, is for the whole family to take their vacation at this time. Less obvious is for one parent to take a vacation with the children during Christmas, the other during Easter week.

Older children present a special problem for working parents, since they may be too young to amuse themselves or to find jobs easily and too old for traditional camp experiences.

Writing in *Working Woman* magazine, psychiatrist Stella Chess provides practical advice for the parents of young teenagers in a quandary about summer vacations. She suggests that they first check into their local People's Yellow Pages or other directory of agencies and programs that serve parents and children, and then offers the following recommendations:

> *Volunteering.* Hospitals, nursing homes, and child-care agencies welcome aides. Youngsters can tutor children, help in arts-and-crafts programs, assist in laboratories—while gaining valuable work experience.
>
> *Summer school.* Not as grim as it sounds. Here's a chance for your child to catch up on problem subjects, or to study photography, typing, ceramics, video, dance, or other subjects she wouldn't ordinarily encounter.
>
> *Part-time work.* Mowing lawns, delivering groceries, baby-sitting give youngsters a chance to earn money and practice independence.

STRATEGIES FOR SCHOOL VACATIONS

Plan ahead. Avoid the panic of last-minute preparations by taking the time well in advance to schedule entertainment, hire helpers, make arrangements. Don't get caught short by an unexpected one-day holiday: Post your child's school calendar in a place you can always see it.

Do your homework. Look into community services—YMCAs often have inexpensive Christmas and summer programs; churches and synagogues operate sleep-away and day camps. Check the classified section of your local paper for parent cooperatives, or try forming one of your own.

Combine forces or trade off with another family. You take Christmas, they take Easter. Sharing a summer rental or taking turns vacationing with a brood of kids is a good way to give your children new experiences—and to save money at the same time.

Hire a mother's helper. This can make the difference between a boring vacation for your children (plus guilt and aggravation for you) and a fun-filled week of activities. You'll need an older student (preferably one who drives) for longer vacations, but even a twelve-year-old can manage to sustain enough interest and assume enough responsibility to entertain small children for a few days.

Cautions Dr. Chess: "Be sure that the activities you plan leave free time. Vacation isn't vacation if every minute is scheduled, no matter how pleasant the program."

THE BOTTOM LINE

As we develop new kinds of relationships with our families and discover new ways of being together, we learn that the road to work is not the road to ruin for our children. We find out that children are resilient; they are far more adaptable than many of us realize. They do not need our constant attention to grow into self-reliant, self-respecting adults. They do need our love and the devotion and protection of other adults in their world. And this we can give them whether or not we hold jobs outside our homes.

But we can also give them something else: models of ourselves as creative, satisfied women, models that will help them make intelligent choices for their own futures. We can, by our own example, show them men and women breaking away from traditional patterns, so that they can ultimately enrich their own lives and the lives of their children. We can give them the space to experience loneliness, to suffer some of life's disappointments, and to learn and gain strength from these experiences.

And, finally, because we must demand their cooperation, we can teach them to take pride in their own efforts as well as the group endeavors of their families. These are valuable lessons.

BOOKS THAT MAY HELP

How Was School Today, Dear? (Fine, What's for Dinner), Sara Ann Friedman (Reader's Digest Press, 1977). This delightful book about how Ms. Friedman and her husband have enriched their three children's school and home lives is filled with practical tips on turning ordinary family events into educational and enjoyable experiences.

What We Really Know About Child-Rearing, Seymour Fisher and Rhoda L. Fisher (Basic Books, 1977). Subtitled "Science in Support of Effective Parenting," this sound work offers much useful information on parenting, from new insights into discipline to fresh ideas about helping children succeed in school.

Parents' Yellow Pages, edited by Frank Caplan (Doubleday, 1978). An impressive and enormously useful five-hundred-page compendium of information on 130 subjects, from emergency medical advice to addresses of YMCAs and zoos.

Baby and Child Care, Benjamin Spock, Revised Edition (Pocket Books, 1976). The venerable Dr. Spock has completely revised his best-selling handbook to reflect current child-rearing practice. Gone—at last—are references to sexist practices (fathers can now share equally in child-raising), as well as a negative bias against working mothers.

Between Parent and Child, Haim G. Ginott (Macmillan, 1965). This now-classic book teaches, through easy-to-understand explanations and examples, a simple way to tune in to your children and to understand what they are feeling. Dr. Ginott's *Between Parent and Teenager* (Avon Books, 1971) offers similar guidelines for parents of adolescents.

How to Help Your Child Get the Most Out of School, Stella Chess and Jane Whitbread (Doubleday, 1974). Practical and reassuring advice on everything from learning disabilities to emotional difficulties at school from the noted child psychiatrist.

How to Parent, Fitzhugh Dodson (New American Library, 1970). One of the most sensible and straightforward child-rearing and childcare manuals. Loaded with important information about children ages one to five.

Books on Child Development

These books offer useful information on how young children develop, both psychologically and physically.

The Magic Years, Selma H. Fraiberg (Scribners, 1959).

Infants and Mothers, T. Berry Brazelton (Delacorte, 1973).

Toddlers and Parents, T. Berry Brazelton (Delacorte, 1974).

The Parenting Advisor, Princeton Center for Infancy (Doubleday, 1977).

The First Five Years of Life, Arnold Gesell et al. (Harper, 1940).

The Child from Five to Ten, Arnold Gesell and Francis L. Ilg (Harper, 1946).

Your Career

Chapter Eight
SUCCEEDING ON THE JOB

THE INTERVIEW: GET STARTED RIGHT

Madeleine Engelson, thirty-two and mother of four- and two-year-old daughters, is nervously carrying off her fifth interview for a job as an engineer—a career she left off five years ago. Her interviewer, the president of a small engineering consulting firm, is a rumpled, friendly man in his mid-forties. His desk is haphazardly piled with reports, but their conversation reveals he's on top of his job. Madeleine is clicking off in her head all the things that have come together, as though this job were written to order: The company is growing and she'll have a chance to advance quickly . . . the salary is right . . . even better, the firm's location will let her drop off her daughters right on the way at the family day-care home she's picked.

Her future boss has spoken approvingly of the college where she was trained and of the large corporation where she worked after graduation.

Then the amiable man lights his pipe and says: "All that looks good. But who's going to take care of your children while you're working?"

Madeleine is caught on the horns of a dilemma that will continue to plague mothers for the next few years.

Legally, since the anti-sex discrimination guarantees spurred by the 1964 Civil Rights Act, an interviewer *cannot* ask you about your child-care arrangements any more than he has a right to probe into your birth control practices, your plans for future children, or your religious views. Should you then sit back secure in your legal protection in an interview . . . or volunteer that you have a fail-safe, foolproof baby-sitter?

We'd certainly like to answer with an unequivocal "give them no

149

more than your name and qualifications." But in this still-uncertain transition time, your best strategy is to plan your answer with a good dash of realism.

Caroline Bird, the noted expert on women and work, advises, "Theoretically . . . an employer has no more right to know a woman's maternity plans or how a woman's children are being cared for while she works than he has to know about the childcare arrangements of fathers who apply. Practically, however, a mother can greatly improve her chances of being hired for a responsible job by bringing up the subject herself."

Cynthia Pincus, job counselor to highly trained women students at Yale, also advises caution if you are asked about your family plans in interviews. If you want the job, she suggests, contain your outrage and give a straightforward reply such as, "Yes, I am planning a family and I've decided to continue working as so many women do." Or, "Right now I'm concentrating on my career."

Many women who've survived in the work world agree that *volunteering reassurance to an interviewer that you're well covered on the home front can mean the difference between getting a job and losing it.* Without loss of professional image, you can offer a confident statement that you're ready to meet office demands. Don't elaborate and certainly don't apologize. A personnel director warns, "The worst thing a mother can do is to act apologetic. She should speak confidently as though she's in control, whether she is or not." You might say, "I'm lucky to have an excellent housekeeper who'll be working full-time." Or, "My husband and I have made arrangements for childcare." (It's good to let the interviewer know that your husband's involved in your family responsibilities, too.)

If you've held a job while mothering or have extensive professional training, you can more easily let your qualifications speak for themselves. "An interviewer has no more right to know how my boys will be picked up after school than he does to know my bra size," says a successful TV news writer. These women are on secure ground not only legally but usually professionally. But even they are likely to find the subject of childcare creeping in as their future employers talk with them. A woman personnel director explains, "No personnel interviewer or executive in most corporations is going to ask you outright about how your children will be cared for. But you can expect subtle probing, because frankly it's our job to get to know a person's motivations, to sniff out possible problems in informal interchange."

Only you can decide in a job-hiring situation what the vibes are, whether the interviewer is fishing—and whether you want to make any statements about your home arrangements. If you're newly divorced and have to support yourself and children, you may decide a principled stand is something you can't afford. Know your rights, under Equal Economic Opportunity Commission (EEOC) guidelines (see pages 151–154), and you'll be able to recognize illegal questions and decide then on your own actions.

If you are clearly abused by an interviewer and want to retaliate, send a written complaint, detailing particulars—date, job applied for, interviewer's illicit questions—to your state's fair employment practices agency or to the EEOC in your area (see pages 175–179 for address). Complaints must be filed within 180 days of the incident. You may also address a letter with a carbon copy of your complaint to the interviewer's superior. It's a good bet the superior knows exactly what's going on in interviews, but the prospect of an official complaint will shake him up. As we've seen time and again as women progress in our society, forcing those in authority to comply with the letter of the law forces them to share some of the spirit as well.

A WORKING WOMAN'S BEST FRIEND: TITLE VII

Your basic protection as a working woman is the Civil Rights Act of 1964 (Title VII), which prohibits employment discrimination on the basis of sex, age, religion, race, or national origin. Followed by the Equal Pay Act of 1972 and important court decisions protecting women, Title VII has spurred far-reaching changes in our employment opportunities.

How does Title VII protect you? The act applies to all businesses employing fifteen people or more, to employment agencies and unions, and to most government jobs—in other words, to virtually all jobs except those in very small private businesses. And Title VII protects you in every phase of your working life—advertising for job applicants, interviewing, hiring, on-the-job advancement, pay privileges, benefits.

The important responsibility for interpreting and enforcing Title VII rests with the five-person Equal Employment Opportunity Commission

(EEOC), which has branch offices in thirty-two major cities to handle inquiries and complaints (see pages 175–179). EEOC sets guidelines for employers, investigates complaints of employees and applicants, and institutes legal action against employers accused of discrimination. Know your rights under this landmark legislation.

Getting a Job

Can I be refused a job because it's a "man's job"? "Men's jobs" and "women's jobs" are legally things of the past. Applicants' sex cannot be specified in want ads or job interviews unless being male or female is a *bona fide occupational qualification (BFOQ)*. A male model, a female masseuse for a women's exercise salon, a woman participant in a research study of women are examples of the very few jobs in which sex can be a requirement.

I've known of many employers who object to women workers in general and claim women haven't worked out on the job. Do they have a case? No. The same conviction behind BFOQ rulings led the EEOC to rule that an employer can't refuse to hire women based on assumptions about women in general—for example, that their absenteeism is higher, or that women with young children will have a higher turnover rate.

One man I interviewed with as a product salesman told me he'd like to hire me, but "the men customers wouldn't accept you selling heavy equipment." Could I protest? Yes, you could. An employer can't refuse to hire women on the premise that customers or co-workers prefer male employees. Nor can an employer bar women on the grounds that they're less able at a certain type of work—for example, selling cars.

Can I be turned down for a job because I'm married? Yes, if the same prohibition goes for men. You can be forced to resign when you marry—*if* the same rule applies to men. Since very few employers want to restrict the marital state of male employees, this usually protects women.

Can I be turned down for a job because I am now pregnant? Not legally, unless the employer can prove business necessity.

If they can keep from hiring me because I'm married, can't they make up some rule about not hiring me because I have young children? It's unlawful to refuse to hire women with young children—unless the employer can establish a BFOQ, which is very difficult indeed. Title VII prohibits companies from having one hiring policy for men and another for women. Thus, women with young children cannot be disqualified unless fathers with young children are also barred.

If it's illegal for an employer to ask for a man for a job, why do I have to fill out forms that ask "Male-Female" or have me check Miss, Mrs., Mr.? Applications can ask these questions, except in a few states, providing the information is not for discriminatory purposes.

Can they ask about my childcare arrangements? That's unlawful, since no such information is asked of male applicants. And, of course, no interviewer can legally ask you about your birth control practices or your plans for future children.

How about age? You do not have to reveal your age, since it is unlawful to discriminate on the basis of age. However, you may legally be asked whether "you are between the ages of sixteen and sixty-five." Remember that these restrictions apply only *before* you are hired. The personnel director's bible, *Personnel Management,* states, "There are no limits on questioning after an employee has been hired." Your boss, for example, might request proof of your age for the company pension plan.

Your Rights on the Job

Can my employer force me to resign or fire me when I become pregnant? No. Under EEOC guidelines, you must be granted a leave of absence (the length of time varies from state to state), and you must be offered the same or an equivalent job when you return to work. You cannot be caused to lose seniority or other benefits. You may, however, be required to have worked for the company for a specified length of time before being eligible for a pregnancy leave of absence. If so, the same length-of-service requirement must apply to any male employees who desire a leave of absence for illness or other reasons.

My boss told me I was a good worker, but he'd never promote a married woman to the job I want because "she wouldn't have her whole heart in the job." It's very important for women to realize that an employer cannot refuse to train, assign, or promote pregnant women, married women, or women of childbearing age.

My company told me that I would have to retire earlier than men or else pay a higher premium "because women live longer than men and the insurance company charges us more." Is that legal? No—and retirement plans are only one part of a larger pattern of discrimination in benefits against women employees. You must be given the same fringe benefits— medical, accident, life insurance, and retirement—as male employees, as well as profit-sharing and bonus plans, leaves, and vacations. Remember these points:

- As a woman, you cannot be forced onto a pension or retirement plan that requires a different retirement age than one for male employees.
- You cannot be forced to pay higher premiums on pension plans than men because of the longer life spans of women.
- Benefits cannot be restricted to employees who are "head of household" or "principal wage earner," a common practice that tends to discriminate against women employees.
- If benefits are extended to the wives of male employees (for example, maternity), the same benefits must be extended to women employees. And benefits extended to the wives and families of male workers must be offered to your husband and family.

Why doesn't our company insurance policy have to cover maternity disabilities? My personnel director says it's because pregnancy applies only to women and that would be discriminatory. But it does cover prostate trouble, and that certainly applies only to men. Unfortunately, because of the Supreme Court's controversial 1976 decision in *General Electric Co.* v. *Gilbert,* an employer can elect to exclude pregnancy-related disabilities from a sick-pay plan. The Court ruled that a company's sick-pay plan was "nothing more than an insurance package, which covers some risks but excludes others." Since nothing in Title VII requires an employer to set up an all-inclusive plan, excluding certain risks incurred only by women is not discriminatory. In practice, this means that when you suffer a pregnancy-related disability, including the normal recovery period after childbirth or even a medical mishap like an ectopic pregnancy, you may not even be entitled to take sick pay you've already earned.

Employers argue that the cost of paying disability or sick pay to pregnant employees would be astronomical. The Aetna Life Insurance Company, for one, however, presented figures to show that only small increases—about 60¢ per month per worker—in insurance rates would result. And male employees generally enjoy benefits for exclusively male diseases like prostate trouble.

We feel that businesses are going to find that the temporary absence of an experienced woman worker after childbirth is much less disruptive and expensive than hiring and training a wholly new employee. Taking care of a good employee *is* a good investment. New challenges to this Court ruling are in the works, and many legal observers feel that Congress will act to allow pregnant women to collect earned sick pay or disability payments during the time they must take off for illness after childbirth.

DO YOU WANT THE JOB?

Just as important as impressing your potential employer is your skill in finding out about the company and the job. You'll certainly need to know if you'll be expected to put in overtime. Many jobs with seasonal or monthly peaks—accounting, retail sales, nursing—routinely require overtime, though an interviewer may neglect to inform you. If overtime is expected, you'll want to ask "Will I be notified in advance?" so you can make arrangements for childcare. (And, of course, you'll ask "Will I be paid for the overtime?") Much as you want the job, if you absolutely can't manage working late, now's the time to say so. Don't hope the problem will magically go away once you're on the job, or that you'll be able to persuade them to make an exception "once they know me."

Find out how pressured the job is. Watch for phrases like "Now there are times when we're very, very busy and everyone pitches in. . . ." Or "We're a little short-handed now, but we're hoping to get up to staff soon." Highly competitive sales jobs, for example, where your salary may depend on beating out other salespeople, have pressure built in. If the job involves pressure and overtime, and your children are still small, you may want to look elsewhere.

Don't forget to ask about benefits: medical, disability, dental, pensions, maternity leave, life insurance for you. Women constantly overlook their need for life insurance, and most companies provide good coverage at minimal cost.

FINDING THE UNDERSTANDING BOSS

Finding a boss who's not uptight about small changes in schedules, who can sense your commitment to the job even if he is inconvenienced on occasion, can spell the difference between a manageable job and one that makes you miserable. Don't make the mistake of assuming that a woman with children is the ideal employer. "The biggest dragon lady I ever worked for was a mother," remembers Sharon, a successful market researcher for a major department store who broke into her highly chauvinistic field fifteen years ago and has collected a colorful assortment of horror stories along the way. "She was one of those women who'd clawed her way to the top, and she thought every woman who wasn't like her was a weak sister that should stay home with the children. Once I got a call from my son's music teacher while she was in my office and she blew her stack. 'If you want to be the little housewife, stay at home,' she screamed. She couldn't understand anything in between."

If your potential boss happens to be a man, consider it a plus if *his* wife works (chances are he'll be up at 6:30 A.M. filling lunch boxes just as you are) or he has been known to stay home with a sick child himself in a pinch.

No one type of boss is necessarily best. A relaxed, easy-going atmosphere usually signals that the person in charge is not rigid or unreasonably demanding. But even an old-style authoritarian who likes his desk lined up with one single file folder and expects all workers at their desks at the crack of 9 A.M. may be fair and supportive. Generally, the best two qualities a boss can have are: (1) he or she is secure in the job and is not likely to be propelled by anxiety or pressure from above to put in overtime or worry over every nicety of office regulation; (2) he or she needs and values *you*.

SELLING YOURSELF

Again and again the advice comes from career experts and from personnel directors who interview and hire: *Act confident.* Says a personnel manager who, ten years ago, was an unemployed, divorced mother of two under-three sons, "I'm constantly seeing mothers who want jobs desperately, but instead of being positive and aggressive about it, they're almost apologetic that they have children and that someone else will be taking care of them. You have to exude confidence whether you feel it or not."

Take a strong, positive stand when you talk to potential employers. There's no reason you shouldn't be as reliable as a woman without child-care responsibilities. If an employer expresses doubts about the depth of your commitment, be ready to state your attitudes clearly and confidently: that you've thought about working carefully and you're prepared to make the arrangements in your home life that are needed. Some women may want to add that their husbands are behind them in their decision to work since employers find that home pressures from an uncooperative husband can force women to quit.

The anxiety women feel about their ability to manage both a job and mothering often creeps out unnecessarily. Many women, for example, feel compelled to spell out their priorities all too clearly, setting limits on the job from the start.

Patricia, a legal secretary and divorced mother, says, "I told my boss before I took my first job that there *would* be meetings at school or sickness or whatnot and I just wouldn't be in then *because my children come first always.*"

Karla, an experienced, high-powered sales manager for a dress company, felt equally compelled to state her priorities. "When we were negotiating, I told my boss Sol that *my children's needs would always come first,* and while he could count on me to get the job done, there might be a lot of interruptions."

Most people don't need to be told that a mother's first commitment is to her children. Men, too, rush out of their offices when a home emergency arises. Karla and Patricia seemed to be speaking more out of anxiety about their new obligations than from a real need to set the record straight. Unless you foresee a clear conflict between your needs and your employers in time, overtime, or job expectations, avoid the temptation to clear your conscience by limiting your commitment to the job.

Once you have the job, hopefully you'll sail right through with no more problems than any employee battles. But you should prepare yourself to deal with several potential roadblocks that lurk ahead for some working mothers, ranging from children's sickness to the persistent notion that a woman with children can't really be committed to her job.

SICK DAYS

No problem troubles mothers more than sickness: *What do you do when your child is sick?* The first impulse is to reach for the phone and call in sick yourself.

"The whole office," says Sara, a middle manager for a big insurance firm, "thought I had pneumonia when my son was the one who actually had it. Then when I got a light case of it myself, I struggled through and missed only two days from work. I told everybody it was a relapse."

Drill-press operator or account executive, mothers fear that staying at home with a sick child is hard to justify to their bosses. "If I had to reschedule a business meeting because of the children, no one ever knew why," says Jo Beth, a divisional merchandise manager at a large Los Angeles department store chain.

Yet the conflict between work and children's sickness is more worried about than actual. "Absentee rates of mothers are just the same as other workers," says a personnel director. National studies back her up. A recent Public Health Survey found no statistically significant differences in illness and injury time between men and women, with men averaging 5.2 days a year off and women averaging 5.6.

Despite all your arrangements, your husband's sharing, or your child's independence, there *are* times when you'll need to take off work to be at his bedside for actual or emotional support. Present some alternatives to your employer for getting your work done during your absence. You can:

- offer to work at home (maybe even catch up on a disagreeable job you've been putting off until "I get some peace and quiet in the office")
- offer to work extra when you return
- have a clearcut backup plan at work

You *can* organize yourself at work to minimize disruption when you have to stay out. Diane, a well-paid executive secretary with two young children, works closely with her boss in a job that is "one-person servicing"—unlike a pool typist or a person who works on her own, she can't really be replaced. So Diane, preparing for her unexpected absences, defied the usual rules of a successful worker: (*Make yourself indispensable, and Never write anything down*). She organized her files so carefully that even a temp could retrieve files her boss needed. For her boss's reassurance, Diane created a slim index in a neat notebook detailing every subject he might need: "1978 Sales Plan," "South Plant Monthly Reports," "Budget for 1980"—with numbered directions of where to find the information (File Cabinet 2, Folder 29). Not only did Diane feel less pressured about deciding when her children needed her at home, but she and her boss also found her meticulous organization helped them both perform better on the job.

Organize your files, records, or management objectives so co-workers can find important papers or follow your guidance by phone. Faultless organization takes time, but you'll feel easier when your son is throwing up two hours before work and you're trying to decide if you should stay home.

If you are like most mothers, you'll probably hoard your own sick days for when your kids are sick. "Mothers don't get sick; we can't *afford* to," say many working mothers. During the years of child-rearing, you simply don't allow yourself to be sick. You may be quite capable of mucking through an office day with sniffles or mild discomfort that would put your co-workers out. You'll then have an untapped reserve supply of sick days to call on in a home emergency.

All of which leads us back to the question: Should a mother take her own sick days to see after her child? While thousands of mothers continue to do just that, some women class this deception in the same category as faking orgasm: a ruse that does none of us any lasting good. Certainly if women's talents are to be utilized at work, employers are going to have to learn to make allowances for occasional home emergencies. Meanwhile, you may edge the movement along by frankness with your employer. If you make yourself valuable on the job, if you're careful to be consistently reliable at work, you'll earn more leverage than you realize. Try using it. (And it won't hurt to keep count of your male colleagues' sick days. Your employer may be surprised to see how they match—or exceed—yours.)

CREATING A GOOD IMAGE

Lisa, a crackerjack saleswoman newly promoted to district sales manager, was the first woman to hold this responsible position in her company, a cosmetics firm. While she was deep into a brainstorming session planning the fall campaign with her force of twelve male salesmen, a call came through on the conference loudspeaker phone for her. And as twelve sets of male ears pricked up, a small voice piped, "Mommy, I let the gerbils out. When are you coming home?"

"I was really mortified. I had worked so hard to build my authority. Here were all these married guys with nonworking wives looking at me and saying, 'Aha, she's just a woman after all.' I've had to start all over, and I don't think they'll ever forget that incident."

A good general rule is to keep your children at a low profile in the office. "Remember," says an executive working mother who managed her dual roles long before it was fashionable,"that people at the office want to hear you have this baby and see a snapshot once and that's all. It shouldn't be a daily event." Be sure your children know how to ask for you in a businesslike way when they call. If other people answer your phone, familiarize them with your children's names. But don't encourage long chats between them and others in the office—no matter how maternal your office mate is or how he or she loves to hear all about your teenage daughter's boyfriends.

BATTLING HOSTILE ATTITUDES

Fran, executive director of a professional society, holds an important job. She represents the organization at professional conferences, handles all inquiries from the press, and puts out the monthly professional magazine. After four years on the job, she was startled when a male member of the society's board, beaming paternally, declared to her one day, "You do a wonderful job, Fran, but of course if something came up at home, if one of your children was sick, you would be the one who had to stay home, not your husband."

"My mouth dropped open. After four years, he hadn't come to terms with me as a responsible worker. I told him, 'I make 50 percent of the income and therefore we split the house and child responsibilities fifty-fifty.' And he looked at me as if I had suddenly turned into a Martian."

The board member did survive his shock, and now treats Fran warily but with new respect. In countering hostile attitudes toward working mothers, a straight, assertive answer like Fran's is usually your best bet.

For women in jobs formerly labeled male, remember that people's attitudes toward a new idea don't usually change overnight. Forget the fantasy of your doing such a glorious job that all your male colleagues instantly accept you and jettison their doubts about your right to their turf. Be aware that for most people, the change from hostility to acceptance of a person usually follows certain stages:

1. hostility, with the firm conviction that one's own way is right
2. veiled hostility, with superficial acceptance
3. defensive acceptance—"Look, she *is* a good worker, but, old-fashioned as I may be, I still think she should be home with her children"
4. acceptance—*real* acceptance

The most important step in this progression is from outright hostility, when a person is convinced you're all wrong and he's all right, to a more open attitude that concedes you may have a point or two (after that, give them time and the rest will probably follow). How can you get bosses and colleagues to take that first step? Obviously, you can be reliable and do as good a job as anyone else (this is laudable proof but, unfortunately, can take years to have effect). More effective, if you're challenged, is a straight, assertive statement of your feelings and motives for working, like the one Fran gave. Women who've taken assertiveness training have learned the simple power of the spoken word in changing attitudes. When someone attacks you, you lose points by being apologetic or overly logical (don't feel compelled to respond to your accuser's words, which are usually loaded and unanswerable by logic anyway). Simply stating your point of view unemotionally and concisely makes the other person stop, listen, and confront your feelings and rights. As an overall policy, this approach should stand you in good stead in most situations.

Hostility and patronizing attitudes can surface in these ways, too:

1. You're a Bad Mother. Janet, a Chicago teacher and mother of two girls, altered her childcare arrangements several times because of her concern for their changing needs. "One of the men teachers used to say every time he crossed my path, 'So who's raising your children this year?' " After nursing her wounds silently for several years, Janet realized she was perpetuating the wrong image by letting others express their negative views unchallengd. "In fact, a friend commented that she doesn't know any other mother who puts in as much time with her kids in the summer and after school, taking them to the zoo, the park, to other events. I got my own head straight about myself as a good mother, and the next time someone did a number about who was raising my children, I said, 'I am. Only it doesn't take me twenty-four hours a day to do it!' "

You don't want to make a crusade of your way of life. But if your office mates openly express doubts about your mothering, quietly state your confidence about the job you're doing. After all, you're the only one in a position to judge.

2. Cute Little You. Sharon, the efficient and well-paid market researcher for a retail store chain, entered her field fifteen years ago when married women with careers were an oddity. "Salesmen and bosses couldn't take me seriously. They kept asking, 'Are you going to quit when you buy the refrigerator and all those little things you want for the house?' " Sharon made the mistake of ignoring the belittlement behind the joshing. "I tolerated it and looked on it as their brand of flirting, a kind of aren't-you-a-cute-little-thing. Professionally, I was dead wrong. I should have said, 'I expect to be here as long as you are.' It would have meant an enormous difference in what I earned over the years."

With women taking less time out of their work lives for family responsibilities (women today average 22.9 years in the work force, as opposed to only 12 years in 1940), employers are less likely to assume that you're only working for extras at home and are going to hand in your notice as soon as your nest is furnished. But they may still see you as having only a secondary commitment to work, and so be inclined to pass you over when promotion time comes.

One of the best ways to combat this is to keep your eyes open to how your talents can be used—and suitably remunerated—with a shift in office structure. For example, with three children aged nine to sixteen, Sharon couldn't handle her retiring boss's job as head of marketing research, which required constant travel to the chain's one hundred stores. Instead, she proposed—and won—a reorganization of the marketing department that put her market knowledge and statistical expertise to work as head of research. She then became co-equal with a new operations head (who does the traveling) and got a substantial raise.

3. No Right to Work. "Why don't you stay home and stop taking a man's paycheck away from some family?" This bald accusation was hurled at Kathy, a computer programmer who makes $14,000 a year, on which she supports herself and her three-year-old daughter. Like Sharon, Kathy made the mistake of not confronting her co-workers' disapproval. "It's their problem if they can't handle it. They're envious because they're stuck with mortgages and have wives home spending the money they earn. I just answer back with a crack, like, 'I've got to fulfill myself.' I never told them I'm divorced and supporting my family."

Married or not, there are plenty of good reasons that you are working, and you shouldn't be hesitant about stating them. "I'm helping support *my* family." "I'm qualified to do the work, and there's no reason I shouldn't be paid for it." "I'm working for reasons that are as important to me as yours are."

Stated calmly, such phrases go a long way in crumbling prejudices.

"I'D GIVE UP MONEY FOR TIME": SEARCHING FOR THE FLEXIBLE SCHEDULE

A job that will let you work fewer hours one week, more the next . . . a job that would allow you to arrive anytime between eight to ten—this may sound like a fantasy to most of us, as we sit drumming our fingers in the 8:30 A.M. traffic jam or racing around searching for Susie's homework while the whole family waits to get off to school and work. True, over 80 percent of all full-time jobs in America are rigidly tied to the forty-hour week, the daily 9-to-5 or 8-to-5 timeclock, five days a week. No major change has occurred in this American work week since the late 1930s, when the forty-hour standard was mandated by the Fair Labor Practices Act of 1938, a New Deal–inspired reform that limits a nonmanagerial worker's week to forty hours and requires overtime pay for longer hours. Surprisingly, while workers' benefits in salary, fringe benefits, vacations, insurance, and job conditions have escalated in the thirty years since, the hours spent working haven't changed one whit. Though most employers still view the fixed forty-hour timeclocked week as being the natural order of work, signs indicate that changes *are* coming.

A resourceful working mother *does* have a few options. And if enough of us press, business will become more responsive to our needs. If you're seeking flexibility, school yourself in these new working plans.

JOB SHARING

More written about than practiced, job sharing is a truly revolutionary concept that pairs two workers who split up a permanent full-time job between them. The pair may alternate mornings and afternoons on the job, work on alternate days, or even share unevenly, one working four days a week, the other two.

What kinds of jobs can be shared?

Most people react instinctively: *Not mine.*

In fact, women are now splitting jobs in such diverse occupations as librarian, probation officer, city planner, secretary, bank researcher, lawyer, teacher, counselor, lab technician, assembly-line worker, administrative assistant, executive. Companies in which this goes on include The Bank of America, the City of Palo Alto (California), Stanford University Medical School, and many smaller firms, from a Kansas community agency where husband and wife split the job of agency director to a small Massachusetts finance company that has job-sharing secretaries. One of the most impressive examples of the system successfully at work is at the Federal Reserve Bank of Boston (hardly a hotbed of innovation), where Carol Schwartz Greenwald, assistant vice president and economist, works a twenty-hour week, dividing her exacting work with Stephen McNees, a bank economist.

The key to getting your employer to consider job sharing is for him to learn about its advantages to *him* (he gets the best part of your work energies: two people may bring more abilities to a job than any one employee). And you'd better bone up on the practical objections, too. Medical insurance and certain other fringe benefits can be prorated between you and your partner according to hours worked, *but* you need a

NEW JOB ARRANGEMENTS THAT CAN BUY YOU TIME

Job Sharing—Two people share a full-time job, usually splitting the hours in half. You and your partner might split days in half, with you on in the morning, your partner in the afternoon. Or you might alternate days.
Advantage: You have a part-time job, with full-time commitment and prestige.
Disadvantage: You go on half salary—but you may make up much of the loss by savings on childcare.

4/40—Widely touted a few years ago, the 4/40 compressed week allows workers to put in ten hours or more of work in four days instead of five, leaving a luxurious three days off for their private lives.
Advantage: For most mothers, nil, though for a few, having three days off is personally preferable.
Disadvantage: You're gone from home twelve hours instead of ten during the days you work—too long for most mothers.

Staggered Hours—You and your co-workers are assigned different shifts for getting to the office, with the first arrivals expected at 7 A.M., the second at 8, the third at 9, the fourth at 10.
Advantage: You may buy time at the hour you need it most, either that extra hour to get the kids to school and arrive at work at 10 A.M., or, conversely, you might be able to go in early and be available at home when your children arrive from school.
Disadvantage: One end of your day is still crowded.

Flexitime—You work forty hours a week, but are only required to be in your office during a "core time"—usually 10 A.M. to 3 P.M. Depending on your personal needs, you can come in early or late, and leave when your eight-hour day is done.
Advantage: You gain far greater flexibility to adjust to your fluctuating demands.
Disadvantage: You may lose the chance to earn overtime on days you work longer than eight hours.

good understanding of the facts to explain why fixed statutory worker's benefits like Social Security and worker's unemployment will cost your employer only slightly more under job sharing. Two pioneering organizations can help you learn about whether job sharing is an option for you:

> *New Ways to Work* (475 Kingsley Avenue, Palo Alto, California 94301). This nonprofit work-resource center shows employers how job sharing can benefit them and counsels individuals on how to find a partner and a shared job. New Ways also publishes informative, inexpensive bulletins about such concerns as how fringe benefits can be prorated and case histories of job sharing. Send a stamped, self-addressed envelope to receive a list of current publications.

> *Catalyst* (14 East 60th Street, New York, New York 10022). This fifteen-year-old, national, nonprofit organization provides information on how to job-share, based on its own experience. The agency also maintains a network of contacts with over 150 women's counseling centers across the country and provides, at minimal cost, excellent guides on emerging careers for women, how to train for them, and how to write a resume and reenter the job market. Write for a catalog of their modestly priced publications.

But you don't need to be trained by experts to persuade your boss that job sharing will work to his advantage, too. Shirley Clowser, a thirty-four-year-old teacher in suburban San Lorenzo, California, had ten years' job experience and a deep love for her work. But when her four-year-old daughter was joined by a new baby at home, Shirley found full-time teaching almost destroyed her family life ("My husband only saw me when I was asleep or frantically busy"). Shirley became the first in the local grade school to switch to a job-sharing schedule, paired with a like-minded teacher and mother, Linda. Shirley had two things going for her when she went to her school principal and personnel director: (1) school population in her area was shrinking, and the school board was oversupplied with tenured teachers who could not be let go; (2) a gifted, dedicated teacher, Shirley was valued by her principal, who said, "If that's what it takes to keep you, that's what we'll do."

Shirley also did her homework. A warm woman bubbling with enthusiasm, she explained her argument to management: "Hiring two tenured teachers for one full-time job is cheaper than hiring two tenured teachers for *two* full-time jobs," she said. Shirley was equally persuasive in demonstrating to the personnel director how the school board would not have to spend anything extra on benefits.

Besides the fear that hiring two employees for one job will cost extra in fringe benefits, the other chief objection of employers is communication: "How will you know what the other one's doing?" Shirley and Linda were well prepared there, too, and they carefully explained to parents at the opening of the school year why their children would not suffer from having a morning teacher and an afternoon teacher, and might even benefit from it. Shirley and Linda have weekly conferences to jointly plan their lessons and confer on students; they also hold joint conferences with parents—where they feel free to express different opinions about the child. The parents are delighted and, in fact, see having two teachers as a plus. "Sometimes one child does not get along with one of us, but gets along better with the other one," says Shirley. "As for us, we're both fresher and more creative than we've been in years. I used to run down by spring. But now, our enthusiasm keeps the children going right up to June."

Carol Williams, a Bronx, New York, vocational teacher, took job sharing one further step. While she and her partner alternated mornings and afternoons at work, they also alternated taking care of their preschool daughters. Exchange of information, lesson plans, and students' papers were simplified—"We could run over the next day's lesson plans while I was getting my daughter into her snowsuit for the trip home, knocking out two birds with one stone," says Carol. "No extra stop at the baby-sitter's."

How can you make job sharing work? Essential to the success of a job-sharing arrangement is a great deal of trust and like-mindedness between you and your partner. Ideally, you should have worked together before, which is a sound basis for knowing about each other's personality and professional competence, and for heading off unpleasant surprises. If you don't share similar work styles—say, you're neat, the other's a paper-piler—devise procedures to assure that you can work in the same space without confusion. You might set up different desks, or, if that's impossible, at least divide your desk areas. Agree on places to post schedules and urgent information. And *build into* your schedule regular times for conferences and information exchange.

If your job requires that you meet deadlines, be sure you can live with your partner's style of organization and pacing. If you're the methodical one who makes weekly goals and sticks to them, you're sure to be annoyed by a partner who slides into deadlines via a last-minute, all-night-with-black-coffee effort. And remember, as in marriage and other partnerships, successful job sharing depends on each party giving a bit more than 50 percent.

FLEXITIME

Another promising option is flexitime, a system under which you work a forty-hour week but have leeway to set your own starting time. Typically, flexitime workers must be in their offices during a "core day" of 10 A.M. to 3 P.M. But they may arrive as early as 7 A.M., and then leave at 3 P.M. when their eight-hour day is done. Since Flexitime has been installed at a large life insurance office in New York, Jo Brown, a forty-one-year-old divorced clerk, has solved her childcare problems. She arises at 5:30 A.M. to make breakfast for her teenage daughter and younger son. After walking her daughter to school, Jane catches a subway that is blessedly uncrowded at that hour. By 3:15 P.M., her work day is done and she is back on her way home, ready to meet her children when they get in from school.

Flexitime doesn't give you any more time free from work. But it does let you shift your work hours to handle changing day-to-day needs at home, whether you have to take a child to the dentist, attend a 2 P.M. school program, or stay home a few hours with a sick child.

Credit for conceiving the idea goes to a West German woman economist, Christel Kaemmerer, who, in the mid-sixties, was looking for a way to lure mothers back to work and to solve bruising peak-hour traffic jams that were delivering West German workers to the factory tardy and exhausted. More than 30 percent of the West German labor force and 40 percent of Swiss workers now enjoy flexitime.

In the past few years in the United States, flexitime has rapidly displaced such other movements for curing worker alienation as job enrichment, staggered work hours, and the compressed 4/40 week (a disaster for mothers). More than three thousand American firms reportedly are dabbling in flexitime, with highly favorable results. The American Management Association recently published a detailed study of progress (*A Flexible Approach to Working Hours,* by J. Carroll Swart, 1978, $19.95) showing that flexitime produces good results at such diverse firms as:

Eastern Air Lines headquarters (Miami)

Scott Paper Company

Occidental Life of California

California State Automobile Association

Nuclear Center of Westinghouse Electric Corporation (Monroeville, Pa.)

First National Bank of Boston

Hewlett-Packard (Palto Alto, Calif.)

Nestlē Company headquarters (White Plains, New York)

Metropolitan Life (New York City)

Lufthansa (in America)

Sun Oil Company headquarters (Philadelphia)

Northwestern Mutual Life Insurance Company headquarters (Milwaukee)

Pacific Gas & Electric Company (San Francisco)

the Social Security Administration

the U.S. Geological Survey

Reporting on the experience of dozens of companies, this study shows that employers whose workers are on flexitime can look forward to an end to tardiness, reduced absenteeism, greater productivity and worker loyalty, and reduced sick leave. And Catalyst's study of flexitime revealed that businessmen's fears that worker-set hours will lead to mass confusion in the office are not borne out. Indeed, communication between the staff *increases,* because managers must plan ahead and develop work schedules with their workers. "Instead of constantly buzzing their people," says Catalyst President Felice Schwartz, "a flexitime manager has to organize himself and collect all his buzzes for one planning session."

Setting her own hours can make an enormous difference in the fatigue and pressure that a working mother must cope with. With a more flexible work schedule, for example, you could leave work at three or four P.M. and clothes-shop with your kids, pick up the laundry, take the dog to the vet, drop off your car for a tune-up, or handle those hundred other chores you usually cram in on Saturday. One caution: unions have often been unenthusiastic about flexitime because it can result in workers putting in ten-hour days with no overtime compensation. And the Fair Labor Practices Act of 1938 and the Walsh-Healey Act prohibiting uncompensated overtime create legal complications in some instances. If you'd like to explore flexitime in your organization, consult Swart's *A Flexible Approach to Working Hours* for a detailed program for instituting flexitime.

BARGAINING FOR YOUR OWN
FLEXIBLE SCHEDULE

While the freedom of these options is far from reality for most of us, working mothers do bargain with bosses for their own "arrangements." The price you pay for these favors, unfortunately, is often stiff. Consider these experiences of mothers who gave up money and advancement in return for flexible working arrangements.

Nancy had an off-the-record four-day working arrangement with her woman boss in a large, staid Massachusetts corporation. While listed as a regular full-time employee, she took Fridays off to cook for the weekend and spend extra time with her two daughters. In return, Nancy's boss Bernice kept her salary budget under the company average by granting her minuscule raises—even though Nancy's efficiency enabled her to do the full week's work superbly in four days. Nancy, like many mothers, was so grateful to have her Fridays that she made no protest. But then Bernice was lured to another company and management examined Nancy's records. What they saw was a worker who wasn't highly valued. And when Nancy tried to explain that she had been on a four-day week by arrangement with her boss but *was* valued and efficient, her superiors discounted her even more—"she's not interested in committing full-time to the job" was their snap judgment. Though Nancy was superbly qualified for Bernice's job, someone from outside the company was brought in over her head.

Nancy's story has a happy ending, however. Forced to canvass the job market, she landed a position with a new company run by enthusiastic young people. To make the switch to a five-day work week, Nancy asked her husband to take over the marketing, which he quickly learned to manage efficiently. She experienced a new surge of energy and excitement in her stimulating new job and made the transition without a problem. "All these years I've been in a place I really didn't like, just to keep my Fridays. And when I look at it, I see I didn't accomplish a single thing on those Fridays off that I couldn't have handled just as well on a two-day weekend if I'd only gotten myself organized. My advice is, four-day weeks are for the birds."

Julianne, director of the children's section of a Chicago model-booking service and herself the mother of an infant, worked four days in the office and stayed at home on the fifth day with her baby son, though she took care of paperwork at home and was available for phone calls from the office or clients. "After a year of this, I've just had a discussion with my bosses about a raise. One of the questions they asked was whether I'd consider coming back into the office for the fifth day. They have no complaints, and they admit that things have gone very smoothly. But they consider the fact that I work at home on the fifth day as reason not to give me the same raise they might have given me if I didn't work at home. Somehow, even though I work full-time, my workday at home doesn't count with them. Of course, my reaction to that is not very pleasant. I thought I was managing beautifully."

To get the raise she thinks she deserves, Julianne will probably either have to give up an ideal situation . . . or be extraordinarily valuable to her bosses. The present reality for most working mothers is that you have to be quite a few notches above your peers in ability to win flexibility without sacrificing either money or career advancement.

Cynthia, a mother of two who got her law degree at the age of thirty-four and was offered a job in a prestigious firm, was elated to get a big concession from the firm's partners who were wooing her: she would work only nine to five, no matter how heated the case, and she would get two months off each summer. Practice proved different. "How can I function as a member of the law team and waltz off at five when my male peers are working on to ten or twelve at night to get ready for court the next morning? There was too much hostility for me to keep up that limited commitment, and I quietly dropped it. What I do is go home at five, and come back at eleven. It wasn't a question of my paying the price of hostility from others. It just wasn't workable," she sighs.

And so we struggle on, crunched by work schedules that often unreasonably demand rigid working hours, or professions that require energies and commitment beyond an eight-hour day. Options are opening up; business is becoming more sensitive to the family needs of fathers as well as mothers. But the responsibility for forging long-range strategies that will let you make the most of your career without sacrificing your family still rests on one lonely set of shoulders: yours.

KIDS IN THE OFFICE

Visits. Holidays invariably bring a few children into every business establishment. You see them buying muffins from the coffee wagon and cheerfully producing great rolls of paper from the adding machines.

When Daddy brings his son or daughter to the office, they're usually greeted with warm smiles and clucks of approval (Daddy's secretary too, can spend the entire day entertaining The Children and doling out reams of paper and Magic Markers for their amusement).

But let eight-year-old Amanda accompany Mommy to her job and the eyebrows rise. Never mind that it's Columbus Day (schools closed, offices open—a combination all working mothers learn to dread), that your sitter who never gets sick just did, that every available teenager in town is at the football game, and your mother lives two hundred miles away. What's okay for a man often doesn't wash for a real-life mother. One woman likened the feeling to wearing a bikini at the company picnic —the men found themselves looking at something they knew she had but were not accustomed to seeing.

Even with the prospect of a chilly reception, you may want or need to bring your child with you occasionally. Unless there are company rules against it, there's no reason you shouldn't enjoy this privilege. Just observe some precautions:

Take it in small doses. Spending only the morning with Mom may be more fun for your five-year-old than trying to be on his best behavior for an eight-hour day. Have a baby-sitter take him home after you and he have a special lunch together. Or arrange to have him meet another mother with children for a movie.

Don't arrive empty-handed. Take along activity books, coloring books, puzzles, snacks—anything that will keep a youngster occupied.

Bring one child at a time. "One child is a visitor; two is an army," says one woman who found out the hard way. Sibling rivalry (and the noise that accompanies it) is a phenomenon best not shared with your co-workers.

Don't assume your children automatically understand office etiquette. Unless he's warned not to, even the most sensible seven-year-old might decide to stroll into the boss's office for a mid-morning visit. (One advertising account executive who calmly went about her work was horrified to discover that her normally quiet son, brought to the office after a Halloween shopping trip, barged into the office of an elderly vice-president baring his brand-new Dracula teeth.)

Have an older youngster do errands for you and your co-workers. Favorite jobs: running the Xerox machine; taking messages "on the double" from one desk to another; answering the phone (but be sure your child can do so in a businesslike manner).

Cribs in the Conference Room. Do you ever fantasize about finding a job where your child could go, too? While children on the work scene was the norm for generations of women in the past, today it seems an option only if you hold one of two jobs: day-care attendant or fifth-grade teacher with a fifth-grade child.

But a few intrepid mothers do manage to take their youngsters to work every day. Connie Vogelsang, a California mother, took her baby daughter right along in a backpack to the roofing-materials firm where she does general office work. By the time her daughter was a toddler and no longer slept quietly, Connie's bosses were accustomed enough to the idea to overlook the interruptions an active toddler brings to a business office. Connie was fortunate; bringing a small child to the office regularly can probably be managed well only in a small, informal one- or two-secretary office.

Illinois Representative Susan Catania made news when she brought along her daughter Amy to sleep in a box under her desk while debate raged around her on the legislative floor. *Ms.* magazine recently ran a cover story about a staff member who brought her toddler to her office, to the enjoyment of the entire staff. And an Oklahoma welfare-agency director not only brought her own baby to work, but invited her secretary to bring hers. "We had two babies stashed in two cardboard boxes—but the work went right along as usual," she declares.

Before you pop your infant into a baby carrier and take her along with your attaché case, ask yourself realistically: How will your co-workers react? Said one woman whose boss's baby became an office fixture, "Crying babies, a child's demands—I went to work to avoid exactly this situation!"

Not all children will flourish in an adult office environment that forces them to subjugate their needs to adult requirements. "Certain kinds of babies and offices just don't go well together," observes a univerity teaching fellow who tried bringing her infant son to work. "Everybody—my office mates, employers, and students—was cooperative, everyone except the baby." She goes on to report that he slept very little, managed to disrupt her own and his schedules, and caught every infection going around the office. "Perhaps the worst effect," she recalls, "was the anxiety I felt when he was noisy, which was often. People assured me that they didn't mind, but I certainly did, and they soon would have as well."

Handled cautiously, however, allowing your children to experience

WORKING AT HOME

For many mothers torn by doubts about leaving their home scene, the perfect answer may seem obvious: Work at home.

Maybe. While it's true that you can more easily sneak away for an afternoon of shopping when your "office" is the attic, you may find that it's not so easy to wear two hats under one roof. The number of career options you can pursue is limited, and the financial rewards are uncertain (remember, too, that you will forego medical insurance and other benefits). You may miss the companionship of an office, the sense of being part of a work team. Most important, unless you happen to be one of the rare at-home mothers who earn a lot of money, both you and your family may have trouble according your work the same respect that you would a job. In any case, you'll probably have trouble separating your working time from your mothering time. A Mommy-behind-closed-doors can be more confusing to small children than one who leaves the house each morning. And, as Cornell University psychologist Urie Bronfenbrenner notes, mothers who are on the premises all day are less likely than office workers to benefit from their husbands' shared participation in childcare and housework.

Despite these disadvantages, it is possible to make working at home work out well. Whether you are a graduate student or an artist, a free-lance writer or the proprietor of a mail-order business, you and other home-based career mothers face strikingly similar problems. Here are some tested solutions that will help you succeed:

- Set aside a work area that's yours and yours alone. Declare this space off limits to the family, and as a boost to your privacy, install a lock on the door.

- Invest in a separate phone and phone number, and discourage other family members from answering your phone. Instead, install an answering device that will record calls while you are away from home or when you want to work without interruption.

- Decide what your working hours will be and then discipline yourself not to waver from them. Follow the lead of novelist Norma Klein, who applies makeup and gets dressed each morning as if she were going to an office. Or adopt the example of countless at-homers who rise at 6 A.M., dash through minimal morning chores, and settle down at their desks by 8:30 A.M. as soon as their husbands and children leave for the day. Not interrupting your work to walk the dog or stir the soup can make the difference between a satisfying career and unproductive busy work.

- Let teachers, other parents, even your friends know that you are not available for conferences, car pools, or chitchat during the hours you are working.

- Schedule all house service people—the exterminator, plumber, appliance repairman—on the same day. Don't arrange to have packages delivered at home just because you'll be around. Manage deliveries just as you would if you were working away from home.
- Combat the isolation of working at home by scheduling carefully planned breaks in the middle or at the end of your workday. Try to combine out-of-house chores with social visits. If your work is sedentary, use your breaks for exercise (try jogging to the corner for the newspaper instead of driving or having the paper delivered).
- Since few children really understand the meaning of "Mommy's working, " don't try to work when they're around, unless you have nerves of steel. If your children are not in school, hire a sitter to entertain them during your working hours.

your work life occasionally is an important way to help them understand the realities of your job. It can also be a humanizing influence on you and your co-workers. But, more important, seeing you in your professional role gives your child a new perspective on you as an individual separate from the family. And, if all goes well, you may be rewarded by a comment like the one made by eleven-year-old Marilyn, who, overhearing her mother conclude a business deal on the telephone, said with surprise, "Hey, Mom, you really know what you're doing."

BOOKS THAT MAY HELP

Everything a Woman Needs to Know to Get Paid What She's Worth, Caroline Bird (McKay, 1973). Informed advice on everything from overcoming resistance on the job to joining a union.

Getting Yours: How to Make the System Work for the Working Woman, Letty Cottin Pogrebin (McKay, 1975). A practical guidebook for today's working woman, filled with advice and inspiration.

The Managerial Woman, Margaret Hennig and Anne Jardim (Double-day, 1976). Sensitively explores the personality traits of executive women and offers insight into the conflicts between business and personal lives.

What Color Is Your Parachute?, Richard Nelson Bolles (Ten Speed Press, 1972; revised yearly). One of the best job-guidance handbooks around. Helps you identify the kind of work you'll enjoy—and how to look for the job that will provide it.

If you meet discrimination . . .

EEOC DISTRICT OFFICES

To get counseling or to file a complaint of sex discrimination, contact the EEOC office nearest you. A complaint must be in writing (your office will provide a handy form) and should be initiated as soon as possible after the incident and no later than 180 days. In some states, the federal EEOC office will defer the case to the local state or city agency which has 60 days to act. If the state agency takes no action in that time, the case reverts to the EEOC.

Alabama

Birmingham District Office
2121 8th Ave., North, Rm. 824
Birmingham, Alabama 35203
Telephone: (205) 254-1166

Alaska

Seattle District Office
Times Square Bldg., 4th Fl.
414 Olive Way
Seattle, Washington 98101
Telephone: (206) 422-0968

Arizona

Phoenix District Office
Valley Central Bldg.
201 N. Central Ave., Suite 1450
Phoenix, Arizona 85073
Telephone: (602) 261-3882

Arkansas

New Orleans District Office
Hale Boggs Federal Bldg.
500 Camp St., Suite 1007
New Orleans, Louisiana 70130
Telephone: (504) 682-2722

California

Los Angeles District Office
1543 W. Olympic Blvd., Suite 340
Los Angeles, California 90015
Telephone: (213) 688-3400

San Francisco District Office
Fox Plaza, Suite 325
1390 Market Street
San Francisco, California 94102
Telephone: (415) 556-0260

Colorado

Denver District Office
Ross Bldg., 6th Floor
1726 Champa St.
Denver, Colorado 80202
Telephone: (303) 837-3668

Connecticut

Boston District Office
150 Causeway St., Suite 1000
Boston, Massachusetts 02114
Telephone: (617) 223-4535

Delaware

Philadelphia District Office
219 North Broad St., 2nd Fl.
Philadelphia, Pennsylvania 19107
Telephone: (215) 597-9350

District of Columbia

Washington, D.C. District Office
1717 H St., N.W., Suite 400
Washington, D.C. 20006
Telephone: (202) 653-6197

Florida

Miami District Office
Biscayne Terrace Hotel, 10th Fl.
340 Biscayne Blvd.
Miami, Florida 33132
Telephone: (305) 350-4491

Georgia

Atlanta District Office
Citizens Trust Bldg., 10th Fl.
75 Piedmont Ave., N.E.
Atlanta, Georgia 30303
Telephone: (404) 526-4566

Hawaii

San Francisco District Office
Fox Plaza, Suite 325
1390 Market St.
San Francisco, California 94102
Telephone: (415) 556-0260

Idaho

Seattle District Office
Times Square Bldg., 4th Fl.
414 Olive Way
Seattle, Washington 98101
Telephone: (206) 422-0968

Illinois

Chicago District Office
Federal Bldg., Rm. 234
536 S. Clark St.
Chicago, Illinois 60605
Telephone: (312) 353-7550

Indiana

Indianapolis District Office
Federal Bldg.
U.S. Courthouse
46 East Ohio St., Rm. 456
Indianapolis, Indiana 46204
Telephone: (317) 269-7212

Iowa

St. Louis District Office
1601 Olive St.
St. Louis, Missouri 63103
Telephone: (314) 425-5571

Kansas

Kansas City District Office
1150 Grand Ave., 1st Floor
Kansas City, Missouri 64106
Telephone: (816) 374-5773

Kentucky

Memphis District Office
The Dermon Bldg., Suite 1004
46 North Third St.
Memphis, Tennessee 38103
Telephone: (901) 534-3591

Louisiana

New Orleans District Office
Hale Boggs Federal Bldg.
500 Camp St., Suite 1007
New Orleans, Louisiana 70130
Telephone: (504) 589-2721

Maine

Boston District Office
150 Causeway St., Suite 1000
Boston, Massachusetts 02114
Telephone: (617) 223-4535

Maryland

Baltimore District Office
Rotunda Building, Rm. 210
711 W. 40th St.
Baltimore, Maryland 21211
Telephone: (301) 962-3932

Massachusetts

Boston District Office
150 Causeway St., Suite 1000
Boston, Massachusetts 02114
Telephone: (617) 223-4535

Michigan

Detroit District Office
Michigan Bldg., Suite 600
200 Bagley Ave.
Detroit, Michigan 48226
Telephone: (313) 226-7636

Minnesota

Milwaukee District Office
Veterans Administration Bldg.
342 N. Water St., 6th Fl.
Milwaukee, Wisconsin 53202
Telephone: (414) 224-1111

Mississippi

Jackson District Office
The Petroleum Bldg.
200 E. Pascagoula St.
Fifth Floor
Jackson, Mississippi 39201
Telephone: (601) 969-4537

Missouri

St. Louis District Office
1601 Olive St.
St. Louis, Missouri 63103
Telephone: (314) 425-5571

Kansas City District Office
1150 Grand Ave., 1st Floor
Kansas City, Missouri 64106
Telephone: (816) 374-5773

Montana

Denver District Office
Ross Bldg., 6th Floor
1726 Champa St.
Denver, Colorado 80202
Telephone: (303) 837-3668

Nebraska

Kansas City District Office
1150 Grand Ave., 1st Floor
Kansas City, Missouri 64106
Telephone: (816) 374-5773

Nevada

Phoenix District Office
Valley Central Bldg.
201 N. Central Ave., Suite 1450
Phoenix, Arizona 85073
Telephone: (602) 261-3882

New Hampshire

Boston District Office
150 Causeway St., Suite 1000
Boston, Massachusetts 02114
Telephone: (617) 223-4535

New Jersey

Newark District Office
744 Broad St., Suite 502
Newark, New Jersey 07102
Telephone: (201) 645-5967

New Mexico

Albuquerque District Office
Western Bank Bldg., Suite 1515
505 Marquette Ave., N.W.
Albuquerque, New Mexico 87101
Telephone: (505) 766-2061

New York
New York District Office
90 Church St., 13th Fl.
New York, New York 10007
Telephone: (212) 264-7161

Buffalo District Office
One W. Genesse St., Rm. 320
Buffalo, New York 14202
Telephone: (716) 842-5170

North Carolina

Charlotte District Office
403 North Tryon St., 2nd Floor
Charlotte, North Carolina 28202
Telephone: (704) 372-0711 ext. 541

North Dakota

Denver District Office
Ross Bldg., 6th Floor
1726 Champa St.
Denver, Colorado 80202
Telephone: (303) 837-3668

Ohio

Cincinnati District Office
Federal Bldg., Rm. 7019
550 Main St.
Cincinnati, Ohio 45202
Telephone: (513) 684-2851

Cleveland District Office
Engineers Bldg., Rm. 402
1365 Ontario St.
Cleveland, Ohio 44114
Telephone: (216) 522-4793

Oklahoma

Albuquerque District Office
Western Bank Bldg., Suite 1515
505 Marquette Ave., N.W.
Albuquerque, New Mexico 87101
Telephone: (505) 766-2061

Oregon

Seattle District Office
Times Square Bldg., 4th Fl.
414 Olive Way
Seattle, Washington 98101
Telephone: (206) 442-0968

Pennsylvania

Pittsburgh District Office
Federal Bldg., Rm. 2038A
1000 Liberty Avenue
Pittsburgh, Pennsylvania 15222
Telephone: (412) 644-3444

Philadelphia District Office
219 North Broad St., 2nd Fl.
Philadelphia, Pennsylvania 19107
Telephone: (215) 597-9350

Rhode Island

Boston District Office
150 Causeway St., Suite 1000
Boston, Massachusetts 02114
Telephone: (617) 223-4535

South Carolina

Atlanta District Office
Citizens Trust Bldg., 10th Fl.
75 Piedmont Ave., N.E.
Atlanta, Georgia 30303
Telephone: (404) 526-4566

South Dakota

Denver District Office
Ross Bldg., 6th Floor
1726 Champa St.
Denver, Colorado 80202
Telephone: (303) 837-3668

Tennessee

Memphis District Office
The Dermon Bldg., Suite 1004
46 North Third St.
Memphis, Tennessee 38103
Telephone: (901) 534-3591

Birmingham District Office
2121 8th Ave., North, Rm. 824
Birmingham, Alabama 35203
Telephone: (205) 254-1166

Texas

Dallas District Office
Corrigan Towers, 6th Fl.
212 N. St. Paul Street
Dallas, Texas 75201
Telephone: (214) 749-1751

Houston District Office
2320 LaBranch, Rm. 1101
Houston, Texas 77004
Telephone: (713) 226-5611

San Antonio District Office
727 E. Durango St., Suite B-601
San Antonio, Texas 79206
Telephone: (512) 225-5511 ext. 4864

Albuquerque District Office
Western Bank Bldg., Suite 1515
505 Marquette Ave., N.W.
Albuquerque, New Mexico 87101
Telephone: (505) 766-2061

Utah

Denver District Office
Ross Bldg., 6th Floor
1726 Champa St.
Denver, Colorado 80202
Telephone: (303) 837-3668

Vermont

Boston District Office
150 Causeway St., Suite 1000
Boston, Massachusetts 02114
Telephone: (617) 223-4535

Virginia

Washington, D.C. District Office
1717 H St., N.W., Suite 400
Washington, D.C. 20006
Telephone: (202) 653-6197

Washington

Seattle District Office
Times Square Bldg., 4th Fl.
414 Olive Way
Seattle, Washington 98101
Telephone: (206) 442-0968

West Virginia

Pittsburgh District Office
Federal Bldg., Rm. 2038A
1000 Liberty Ave.
Pittsburgh, Pennsylvania 15222
Telephone: (412) 644-3444

Wisconsin

Milwaukee District Office
Veterans Administration Bldg.
342 N. Water St., 6th Fl.
Milwaukee, Wisconsin 53202
Telephone: (414) 224-1111

Wyoming

Denver District Office
Ross Bldg., 6th Floor
1726 Champa St.
Denver, Colorado 80202
Telephone: (303) 837-3668

Canal Zone

Miami District Office
Biscayne Terrace Hotel, 10th Fl.
340 Biscayne Blvd.
Miami, Florida 33132
Telephone: (305) 350-4491

Guam

San Francisco District Office
Fox Plaza, Suite 325
1390 Market St.
San Francisco, California 94102
Telephone: (415) 556-0260

Puerto Rico

New York District Office
90 Church St., 13th Fl.
New York, New York 10007
Telephone: (212) 264-7161

Samoa

San Francisco District Office
Fox Plaza, Suite 325
1390 Market St.
San Francisco, California 94102
Telephone: (415) 556-0260

Virgin Islands

New York District Office
90 Church St., 13th Fl.
New York, New York 10007
Telephone: (212) 264-7161

Wake Island

San Francisco District Office
Fox Plaza, Suite 325
1390 Market St.
San Francisco, California 94102
Telephone: (415) 556-0260

Chapter Nine
PACING YOUR CAREER: LONG-TERM STRATEGIES FOR SUCCEEDING ON THE JOB

If you're shouldering the dual responsibilities of work and family, expect a few of those grim, soul-searching times when you look around at your old schoolmates, your husband and colleagues and see them all Moving Ahead—finishing a thesis, landing an exciting promotion, taking on new job challenges—while you're hoarding your daytime office energies to cope with diaper rash and 2 A.M. feedings. Even if you've *chosen* to devote your energies to family, you will still occasionally feel those jealous pangs of "What-am-I-doing-with-my-life?" These moments need only be fleeting, for the first requirement of pacing your career is a good dose of courage about not following the pack.

Certainly there can be no sense of worth in working without a real commitment on your part. But that does not have to mean a career with no breaks, a rise to success patterned after and paced to a man's. It *does* mean that you may have to be more energetic, flexible, and risk-taking than others without parental responsibilities. But working mothers—as we admiringly saw again and again—are nothing if not versatile.

And a great many of us manage to enjoy a more rewarding work life than those plodding single-mindedly in the rat race. For one thing, because a mother's duty to children is widely accepted, you will enjoy a few time options that men don't. "When a man comes in with five years blank on his resume," says a veteran executive recruiter, "my guard immediately goes up. I may understand perfectly well why he took time out to travel, try out a creative endeavor, or just find himself. But my corporate clients don't always share my understanding. They're worried that he might be too individualistic, unstable. But with a woman, it's no problem to explain, 'She took time off when her children were young.' Sometimes it's even a plus. The employer regards her favorably as stably married, settled.

180

Since she's had her kids, they don't worry the way they would with a younger woman that she'll eventually quit to raise a family."

Having a professionally acceptable reason for dropping out of work in a world that expects us all to be gainfully employed from age eighteen to sixty-five (no gaps on the resume!) is only one small reason, however, why a mother can achieve a more humane and balanced career. Having other strong commitments besides your job forces you to wrestle with your deeper needs and make choices that men and childless women aren't forced to confront until it's too late. The magnets of success and ambition are powerful in our competitive, individualistic society, and, until recently, few of us questioned the work ethic or the price of job achievement. Pursuing such goals single-mindedly for the first twenty years of their careers, American men typically suffer a crisis of doubt about their work lives in their late thirties. Many working mothers long before that age, in fact, in their mid-twenties, thrash out their personal balance between their ambition and fulfillment with family and avoid being pressed into an over-investment in career success, to the exclusion of other human values. Says the powerful woman head of a publishing house, who has risen to the top of a field dominated by men and childless women: "Having children tempered my ambition in a useful way. I haven't pursued success with the same anxiety I would have otherwise."

One good question to ask yourself along the way: are you pursuing a career or is it pursuing you? Are you following deep impulses within yourself that require fulfillment in work—or driving yourself in a need to "perform" for the world? In school, we, far more than men, tend to perform as "good students" for teachers—studying for tests, giving the "right" answers we know are expected, hinging our self-worth on teachers' approval. When we work, many of us continue right along in that path of passive performing, exchanging teachers for bosses as judges of our work. A hard-driving magazine editor who's pushed to the top of her field surprisingly confesses herself a victim of this hang-up: "Even if I think I've put out a terrific issue, I never *really* think so until my male editor-in-chief pats me on the back and says 'terrific.' I still perform for his approval. I don't trust my own judgments."

Bosses certainly have to approve of us; work must certainly be done according to our boss's needs; but a woman who always depends on her superiors to set goals and tell her how good she is isn't likely to ever have the independence to take control of her own career. Deciding how much energy you want to put into work just now . . . whether that new title and raise are really what you want (and whether you're willing to pay the price of having less time for your family) . . . deciding whether the lock-step achievements your profession prescribes can be shortened or omitted —these are the gut issues you have to wrestle with. In the struggle, you just may discover that you can defer some of the demands of your career without feeling guilty about cheating yourself or achieving less than you've been educated for.

No one says it will be easy to make choices, but one thing is certain: decisions about your career ambitions are not something you can tuck behind you until next year, as the childless can. Elizabeth, a brilliant, divorced, thirty-five-year-old law professor who's managed to publish several important articles, win a landmark case in her state, and hold down a full-time teaching job while raising her three sons alone, told us, "When you're forced to make daily decisions about how you're spending your time—you either are going to the PTA tonight or you're staying home to work on a professional article—you have to stop a minute and say, 'Look, is my career important to me because I *want* to be working so hard at it right now? . . . or is it because everybody else says I ought to be working so hard at it right now?' "

An intense, fragile-boned woman who's never without her leather briefcase bulging with such miscellanea as a Little League sponsor pin, an hour-by-hour schedule book, and a sheaf of papers from a law case-book, Elizabeth formed a small rap group with other teaching mothers to confront their common problems. She is convinced that professional women have the clout to make their careers more flexible and less con-suming. "I think there are real deficiencies in the male model of successful work, and women have got to feel strong enough to put their families first when it's important.

"We don't need," Elizabeth says angrily, "to feel defensive about wanting to be with our kids at important times as they grow up. I *am* good at my job, and I think it's fair to say they're lucky I'm working for them, but my family right now comes first for me. That doesn't mean that my profession isn't important, but it's going to have to give in some ways for the time being."

Because Elizabeth has managed to be highly successful while staving off many career pressures, she is often called upon to advise other women who are reluctant to sacrifice their personal lives and time with their chil-dren for getting ahead. "Sometimes," she says, "women just need someone to say it really is okay, your personal life is more important than your professional." Or, we hasten to add, that you *can* space your commitments, you won't necessarily destroy your professional investment with unorthodox decisions or gaps. Working mothers—and many younger men—are developing new strategies for working without sacrificing their families. We're convinced that within ten years, management specialists will be writing their doctoral theses on "career pacing" and "the new laid-back executive"—all patterned after such successful working mothers as Elizabeth.

CAREER PLANNING

One of the most useful and effective precautions you can take in planning your work life is to find out how the job market will develop in coming years. Despite bows to career counseling in high school and college, this simple act is one most women neglect. If you're taking time off or working while maintaining a family, you don't want to face the added disadvantage of a tight job market with two job openings and two hundred candidates.

Where Will the Jobs Be? Women have notoriously been educated for impractical fields. Two hundred years ago, our great-grandmothers studied needle arts while their brothers mastered the practical math and spelling needed to earn a living. Today, bright women tend to study Russian literature while men march off from college with a useful business or engineering degree. Whether you've been trained with a practical eye or not, nothing could be more essential to pacing your career than *realistically assessing where your field's going in the next five or ten years.*

We're living in a time of rapid occupational upheaval. Technology and slowing economic growth are drying up many traditional fields and creating new professions overnight. Getting a college degree—once the ticket to jobs and upward mobility—will no longer guarantee that a position is waiting for you. For example, 43 percent of all professional women are now employed as elementary or secondary-school teachers, an occupation that has historically offered upward mobility to thousands of women. But, as the American birth rate drops, the increasing number of women college graduates are running smack into a dramatic slowdown in the teacher market. Women who look to this established women's field will have to retrain. Many a young woman is already learning, to her sorrow, that having a teacher's degree is a good qualification for getting her a job —as a cocktail waitress.

The number of *clerical jobs*—the field where one out of every three working mothers now works—will jump by 30 percent, rising from 15.6 million jobs in 1976 to 20 million in 1985.* Both the largest and fastest-growing occupational group, the clerical field will continue to offer nationwide job opportunities. But computerization will eliminate many routine, repetitive clerical jobs, and the desirable clerical worker will be someone who can prepare material for the computer (a shift you can train for). Typists, secretaries, and receptionists will also increase in number.

The *service-producing industries* will mushroom by 26 percent as our society increases in income and leisure, with workers jumping from 56 million in 1976 to 71 million in the mid-1980s. Examine the array of jobs that fall into these industries—beauty operators, police officers, fire fighters, cooks, mail carriers, occupational health and safety workers, accountants, insurance adjusters—and you're likely to find a job you'll like in a field that will offer continued good opportunity. Business and banking services, for example, will expand rapidly. A woman who trains as an accountant, data processor, or in the banking or credit agencies will have a strong job market to shop in. You'll also be in demand if you specialize in health services, which will have thousands of new openings for nurse assistants, technicians, paraprofessionals, occupational therapists, and other skilled health workers with two-year training. In the service occupations, only jobs for household workers will shrink.

The number of *managers and administrators*—jobs now held by a mere 5 percent of all women—will increase 21 percent to over 11 million by 1985, and, as women make inroads, will offer great financial opportunity. But good training in a particular business or in management skills is essential if you're to advance to financial reward and a title on your door.

Despite the shrinkage in teaching, which currently employs the lion's share of professional women, *professional and technical jobs* will grow by 18 percent as we reach the middle of the 1980s. Strong new professions: jobs that focus on energy conservation, urban planning, and the environment.

If you've earned your living as a *salesperson,* expect uneven growth.

* All figures according to the authoritative forecasts of the U.S. Department of Labor, in the 1978–79 edition of its bible, *The Occupational Outlook Handbook.*

25 GOOD JOB PROSPECTS FOR THE 1980s

Job	Current Average Income	Future Demand Prospects
Accountants	$15,400–23,400	Excellent. Jobs for accountants will increase to 1,000,000 by 1985.
Advertising copywriters, design artists	$10,000–50,000+	Good. Advertising services will increase markedly.
Banking clerks and tellers	$6,000–9,000	Excellent. Banking services are growing.
Computer-console and peripheral equipment operators	$10,400–13,400	Good. Jobs will rise to over 300,000. Note: Jobs for less-skilled keypunch operators will decline.
Computer programmers	$18,000	Very good.
Dental assistants	$9,000+	Excellent, with very good part-time opportunities.
Dental hygienists	$12,900	Good—also excellent part-time opportunities.
Dentists	$39,500	Very good.
Dieticians	$14,000–25,400 (for experienced dietician)	Good.
Doctors	$54,000+	Good, but growing numbers of graduates and foreign medical students will offer more competition and push some graduates to practice in rural areas.
Insurance agents and brokers	$15,000–30,000+	Good.
Market researchers	$19,000+	Good.

Job	Current Average Income	Future Demand Prospects
Medical technicians: optometric assistants, emergency medical technicians, medical laboratory workers, respiratory therapy workers	$7,000–10,000	Good.
Medical record administrators	$15,700	Good.
Landscape architects	$15,000–20,000	Good.
Lawyers	$18,000–50,000+	Good, but increasingly competitive.
Licensed practical nurses	$9,000+	Very good. Currently, 1,500,000 jobs.
Personnel and labor-relations workers	$19,200	Good.
Pharmacists	$14,000–17,000+	Favorable.
Real estate agents and brokers	$13,000–40,000+	Favorable.
Registered nurses	$15,500	Favorable, but nurses will have an increased need for specialized training.
Social workers	$13,000–$16,000 to start (with MSW)	Favorable.
Technical writers	$18,000	Favorable.
Urban planners	$11,000–28,000	Favorable.
Veterinarians	$24,000+	Favorable.

Suburban stores and expanding trade will spur some increase in retail-store salespeople, but self-service and central checkout counters will eliminate other positions for cashiers and related workers. The answer can be to switch to sales jobs traditionally held by men—selling cars, equipment, and other hard products that will pay you better commissions.

Now that women are bringing home good paychecks from *crafts,* they can look forward to a strong increasing market, with the number of craft jobs (carpenters, electricians, automobile mechanics, to name a few) growing by 22 percent. Regular *blue-collar jobs*—assemblers, packers, truck drivers, machine operators—will have a dimmer future as, overall, American jobs move into white-collar fields. Once a small proportion of the total labor force, white-collar workers will number about 55 million in 1985, compared to only about 35 million blue-collar workers by that time.

Where Is the Money?　You're probably not just looking for a job; you're looking for a job that will pay you well. The direction? It will usually lie in a field that is now male-dominated. Consider this grim statistic: The median income of women in 1975 was $7,504, compared to $12,758 for men. In other words, *women take home, on the average, only 59 percent of what men workers do.* There is a marked correlation between occupations in which women predominate (teaching, social work, library science, clerical work) and low wages. "Women's work"—even if it's in the office—is consistently paid less than male-dominated occupations.

Do finance, insurance, and banking strike you as dull "men's" jobs? Actually, these areas already have a predominantly female work force at the lower levels, and all three areas will grow sharply in the 1980s, offering a decidedly good market for the woman who wants to work her way into the male-held higher levels.

Law, medicine, and dentistry, the golden occupations, are finally becoming more feminized. The number of women receiving law degrees more than quintupled between 1970 and 1976 (average income of lawyers with only a few years of experience: $30,000). And women currently comprise 20 percent of all medical students (average M.D. income: $54,000). A good rule of thumb for a woman who wants to earn high wages is to look to male jobs like accounting, restaurant management, retail management, banking, insurance, industrial management, engineering, government, and politics. And don't get stuck in the "woman's" side of your field—if you're interested in getting as much pay as a man, don't sell dresses, sell *cars.* Don't aim to manage the secretarial pool, aim to manage the *factory.* Don't file the insurance policies, *sell* them. Don't remain at the social-worker case worker; move on to the *administrative job above.*

Where Is the Information?   If you'd like to find out about the future of your own occupation or job possibilities you haven't thought about, one of the best sources is *The Occupational Outlook Handbook,* a huge but readable tome of job information published every two years by the United States Bureau of Labor and available in any library. If you can't locate a copy, order one for $8 from the Superintendent of Documents, Government Printing Office, Washington, D.C. 20002.

The *Handbook* is our most authoritative forecast of rising and shrinking occupations, as well as a fountain of information on salaries earned in an occupation, the nature of the work, training required, and working conditions. Another good source to check is the monthly magazine *Women's Work,* usually available in local libraries, and chock-full of authoritative information on unusual or overlooked careers for women and how you can train for them.

LONG-RANGE STRATEGIES

Pacing your career is a mixture of attitude and specific ploys. Here's what the women who are managing have discovered.

Establish Yourself.   The best plan for combining a career and family is undoubtedly to *establish yourself first.* Get a good basic training and several years of work experience, and you'll have a firm foundation for returning to work without sliding backward on the job ladder. Or, if you plan to work through your child's infancy, you'll have the clout as an experienced employee to ease off in your work while your toddler demands your energy at home.

Whether you're a telephone operator, a typist, or a TV writer, having a few years of job experience before you take on family responsibilities that will last for eighteen or more years gives you an important chance to test yourself in the work world and absorb its rules and mechanics. Experimenting in several fields or with different companies can teach you more about yourself than the best planning or training.

But don't assume that this means you must deny yourself children when you want them. Many women in their twenties now tend to postpone motherhood. But other couples, like Jill and Harry, both engineers, are agreeing to take time off alternately. "I took a year off when our daughter was born," says Jill. "And then I went back and Harry took a year off to stay with her. We realized it's much easier to take one year off than two." And easier to take two years off than five. Jill and Harry are part of a growing number of couples who both want to be with their children for extended periods, without unduly delaying their careers.

Avoid Either/Or Thinking.   Janet, a bright, hard-working M.B.A., joined a Chicago conglomerate after graduation, and moved up the ranks. On her way up, Janet married, bore twin boys, and went right on rising, winning an assistant vice-presidency on the twins' fourth birthday. When her boys were six and in public school, her company president offered Janet a plum: developing a new branch of the company in Atlanta. The job was one Janet was logically working up to in her company, and turning down this spectacular offer seemed unthinkable. Refusal would tarnish Janet's winner's image in the company she had worked for during her ten years since school.

Janet was torn. "Our community was ideal for raising kids, and our boys had the same housekeeper they'd always known. My husband was very settled in his job, and we felt very happy in our surroundings. I really went through agony for a week. Accepting the promotion would have meant one of those long-distance marriages you read about, or else taking months or years for Jim to find a job in the South. It was very painful. I had to rethink my values." In the end, Janet turned down her promotion.

Within six months, Janet accepted an offer with a smaller local firm that offered her a wider range of responsibilities. "I don't think most men would have had the guts to turn down something they'd worked toward so long. But when I really got down to what means the most to me, my family happiness does. I know over the long range of my work life, I'll move up. And as it's turned out, this crisis forced me into a good move. I had my sights too narrowly focused staying with the same company."

Janet's experience is instructive for other mothers who are torn by an attractive offer that interferes with their commitment to their families. Does the job offer seem so fantastic you'll never get another chance like it? Perhaps so. But the statistical chances are that an equally attractive offer will come your way again. A woman long experienced in affirmative action muses about a young woman with two small children who recently was offered—and accepted—a heady job as college president. "I think probably she made a mistake," says the affirmative-action official. "If she's really got the stuff, she'll be even riper and will succeed on the next round when she's older. And if she doesn't, then she won't succeed now either."

She offers reassurance to business women as well: "You're really not likely to get only one great offer in a career. Usually the offer you get is commensurate with your particular worth. Moreover, you learn an awful lot between the ages of thirty and fifty. Whatever makes you attractive to an employer now will make you even more attractive in five or ten years."

When you feel ambivalent over a difficult career choice, avoid the bleak, short-range either/or view. "Either I take this promotion, or I'll never move up." "Either I push myself to do this, or I won't be taken seriously."

Establish That Your Years of Limited Work Responsibilities Are Limited. No employer is going to automatically look favorably on a woman employee who is reluctant to take on wider responsibilities. How can you avoid being disregarded—or stuck in a dead-end job or at the same salary? Tell your employer frankly that you'll be ready for greater responsibility in a few years. That you're continuing to perform dependably in the job you have, but that you definitely don't plan to vegetate. When your children go to school (or to high school or whatever milestone you're looking toward), you'll be ready and eager to move up and out. Many working mothers are amazed to discover how simply reassuring their bosses of their long-range ambition produces a different attitude toward them. "My boss is very tight," says a secretary who plans to move into a more demanding sales job as soon as her three-year-old son goes to school, "and he loves having an overqualified secretary who can analyze sales reports and knows the products so well he doesn't have to spell out everything when he dictates. But I've let him know that I expect to be rewarded when my time comes to move on. Right now we both feel we're getting something we want."

Making a deal with your boss to hold your place in the promotion line can be tricky. Veteran career analyst and Catalyst president Felice Schwartz warns, "You can't expect an employer looking for his return on investment to settle for less from you than he would from a man. However, you *can* make a deal by saying, 'Listen, I'm a high-potential person who's willing to work in a lower-potential job for the next two or three years. But let me stay abreast of what's happening during these three years so that later I can maybe make a quantum leap.'"

Peaks and Valleys in Work Life.   Many working mothers are determined not to follow the model that male workers have traditionally set—strict adherence to a career immediately following college. Recognize that there may be periods when you'll ease back from work, perhaps take a couple of years off. Once you've proved that you can make it in the business world, you'll feel less anxious about pulling back when your children demand more time. Consider how Jean de Boskey, a thirty-two-year-old Colorado lawyer who's gone far, is pacing her career.

Jean spent her first pregnancy campaigning all over her state for a reform candidate for attorney general. Her man won, and Jean was appointed to the number-two position of assistant attorney general. While in the last stages of pregnancy, she set up her office staff, and then, with the help of a cooperative husband and a dedicated sitter, made it neatly through the next two years, balancing her pressured job with the needs of a young baby. But now Jean's expecting a second child. She's resigned her job to stay home with both babies for several years. Does she regret sacrificing the momentum of her career, a withdrawal that startled her colleagues?

"Not really," says Jean, still slender in her jeans despite being six months pregnant. "If you want a balanced life, you have to plan for it. Women more than men. That's all right. Maybe I won't zoom ahead as fast as I might. But I can go back in two years. Meanwhile, I plan to do a lot of professional catching up on my reading and studying. Right now, my son needs to know more about his mommy, whom he's only seen at night and on weekends."

Take Time Off When It's Meaningful to You.   As part of your independent attitude, take time off from working when *you* think it's right. We generally assume that the time to stop working is when your baby is born. Not so for everyone. Ellen, an assistant buyer for a West Coast fashion house, worked straight through the babyhood of her two girls. But when the elder reached three, Ellen quit to stay home for the next three years. "I feel that's the age when you really instill values in your children, when they're able to talk and learn about the world. That's when I want to be with them, to take them to zoos and play with them and read books and answer all their questions myself. I don't think they would have gained anything from *me* as an individual during those first years, when they just needed someone to change the diapers and feed them." Set your own pace and timetable.

Late-Thirties Creativity.   One of the secret weapons you have in pacing your career is the extra burst of creativity that many women experience in their late thirties and early forties. (A recent fascinating cross-cultural study by University of Michigan psychologist D. L. Gutman revealed that as women age, they become less passive and assume more active, dominant roles in their societies. And women past child-bearing age seem more comfortable about expressing aggressive impulses.) Perhaps biologically based, this outward turning of a woman's energies seems to erupt when her physiological childbearing functions are ending. Of course, her mothering function is also usually less demanding, and her new energies could come simply from having more time for herself. Men at forty, on the other hand, are often worn down by years of work and restive to shed job pressures.

Whatever the reason for this phenomenon, this sudden energy and confidence transforms too many women not to believe it's a common pattern. A woman novelist who's puttered around finishing her long-overdue second novel suddenly hits her creative stride . . . a thirty-eight-year-old woman who's drifted from one career to another opens her own boutique and finds a vocation . . . a forty-two-year-old woman stuck in office managing suddenly gets a chance to join the executive ranks and discovers she loves it. . . . Your late thirties and early forties can be the beginning of a whole new work life. If you're forced to hold back at work during some part of your children's growing-up years, you can still look forward to being a successful late bloomer.

ELIZABETH'S STORY

One of the women most successful at juggling home and work whom we talked with was Elizabeth. Her career as law student and now as law professor demonstrates several pacing principles.

Elizabeth's first hard choice came when she discovered that top-flight law schools refuse to allow part-time study. She still gets angry remembering how her family-law class was always inconveniently scheduled at four in the afternoon—"Here I was supposed to be studying family law just when I needed to be getting home to my family." But because her choice of a school would determine her career future, she decided "it was going to be hard enough being a woman in law. I didn't want to face the double disadvantage of being a woman and not having gone to the best school possible. So, although it took a lot of sacrifice from my family, I went full-time."

As Elizabeth's children grew older, the strain eased (even though she was divorced in her last year of school), and on graduation, she was offered the biggest plum: a coveted clerkship with a U.S. Supreme Court Justice. Elizabeth put in ninety-hour-weeks at her Washington job (with the help of a carefully chosen live-in baby-sitter), but won "the kind of insight into the judicial process that you get *nowhere* else in American law."

Once her two years in Washington ended, she made a dramatic switch, not derailing her career but not taking the next obvious step up the ladder either. "I was hot property then and happily I had job offers from lots of good schools." The most tempting bid came from a major urban university set in a ghetto area. Elizabeth would have had to establish her children miles away in the suburbs—and spend a minimum of an hour commuting each way. Demonstrating unusual self-awareness, Elizabeth simply refused to go to the interview. "I knew my ego would get involved and I wouldn't be able to turn it down."

Instead, Elizabeth job-shopped carefully, finally accepting an assistant professorship at a West Coast university located in a small town. This relaxed, child-centered setting puts her next door to her work. "I can bicycle to work in ten minutes, which also means I can get back in ten minutes if I need to. It was important to me, since I am divorced, to have an atmosphere where the kids can get around on their own safely and know our neighbors. We have a house and small-town friendliness. But we also enjoy the culture that exists in a college town."

After her intense involvement in Washington, Elizabeth is delaying some obvious professional moves she could be making—but with full confidence that she can recover the ground when her children need her less. "I'm good and I'm well trained, and nothing's going to hold me back." In fact, she stunned her college superiors recently by asking them to delay reviewing her record with tenure in mind. She explained that her family responsibilities as a single mother prevented her from researching and publishing as she'd like, and asked the committee to let her proceed at her own pace. She won her request—and has been besieged ever since with admiring inquiries from women and men colleagues who'd like to do the same thing.

As a result, Elizabeth can spend a good part of her weekends not holed up in the library, but cheering on the Little League where her middle son plays shortstop, baking a birthday cake for her youngest, and embroiled in the other activities of a child-centered town. She's confident that her priorities are in the right place.

Elizabeth has acted on our basic principles of pacing a career. She established herself, and when she needed to take a step essential to her career—attending school full-time to get a prestigious degree—she asked her family to accommodate. Now, secure with a degree and professional credentials, she has the flexibility to take time off from her career when it's important to her. And she's avoided the grim either/or route—instead, forging her own unique way that's sacrificing neither her motherhood nor her professional talents.

DROPPING OUT

If you do decide to drop out of work for a while, don't expect the world to stand still waiting for your return. Take out insurance that you'll be able to reenter with a minimum of strain. As a start, be sure to collect a letter of recommendation from your boss, who'll most likely have moved up or away when you return.

Keep Your Hand In Part-Time. Most people prefer to hire a proven quantity, someone they already know, and for this reason, you'll be wise to work part-time in your field. A Texas accountant kept up her career by working part-time during the overflow tax season, not only for her former employer but for several other firms. When she was ready to resume full-time work, she had her pick of jobs in six firms, all of which knew, firsthand, her competence. "If I'd just dropped out," she says, "I would never have gotten back in at the salary I did. And I probably would have been scared to death to even try."

Contacts with people in the work world are also priceless when you're reentering. A kind of law of conservatism seems to work in most job markets, where an inner circle of people who know each other hire and get hired. Having contacts with those who are working assures that you'll learn about new jobs when they occur and have valuable sponsors.

Look Ahead. Don't wait for the morning your child walks off to first grade to start searching the newspaper want ads. Use your years at home to prepare. If you can't spare time for evening classes, you can take correspondence courses in your home, in almost any field from basic accounting to designing, business writing to shorthand and typing. ("The smartest thing I ever did," says a TV producer who finished Wellesley with honors and won a Woodrow Wilson scholarship, "was learn shorthand and typing." Whatever your training, learn how to type; it's a basic business skill.)

If you can't afford tuition, take advantage of free classes offered in your community. Check at your local Y, church groups, and publicly funded colleges.

Bone up on job fields that are growing (see pages 185–186). Now's the time to get career counseling. An expert can be particularly helpful in guiding you to areas that will be most rewarding to you—and then helping you lay out a program to prepare.

A cost-saving word on career counseling: At least for your first try, scout around for one of the many helpful *free* career-counseling services being offered by Ys, university women's centers, and other groups. Remember that the value and quality of career counseling need not bear a relation to the size of the fee charged. And, of course, when you use a counselor, be *sure* you know beforehand what it's going to cost you.

Keep Up. Maintain your membership in any business associations you've joined, whether it's your city-wide accounting group or the women's baseball team of Union Amalgamated. Lunch with old friends from work occasionally. Many a job has been heard of and won over a martini.

Develop a Specialty. One of the best techniques for insuring your profitable return to the job market is to develop a skill that's in short supply. Dottie, a lawyer with four children, worked three afternoons a week when her children were small, "at a job no man wanted—state bankruptcy official. It paid very little and had no prestige." Now that Dottie's children are in school, she's in the enviable position of being one of three top bankruptcy experts in her state and has her pick of offers from a number of large law firms who need her specialty.

Teachers might use their time at home to prepare for a specialty insulated from the academic slowdown, such as special education or guidance. Professional women can use their freedom from the job to complete research projects that will add to their credits.

Volunteer. Unpaid volunteer work is much maligned these days as exploitative and time wasting. But many a mother unsure of her abilities can benefit from well-chosen volunteer work. Performing any job well will give her a good dose of confidence, and she may also get a chance to demonstrate high-level managerial abilities that will be impressive on her resume when she decides to reenter the business world.

Evelyn, a forty-one-year-old mother of two boys, married to a psychiatrist, hadn't worked for fifteen years when she volunteered to help the local fund-raising campaign for the public television station. Her energy, imagination, and organizational skill propelled her to take charge of the entire campaign, supervising a staff of thirty-five solicitors, cajoling local merchants to devote prizes, and devising a new marathon appeal. One of her volunteer phone solicitors was a newspaper owner who was looking for a bright advertising manager to revamp his chain of small neighborhood newspapers. He offered Evelyn the job, based on the showcase of talent her volunteer work had provided.

Reentry. If you plan well and are determined, a return to rewarding work is possible. And don't give up too soon: Finding your way back into a good job after absence from the job market can be a disheartening, arduous, and lengthy process. Smooth your search with one of these tactics.

Pick a job that requires maturity. Employers are increasingly aware that the experience of women in mid-life equips them to perform some jobs more effectively than a younger woman. Catalyst president Felice Schwartz, who's turning her organization's efforts to searching out jobs where mid-life women are welcome, cites two opportunities. One unexpected one: managing a McDonald's restaurant. "McDonald's does *not* want someone just out of college," explains Ms. Schwartz. "They want a thirty-five-year-old woman who has the authority and presence to manage the average McDonald's staff of sixty-five kids. Someone who appreciates a good career opportunity, but doesn't mind the tough work. Their favorite candidate is a thirty-five-year-old divorced woman with kids, who was a teacher!"

"Insurance sales is another excellent area," continues Ms. Schwartz. A mature woman can be far more effective in selling a product, like life insurance, that requires authority and responsibility.

Taking the time to master basic skills before you reenter is essential. "My advice," says dynamic film producer Linda Gottlieb, "is to learn to type and take shorthand so that there's something you can do that people can pay you to do. Get over the ridiculous attitude that it's beneath you. Once your foot is in the door, you can absorb what goes on and advance to bigger and better things."

Another suggestion for women trying to break in: *offer to do a job without pay*. Linda has helped ambitious women get nonpaying jobs on films because any sort of experience there is valuable in the long run. But she adds this caution: Even though you're working for free, do so with a sense of your own worth. Communicate that you're convinced you have something to offer and that you'll prove it on the job.

DOES BEING A MOTHER HELP YOU ON THE JOB?

No look at your long-term career plans can be complete without thought about one deep issue that unites your personal and professional life— how being a mother may eventually help your career. Many women who sacrifice getting ahead in the short term discover it well worth while in the long run. For they discover that being a mother can help them uncover new talents or impel them to greater accomplishments in work.

We gain confidence when we have children because childbirth, the ability to produce life, confirms our womanhood, putting to rest the fears we all have about performing inadequately in our sexual roles, whether we're male or female. Having fulfilled these personal goals, many of us then become more outwardly motivated toward career achievements. Harder to summarize is the emotional widening that motherhood can confer, leading a woman to deeper understanding of people and human relations. And from this widened knowledge comes the confidence to pursue work of her own.

What do women take from their mothering that helps them in their careers? And why do the very women who seem most taxed—running a job at the office, another at home—often prove the most efficient workers?

A high-school teacher: "Maybe what makes us such good workers is that we learn to juggle so many things, to grab opportunities to make time for ourselves, so we become proficient at handling many things at once, to switching gears all the time . . . and that makes us extra versatile and adaptable at work."

A professional writer: "I have more energy, more drive. I'm even writing a book besides my regular job."

An actress: "I always thought I was good at my job, but I found the depth and scope of my work has improved enormously."

A former editor, now managing her own bookstore: "Having a child made me reexamine my whole career and why I was unhappy with it. There's nothing like a little kid to make you grow up fast. All the old identity problems come to the fore and you have to face them honestly. It gave me the courage to take the risk and try something new that was better for me."

A college history teacher: "Being a mother has made my teaching far more human. I had had a rather cold, intellectual vision of history. Now I'm concerned with the human emotions behind the events—I can communicate that excitement and force to my students, not just the treaties and the politics and the economic changes."

A thirty-seven-year-old politician who's just won a city-wide election: "I would never have dreamed of going into politics unless I'd mothered three children. Probably I would have ended up with a technical job, like a city planner, because I'm interested in social action. But the experience of being intensely involved with—*responsible*—for three little human beings made me realize I could help people grow. I was a person able to do something constructive for myself and others as well."

Some women even discover that having a child releases a painful block that has barred them from being successful in their work. In *Working It Out*—a collection of fascinating stories by twenty-three women writers, scientists, artists, and scholars who tell their difficulties and triumphs in establishing themselves in work—scholar Sara Ruddick describes how, in her early twenties, she remained painfully paralyzed trying to complete a thesis, despite idyllic conditions: a husband who supported her emotionally, months untroubled by financial worries, and no mothering responsibilities to distract her. Strangely, her recovery came only when she bore a child.

"I began to organize my thesis almost the day I learned I was pregnant. I outlined it in the early months of pregnancy, writing it in the last months. I worked long hours, then lounged in the bath . . . with Gutmacher and Spock. At home with a new baby, I revised, then defended the thesis. . . . In my second daughter's infancy I returned to my desk [and] for the first time in a decade, I developed new intellectual interests which brought new life to my work."

Ruddick was puzzled and troubled by the release brought by maternity. "Why should new parenthood, which subtracts enormously from the time available for work, nonetheless make work more likely? . . . One obvious explanation is that with conventional feminine desires obviously satisfied, the fear of success in 'unfeminine' work is less acute." Ruddick adds that she resisted accepting the experience since it offended her intellectual pride. "Only recently have I been able to accept the fact that strength came from such a common and womanly experience."

Even those of us who do not experience a release through motherhood invariably find being a parent gives us new authority. It enlarges our perspectives and makes us look at our own lives more purposefully. Zane Kotker, novelist and working mother, says, "Parenthood is the great watershed of life, the great changer and transformer. It's as though you used to see through the glass darkly and then all of a sudden you see it all from the other point of view. It makes you a different, fuller person."

When a woman can draw from her experience of mothering, feelings that overflow and make her a more confident worker, and when her work feeds back into her mothering, she realizes a dream that all of us have: to unite the worlds of love and work; to join seamlessly the purely individual needs that each of us carries throughout life along with the needs of our family; to balance our powerful complex of demands so that neither robs the other and we can better enjoy both halves of the fully human person—caring and achieving. An elusive marriage, but one well worth working and fighting for.

Yourself

Chapter Ten

WILL WORKING HELP YOUR MARRIAGE?

"How does working change my marriage?" muses Abbie, a reporter for a suburban Florida newspaper. "It makes me a more interesting person, more attractive to my husband, and gives me more power in the marriage."

Abbie's swift summary capsulizes the experience of many women. Until recently, social researchers found a higher degree of conflict in marriages where the wives worked, and, in the fifties and sixties, "working wives" were popularly blamed for the rising divorce rate. Newer studies in the late sixties and seventies reflect a new reality: Middle-class families where both husband and wife work do *not* seem to experience more marital conflict than those where the wife does not work.

Indeed, some evidence suggests that *women who enjoy their jobs appear more satisfied with their marriages than wives who stay at home.*

Most of the working mothers we talked to clearly felt that working had a profound, though often subtle, effect on their marriages. None of them thought having a job would directly cause divorce. As Tina, a Chicana government worker, reflected on the dissatisfactions she was experiencing with her husband: "Working hasn't broken up my marriage. It's given me the option not to have to *stay* in the marriage. And that's encouraged me to reexamine things and try to make them better."

HOW MUCH CHANGE?

But some women, feeling conflict about what will happen when they leave their homes, end up ignoring good opportunities for change in their marriages. Sometimes these wives have husbands who distrust the whole idea of working wives—those magnanimous chaps who declare,

"Sure, I don't mind if she works—so long as I get my supper on time as usual." Confronted with such opposition, a wife may drive herself so that no one suffers inconvenience from her job—no one except herself.

Yet a good number of women with successful careers struck us as going out of their way to avoid allowing any change in their marriages. Long after they prove themselves to be valuable, competent workers, they cling to traditional arrangements in their homes. This is true even when their husbands are quite willing to accommodate to change. It is as though, frightened that any change in the status quo might wreck their marriages, they go overboard to be sure everything stays *exactly the same*. Each of these women continues to defer to her husband's opinions, run the household, take all the parenting responsibility, and insist that *his* job is the really important one in the family.

Certainly the road to a more satisfying, equal marriage is not smooth. Even if your husband is a rock of supportiveness, you'll probably suffer strains as your mutual expectations shift. One of the more intriguing findings of a broad-based 1972 study was that while working wives experience more conflict with their husbands, they also express more satisfaction with their marriages! Conflict and tension are not necessarily incompatible with marital happiness.

In fact, our talks with women revealed that the very areas where working wives say their marriages eventually improve—shared decision making, more trust and respect, a healthier emotional balance for the wife—*at first prove the worst areas of fighting and conflict with their husbands*.

Changing the assumptions under which both of you have been living together is unsettling and often frightening. But remember that all marriages change in time. And change does not necessarily mean that things are falling apart.

MONEY AND POWER

Money is the fulcrum around which your marital world can change—partly because of how earning money will make *you* feel. Ask almost any woman why she works and you'll get a fast "for the money." Ask her what her greatest moment of satisfaction is and she'll answer "when I get my paycheck."

A paycheck confers more than the money. It bestows a new power on you—tangible proof that society declares you a useful person—and engenders feeling like these:

"My paycheck is proof that I'm a productive person, that I can earn my way in the world."

"It shows I'm pulling my weight in the family. We have four kids and before we were terribly strapped and my husband was always nagging 'I have to carry all the responsibility, you don't help at all.' Now my paycheck is my contribution to our family and I feel respected."

"It gives me a right to a say in the decisions. Now I feel I can make decisions with my husband—and even disagree with him—about what to buy and how to live."

"It's a tangible reward for my time, not like housework."

As you begin to feel that you, too, are a person whose time is valued, you can expect that your attitude will affect your husband and children as well. It may even prompt a bit of revolution in your household. If you've been solely responsible for all the work, acting as full-time maid, cook, and nurse to your husband and children ("after all, that's my job, they go off to work and school" you probably felt), your financial contributions to the family welfare, along with the fact that you are spending less time at home, may now spur you to ask them for help.

You may cut back on the personal services you provide your husband, like sorting his laundry or shopping for his clothes—leading him to self-righteously remind you of how Joe down the street started straying when *his* wife dished out this treatment.

You may change the behavior expected of your children, letting them become responsible for their homework or go to the dentist alone.

And you'll surely participate more in decision making on everything from what color to paint the house to whether your husband should replace the two-year-old Chevy. Research studies of working wives in almost every Western country show that a woman who earns increases her power in decision making in the family's economic choices, like what car to buy, where to live and vacation, and what clothes to wear. It's not hard to see why.

Men, far more than women, tend to be pragmatists about money. Long accustomed to judging a person's worth by his wage-earning ability, they see a straight-line connection between money and power. They know the difficulty of earning money. And they respect those who can do it. Men seldom are troubled by the hang-ups that women have about the vulgarity of money. So it's no surprise that a wife usually discovers her paycheck is the strongest wedge she has in changing the balance of power in her marriage.

A word now on power: most of us prefer not to use this term in our love relations. Yet power *is* an issue in all human relationships, even those with your children. The trouble with the traditional dominant husband/submissive wife relationship is that it makes any open give-and-take very difficult. Locked into powerlessness within their own marriages, women have often been forced to resort to manipulation and deceit to express their wants, in acts that can range from an innocent calculation to "wait until he's in a good mood to tell him about the sofa we need" to the out-and-out use of sex.

Developing a more honest method of discussing and settling problems together only leads to a richer relationship between you and your husband. Feeling better about making decisions—feeling *entitled* to have feelings and act on them—should not make you afraid of turning into an insensitive person. Quite the reverse. Women who harbor resentment and anger against their husbands often find release and see their problems in a different light when they can act. They find themselves feeling more compassionate and understanding about their husbands' feelings and able to find new solutions to long-time conflicts.

HOW TO INCREASE YOUR
FINANCIAL DECISION MAKING

Working through to give yourself more control of the family money can involve painful or even humorous readjustments. One woman, angry at not having any say in the family budget for years while she stayed home, radically changed her view of herself when she began to work and demanded that her husband stop putting out the grocery money for her on "his" bureau. Instead, she insisted he leave this family fund in a "neutral place" on the refrigerator, one that didn't announce his "ownership" of the money.

A woman who'd never been allowed to write checks began to work and demanded that her husband open a joint checking account (and she's never had an unbalanced checkbook). Another young woman who'd worked before her marriage but turned over all the financial responsibility to her husband when she became a full-time mother, took a job and decided she would take charge not only of buying the car she needed to commute to work but getting the loan as well.

When both you and your husband earn, one of the simplest ways of giving each of you breathing space and autonomy is to agree on different areas of responsibility. Couples typically still split along traditional sex lines. For example, Ann and Larry, whose combined earnings of $28,000 are almost equally split between them: Ann, a speech therapist, pays for the groceries, the household expenses—from light bulbs to slipcovers—and the childcare help. Larry, a salesman, pays all the major shelter expenses —the house payments, car, medical bills, life insurance, vacations.

Don't be timid about formalizing your separate areas of responsibility by setting up separate checking accounts. Sometimes this simple step can produce peace overnight. Lucy's husband's $35,000 salary should have spelled financial ease for their family, but instead he complained constantly about her supposed extravagances: "He's always under a lot of pressure on his job. And just after the baby was born, we had a whole new scale of expenses—a full-time housekeeper, a new co-op apartment, and all the baby's expenses. He kept nagging at me—'Why do you need the housekeeper full-time? Can't you manage with part-time help? Why did you buy steak last week? Why does the baby have to go to the doctor every month if she's not sick?' He was driving me crazy until I put my foot down and opened my own checking account where I deposited my salary and agreed to pay for the food and housekeeper. Almost overnight, when he stopped actually counting the money going out, we stopped quarreling."

Lucy and her husband had different spending styles—hardly unusual, since money is not only a practical matter of living but a highly emotional element in how one copes with life. Most of us are more private about money than any other subject. We'd rather talk openly about our sex lives than about the salaries we make. Whether you're a spender or a saver, your personal style of handling money represents emotional security for you.

Maybe you like to carefully budget every penny, so you'll have the cash to splurge occasionally when you really want something . . . while he hates daily budgeting and considers it small-minded. Sharing every outlay of five dollars from a joint account only throws salt on your differences. Separate checking accounts (or maybe just separate coffee cans of spending money) can give you the autonomy you each need.

Having separate accounts doesn't mean you are disloyal, selfish, or mistrustful of each other. Indeed, the arrangement can help each of you develop your budgeting skills and maybe even create new respect for the other's methods. Linda, a twenty-five-year-old computer programmer, describes how she worked through her husband's indifference to her input about money matters: "He would never listen to me when I told him we should wait to buy something. So finally I put part of my salary in a separate savings account and refused to show him my passbook. When he'd ask how much I had, I lied and said it was less than it was, for fear he'd go on a spending spree. But lately I seem to have become more important in his thinking. He's listening to what I say—like our TV is wearing out and he wants to buy a new color set and I keep saying no, no, we need other things more. And he surprised me—he hasn't bought it. I think the way I've budgeted and saved part of my salary impressed him. Now I've decided I don't want to ever have to lie about my savings book. It's a whole new step in our marriage. . . ."

The Next Step.   One more trap lies down the road for the woman who takes over the spending of her paycheck. She may be so pleased at how far she's come that she doesn't take the next step—becoming fully included in all family financial planning. Even women in responsible professional jobs often feel ambivalent about sharing money planning with their husbands. In fact, this hesitation occurs more frequently among wives who, with their husbands, enjoy above-average incomes. Why? The answer lies in the fact that, traditionally, the notion of finances and financial investment are shrouded in the myth of masculine expertise. Charlotte, a gifted teacher who is particularly perceptive about motherhood and her own evolution as a woman during her forty-two years (an age that she felt prevented her from enjoying all the changes of the women's movement), confessed to us that she plays no part in her family's money management. "I sign my check and turn it over to him and he gives me a certain amount back. I pay for my own expenses, the babysitter, the children's clothes, and food out of that. I would never dream of asking him for more."

Charlotte is equally reluctant to press her husband, who earns half his income from fast-moving real-estate transactions, to tell her their total financial worth, exactly what investments he has, or whether their assets are going up or down. "Sometimes he's very irritable, and when I ask what's wrong, he just snaps, 'The property; don't ask.' "

Ignorance about your family's financial resources is bound to leave you feeling incompetent when it comes to jointly making plans like where you should live, whether you can risk a job change, how to plan your children's schooling. A husband who refuses to explain why "we can't afford it" or insists "let me worry about that" is pushing his wife to become either frivolous with money or needlessly anxious (*not* knowing your financial situation can be worse than knowing, no matter how shaky it is).

Couples can also fall into a his/hers separatism in various arrangements that seem to be fair to both but, in fact, limit the woman's say in financial decisions that affect her and her children. Audrey, a dynamic midwestern woman lawyer who has just masterminded a million-dollar settlement for women workers in a discrimination suit, is typical. She told us that her husband had a large amount of savings and investments when they were married ten years ago, but to this day, she still doesn't know how much or where the money is. And while she's politely asked her husband, she's never insisted he tell her. "I accept that what he earned before he had a family is all his. I think of his earnings as his, too, and I'm careful to live on my income for my personal expenses, the sitter, and the children's needs. I would never dream of asking him to pay for a dress for me."

Both Charlotte and Audrey—highly aware and successful—were astonished as they heard what they were saying. If you realize you've been backing off from making decisions about your family's finances, are you using these excuses?

1. *You really don't know anything about money.* That's easily remedied by taking one of the many free courses in money management being offered to women at your local Y, church, or brokerage house. One woman started her education by investing $1000 with a broker. She soon became familiar enough with Dow-Jones averages and other market terms to talk knowledgeably with her husband.

2. *You really hate talk of money and hate pushing your husband about it.* There are no excuses for being incompetent or ignorant when you must make decisions together affecting yourselves and your children.

3. *You really think money is one last male preserve of identity and you're reluctant or afraid to take it away from your husband.* Maybe so. But unless you test the waters, you'll never find out.

EMOTIONAL CLOSENESS

*My base, my center in life is my marriage. My core is to be
happy with my husband. When that feeling isn't there, I'm
desolate.*

—CARRIE, AN EXECUTIVE SECRETARY

That gut feeling governs most women's lives. And they deeply fear
that taking a job will damage their emotional ties with their husband.
*Will it change the way I need him? Will it change his feelings toward me
if he's jealous or feels left out?* And this one cuts deep into women's
insecurity: *Will he love me if I'm not his idea of feminine?*

The fact is that too much emotional dependence on another person
can be as damaging to a marriage as too much independence. And the
isolated lives that housewives are forced to lead contribute to that lop-
sided investment of emotions in a husband.

Carrie, a twenty-eight-year-old secretary who took her job two years
ago, reports: "When I was just a housewife, my whole world centered on
him. Every night at six, when his key turned in the door, it was the joy
of my life. My day only started then. I depended on him for everything,
even my information about the world. I was demanding too much from
him. Now that I have a job, my own little sphere, I'm much more balanced. And he's happier not to have me so clinging."

The ideal woman-man relationship we have been imprinted with is
that of the gentle, wise, supportive woman, smart enough to minister to
her husband's needs. If you think this ideal is passé, consider the powerful appeal of Edith Bunker, who holds sway in "All In the Family" as
the gentle power-behind-the-throne. In episode after episode, Edith's
kindly instincts puncture Archie's bluster and persuade him to do the
right thing. But can anyone envy Edith for her total dependence on
Archie to tell her what to serve for dinner, what to feel, even where to sit?

In real life, women with Edith's dependence don't have the resilience
to keep in touch with their feelings, much less assert them. Instead, their
lack of control over their lives expresses itself in a roll call of feminine
complaints: headaches, nervousness, anxiety, fatigue—all symptoms of
rage turned inward, the only response of powerless persons to frustration. "The cultural roots of depression among women," writes Helen
De Rosis in *The Book of Hope*, "center around learned helplessness and
a position of self-effacement."

When a woman is house-bound with young children, she must put heavy demands on her husband for emotional excitement. Locked up all day, confined to the routine of childcare, she feels her world shriveling—and clings to her husband with desperation that may repulse him. Many women report this tipping in the balance of their relationship when their children are young. Husbands caught in this tight grip cannot be blamed for backing off. All of us withdraw from loved ones who threaten to tie us up with consuming emotional demands.

Women who've experienced being both at home and at work report dramatic changes in their feelings toward their husbands. Sandra, a dynamic head nurse in a Southern hospital, was appalled at her own personality change when her husband was transferred to another city and she quit working, planning to spend all her time with her daughter and husband. "Instead I turned into a jealous wife. I would spend my whole day by the pool in our apartment complex—never reading all those books I promised myself I'd catch up on. Then I'd bathe and anoint myself, waiting for his return. If he didn't get home on time, I went crazy. I wouldn't believe any excuses. I decided he was having an affair with his secretary. After three months of this, my husband begged me to go back to work."

Mothers who share wage earning and parenting often report a greater closeness and companionship with their husbands. This closeness develops naturally when you come to understand each other's concerns. Let a father stay two hours with a baby on a regular basis and he'll understand why you are exhausted. Let him be responsible for getting your twelve-year-old baseball-crazy son to do his homework and he'll grasp the psychic strains of being a parent. Let a wife put up with the givens of earning a living: coping with a boss, performing when you'd rather be home catching up on your sleep, competing with others in your office —and she can understand his strain when problems arise at work.

Sociologists offer a sound explanation of why wives and husbands who share in each other's worlds can be closer emotionally. Distinguished sociologist Lee Rainwater and others have long hypothesized that role sharing between spouses is related to close, warm, rewarding relationships. Role segregation—where the two sexes seldom share work or pleasures—is associated with social distance and a lack of positive emotions.

By the scheme of things, the wife who stays at home is pressured to live not with or beside her husband, but *through* him. But intimacy based on one person calling all the plays is fraught with the danger of exploitation.

Changing Is Not Growing Apart. Carrie, who earlier spoke of her extreme dependence on her husband, was a bright but shy woman who had been deeply attached to her mother. When she married Ed, a young businessman who possessed the decisiveness and aggressiveness needed to advance in the corporate world, she exchanged mother for husband as the emotional force of her life. She let him set the patterns of their lives.

When their daughter and son were babies, Carrie made herself into what she thought of as the perfect wife for Ed. She entertained his business and social friends at beautiful dinner parties ("I started planning on Monday what I'd serve on Saturday"), rejoiced in Ed's success, quoted his opinions ("I majored in French literature, so I knew nothing about the rest of the world"), and let all her emotions revolve around him.

"It was the high point of the day when he came home. If he was out of temper, I felt terrible. I had to force myself not to be all over him demanding love. It got so I would sneak a call to his secretary at four, asking how Ed felt today. *She* had to tell *me,* his wife."

As Ed's growing commitments to his work took more time, Carrie experienced many signs of unhappiness—anxiety attacks, accidents, headaches. The low point came when she accidentally learned that Ed had briefly had an affair with a secretary in his office. "I felt I was the lowest person in the whole world."

This painful reaction caused Carrie to seek psychotherapy and eventually to take a job as a secretary.

Elaborate dinner parties disappeared as she started to channel her energies into activities for herself. She became friends with a circle of single women at her office and joined them in a tennis group. To her surprise, Ed brought their eight- and ten-year-old children over to watch Mom's game. "It was the first time I'd ever been the center of *anything* in the family. I was always the cheerleader on the sidelines at the dance recital or the Little League or the Junior Chamber of Commerce Young Man of the Year dinner."

Now Ed, an intense thirty-four-year-old man with a commanding manner, became resentful of his wife's newfound energy and enthusiasm. "She had all this time to have drinks with her girl friends after work or play tennis, when she should have been with the children," he complained. "I certainly didn't mind her going to work—I thought she needed that—but when she started going out nights, that was too much. She says I never told her how I felt about all those nights out with her girl friends, but I didn't see why I should have to tell her I wanted her home. She should have *noticed* it."

Ed sees no contradiction in his feeling that while he was careful not to reveal his hurt, his wife should have been psychic enough to know about it anyway.

Feeling left out, Ed took up running in the evenings—and became addicted. Now it was Carrie's turn to feel jealous. But at her insistence, they planned to spend more time together. Over the months, they forged a new companionship, different from the strong husband/adoring wife of the early years of their marriage.

"Carrie's more interesting company than she was. One of the things I discovered about myself is that I'm a controlling person. My mother made me the center of her world, and I expected Carrie to be the same way. But I've come to love her more as her own woman. It's been good for me *and* her. The truth is, it was pretty dull having her just reflect me."

Carrie feels both she and her husband have grown enormously from the changes that have taken them four painful years to adjust to. "I am still very dependent on Ed—and he needs that in me. But now that I no longer see marriage as my only positive thing in life, I don't cling so much and I feel better. And, most important, our feelings go much deeper than they used to." Without changing their basic relationship, Carrie and Ed's commitment to each other has deepened because she allowed herself to grow and develop in her own right.

BUT WILL HE LOVE A STRONG WOMAN?

This is a very real fear for many working wives. Assuming more control over your life can be threatening to you and your husband—and realistically so. He may fear that you will need him less. You may worry that your ability to make decisions or earn part of the family income means you don't have a strong husband. No matter that you're growing and doing these things because you want to—at some subterranean level, you may still think: but he shouldn't *want* me to. That's *not* realistic. You're lucky to have a husband who is loving and strong enough to give you the space to expand and develop.

But the images of disaster that follow on the heels of a strong woman are powerful. Are you wondering that maybe he's not as smart and capable as the man you thought you married . . . if maybe he lets you do as you like because he really doesn't care about you . . . if he's a bit weak and maybe you need a stronger man? Even the most self-confident woman can have these thoughts. For all of us have been shaped by the ideal of a love in which the male is magically superior in affairs of the world, leadership, and sexual knowledge.

Consider that timeless love classic, *Gone With the Wind*. After singlehandedly carrying her family from poverty to wealth, strong-willed Scarlett O'Hara eventually totally succumbs to the domineering but all-wise father figure Rhett.

We might think we're living in more progressive times, but today's best-selling paperbacks still present the same fantasy of lover as father. Typically, the woman plays a masochistic role, being raped in the early pages by none other than Mr. Right himself (who's so overcome by passion that he forgets himself). Immediately, he sails off over the seas, while the heroine suffers a Perils of Pauline series of rapes, beatings, tortures, and close brushes with death before being once more clasped in the strong arms of Mr. Right. Though the spunky girl has managed to survive on her own wits through all this, the last cloud of prose shows her being carried off by her powerful daddy figure, who will make everything all right in the future.

Behind much of this romantic tradition—even including such classics as *Jane Eyre*—lies the Victorian reality in which women were as economically dependent on men as were children. Lacking the right to own property, vote, or even control the dowries handed over to their husbands, a Victorian woman could do nothing better than attract the loyalty of a fatherlike husband, who would take care of her for life.

In another form, today's pinup magazines perpetuate the image of the childlike female sex object, embodying the supposed fantasies of men with provocative pictures of infantile girls with pouting lips, large childlike eyes, and hairless bodies, all characterizing a love object closer to child than to a grown woman.

With all these messages from the past and present bombarding us, we'd scarcely be human if we didn't take some of them in. No matter how much a woman enjoys her increasing confidence, she may secretly fear that there's something unnatural about her, that maybe she's castrating, aggressive, or doesn't love her husband.

It helps to analyze what you *really* feel, not what you're supposed to feel. Do you feel closest to your husband when you're sharing a pleasure, when you're pursuing a goal together, when he listens to what you say? Or when he's coming on like the macho head of the family, you're saying yes-dear, or in more subtle form supporting the male ego?

Certainly there are times you appreciate being able to draw on his strength. But the exchange is evened when you can offer him strength, wisdom, and confidence at the times *he* needs them, as well.

If you feel conflicts about being strong in your relationship with your husband, consider the roots of this dilemma that psychologist Ellen Berman has traced. As counselor to troubled couples visiting the University of Pennsylvania Marriage Council, Berman discovered that many a high-achieving woman unconsciously demands that her husband be superior to her. This is because, although she is likely to see herself as intellectually competent, she still feels somehow unfeminine. Her need to feel desirable as a woman depends on her attracting the love of a man she regards as in some way superior—older, smarter, or more popular. As she starts to attain professional success and finds herself on a more equal footing with her husband, she begins to doubt her husband's superiority. And if he isn't superior, how can his love for her prove she's lovable?

Much as a man unsure of his masculinity feels the need to prove it with a string of conquests, she looks around for a superior man who can assuage her feelings of unworthiness as a woman by bestowing his love on her.

The irony, says Dr. Berman, is that the woman who goes looking for a strong man to "prove" her desirability is often in a marriage of real equality—surely a situation that proves her strength and worth far more than plunging into a new dependent relationship.

Sometimes the ways in which we persist in thinking our husbands are stronger and brighter conveniently deny reality. Joan, an accomplished pediatrician, demonstrates this point unfortunately well. She and her husband jointly head a large diagnostic clinic located in Pennsylvania. They have arranged that her husband works forty hours a week, while she works twenty-five, spending more time with their three children. Despite Joan's popularity with her patients and the respect she commands among nurses and other assistants, she insists her husband "is a better doctor than I am. In school, I was better at manual things—like drawing specimens," she concedes. "But now that we're in real practice, he's much better than I."

But doesn't she have a slight edge in talking to mothers? Well, she admits, she might be more patient, more intuitive in understanding their problems. Probably mothers ask her questions more easily, are less afraid of appearing stupid with her than with a male doctor. But, Joan declares firmly, her husband is better at diagnosis, brilliant at theory, and a far better doctor than she will ever be. Her colleagues disagree, but Joan sticks to her guns. Clearly she's more comfortable playing a secondary professional role.

Unlike Joan, many women *are* learning to get their own heads straight about being successful, decisive, and in charge. Do their mates then feel threatened by the new woman who's no longer the sweet little thing he married?

Increasingly, women are discovering that the qualities that make successful men attractive also seem to make women attractive, too. A woman who's alive, interested in the world and in her work, is likely to generate interest in both men and women. As a divorced Tennessee boutique owner says, "If you're attractive, you go through life having men say things like 'You're very pretty tonight' or 'You look very sexy.' That only goes so far with me since I've gotten absorbed in my business. Now, when a man is impressed with how well I do my job, it makes me feel terrific. That's the kind of admiration I need. The men who date me like me because of *all* of me, and that goes a whole lot deeper than just being the pretty-looking girl they want to show off."

WHEN SEX REARS ITS . . .

Of all the doubts and anxieties expressed about working mothers, none is so paradoxical as the fear that a job will undermine her marital fidelity. Paradoxical, since not long ago, the secret feeling about the career woman was that what she really needed was a good dose of sex. *That* would put her back in her place, at home in the kitchen and nursery. Now the fear is that a mother going out to work is sure to be lured away from her marriage by having too great an opportunity for sex.

The common thread running through both fears is that *women can't handle sex.* Too little or too much—either way, anything above or below a standard controlled portion is likely to drive us bananas. No one in history, however, has ever worried about men having too much sex. And, needless to say, the exposure of men to sexual temptation on the job has never launched the idea that men would be better off at home sheltered from temptation.

All these contradictory feelings reflect a double standard that is still widely accepted—the feeling that a woman's infidelity is far more dangerous and explosive in a marriage than a man's. This double standard lies behind many a husband's objection to his wife's working. Even while he protests that taking a job will mean that you won't have time for the children, that the house will be neglected, that his friends will think he's no provider, his real objection may be the prospect of sexual competition. And the question must be confronted: Is a working mother more likely to have an affair?

Realistically, working usually does place you in an environment that offers more chance for getting together with interesting men. The housewife has good reason to spend time with the pediatrician, the plumber, the washer-repair man—and that's about it.

But working, as a thirty-year-old woman college professor points out, "legitimizes your spending time with men. It's even expected that I will spend hours talking to men, attending meetings with them, working together on projects. And if something does spark, it's much easier to arrange the unaccounted-for time to do something about it. You can always say you were at a meeting."

A recent *Redbook* magazine study of 100,000 women produced this startling picture of greater infidelity among working wives. Here's how the percentage of women who confessed to having affairs broke down according to age:

WOMEN WHO HAVE HAD AFFAIRS

Age of woman	Employed	Not employed
Under 25 years old	21%	17%
25–34	40%	23%
35–39	53%	24%
40 and over	47%	33%

By the time employed wives reach their late thirties, they are more than *twice* as likely as housewives to have affairs!

These are startling figures, and some of the women we talked with told us how they became attracted to men and how the experience affected them. But their experiences were so different that they do not add up to any stereotyped pattern.

Rosemary, thrty-two, returned to work two years ago as a magazine-space salesperson after having spent ten years at home raising children.

She fell into two successive affairs as a result of what she now sees was naiveté about how to handle herself in business socializing.

"All I knew about being with men was what I knew from dating fifteen years before. I didn't understand the etiquette of business or how you maintain your distance while being friendly. All I knew was here I was all dressed up in the middle of the day, taking these successful, self-assured men out to lunch on my new expense account. I would have a drink and carry on this social conversation simply because I didn't know the language of business conversation. One of the men I had to see regularly was going through marital problems and I listened and was sympathetic. I didn't really mean to push it that far, but the talk and everything finally brought us together in a hotel room."

Rosemary's affair was not based on a deep attraction and didn't last long, but the next time she was deeply attracted to the man she had an affair with. Unfortunately, word got back to her boss, who called her in and told her this wasn't good business and to choose: the man or the job. "I chose the job and I realized that I had been dumb about myself and my own reactions and everything. I would advise any woman to make a little rule to herself—don't let yourself get involved in *anything* for the first year."

The first year back at work does seem a dangerous period. Patsy, a twenty-eight-year-old mother married five years, described being smitten with hero worship for her architect boss when she resumed work as a draftsperson in his office.

"He is a very gentle, loving man and all his staff adores him. At first, I was overwhelmed just to be working there—he's already recognized, a name written up in the architectural magazines. I felt part of this fantastic work and that he was leading us all.

"When he started paying attention to me, I figured he was just being extra nice. And when he began to tell me little things about himself or squeeze my shoulder or brush my hands, it was like a dream. Here I was loving my job and having a wonderful man to boot. The whole physical affair was like a fantasy it was so wonderful."

The fairy tale didn't last. Patsy discovered that her dream lover runs through some kind of flirtation with every new person in his office. "He needs to know we all need him. And I finally opened my eyes and saw that our wonderful hero turns his charm on and off as it suits him. And how he woos clients. And that he's even taken credit for a talented junior's work on occasion. *And* that his work is the only thing that means anything to him. I crashed down to reality in about three months."

Interestingly, she adds this reflection: "I became much, much wiser about the world as a result. I don't regret that."

Selma, another mid-thirties woman who returned to work after eight years away, credits several affairs she had with benefits to her marriage. "During all those years at home, I was as secluded as if I were in purdah. We always saw other men in married couples. The women paired off to talk about Kuchen, Kinder, Kinde; James and the men would talk about business and baseball. I spent from twenty-five to thirty-five not really knowing any men except my husband. When I went back to work, I had two brief affairs, one with a man in my office and one with a man I met at a convention. I came out of both experiences knowing much more about the opposite sex and feeling more attached to my husband. I discovered that we were better suited to each other than I had realized."

Selma would probably have a hard time convincing her husband that sleeping with other men helped her appreciate him more. But Selma has no doubts: "I wouldn't *recommend* it, because you can't tell how it will turn out. But it taught me fast about men, helped me catch up on ten whole years of vegetating."

MONOGAMY ISN'T DEAD

But stacked against the statistics is the conviction of many couples that the *quality* of a woman's marriage determines her fidelity far more than opportunity. Husbands repeatedly told us, "I figure if she wants to do it, she will whether she's home all day or in an office. Housewives run around too." In many marriages, just being aware of the potential for attractions leads wives and their husbands to take extra care to maintain their closeness.

Sandra, a twice-married nurse who heads the intensive-care unit of an important Washington hospital, describes her decision to avoid sexual byplay on the job. A vibrant woman who loves her work and is strikingly attractive, she says candidly: "People assume that doctors and nurses are always jumping into bed. Well, it's true. When you work with people intensely in life-and-death situations, you develop strong emotions toward each other. Sometimes when you've lived through a tense night together, you can't just say good night and end it there. You have to share something physical. During my first marriage, which was unhappy, that happened easily and it happened frequently to me. In fact, I still stay in touch with one man and I'm sure we will always care for each other."

But Sandra has been happily remarried for four years. "This second marriage is a deep commitment for us both, because we survived terrible times in our first marriages."

She looks across the living room of her apartment to the terrace where her muscular, sunbathing husband lies stretched before the Sunday football game. "We still have a very physical thing between us after five years. I truly do not believe that Bill has anything going on the side. I certainly don't, though guys do cute things constantly and I have to discourage them. At times, it becomes a hassle. But Bill knows he can trust me and I plan to keep it that way."

Neither frequent advances from attractive men nor a history of affairs shakes Sandra's determination to remain faithful. That same deliberate decision was expressed to us by many women, both for business and personal reasons.

Linette, a hard-driving film producer, acknowledged the sexual temptations in her job. "My husband and I realize that mine is a very sexual business. You get intensely involved with your crew and you go off on location, where the spirit is anything goes. That's why marriages don't last long. If men want to stay married, they bring their wives along on location. But my real affair is with my work. If my husband's jealous of anything, it's certainly not other men, but the turn-on I get from work."

But surely attractions do bud with men even when she's obsessed with work? "Sure. About three years ago, my director and I were very sympatico. We worked together fantastically. It was a real high for us both."

After spending six weeks intensely working side by side, Linette did end up one night in bed with her director. "I felt so guilty about what I'd done that I flew home for the weekend across the country. I decided to end it right away. The man was bewildered and hurt. But I controlled it. I didn't just let things happen. I expect to do exactly the same if that situation comes up again."

Jeanette, marketing director for an Oregon firm, travels with her male salesmen, and last-minute show preparations often involve working late at night in hotel rooms. Jeanette is plainly irritated at being asked what happens.

"*Nothing* happens. I simply don't think about it and neither do they. I read somewhere that Margaret Mead suggested that we develop an incest taboo banning sex among women and men who work together. I endorse that. That's exactly what I've done. If you start with the attitude that your husband is important to you, you just use a little sense and don't let anything compromising or dangerous develop."

Sandra, Linette, and Jeanette have different occupations, but they all share the quality of being highly self-aware women. They are in control of their work and their emotional lives. They don't "just let things happen."

Other women may be less iron willed than they. But one thing's for sure: Failing to think about what you want and value will lead to drifting. As we move from the ideal of monogamous marriages to a society that encourages sexual variety, as women break out to lives that allow them more experience and choices, each of us will have to develop the awareness of her own sexuality and values to steer a course that seems personally right.

And there are plenty of good reasons why a woman may well decide that a few moments of excitement hold little appeal in comparison to the unity of her family life. Nor is every attraction between you and a man necessarily momentous. Says a woman who owns her own crafts business: "Every woman knows that there's a certain kind of harmless attraction and flirting that just makes you feel good about yourself and men. It doesn't stop just because you're married. I call them my Subserious Attractions."

A woman may also decide that her family responsibilities have been too hard won to endanger for an attraction. Says the same woman who enjoys flirting, "Marriage is a responsibility. It's not the most exciting life in the world but it works. Everybody is relatively happy—the kids, me, him. Marriage satisfies all our needs and it allows us to grow and change as well. Why destroy that?"

Others may find that the effort her husband and children make to adjust to her working create an obligation she won't break. Says one woman, "My family and I have worked so hard together to establish a work life for me. I could never betray that."

Hard business sense can also tell you that getting involved with the men you work with is not only dangerous to your marriage, but can also jeopardize the career you've fought so hard to have. Most businesswoman have seen the double standard at work when a man and woman in the same office have an affair. The man (who's usually superior in seniority or position) gets a wrist-slap or good-natured ribbing. The woman gets fired if the situation becomes awkward for management.

Finally, one of the biggest advantages of your working is that you just may discover it acts as a turn-on for you and your husband. All the stimulation and excitement that go with working can produce changes in you that improve the quality of your sex lives. "None of this happened overnight," says Penny, a twenty-nine-year-old mother and store buyer, "but our sex life has become much better."

She explains: "Before, I was a *mother* first and foremost. There's something very antisex about that. You're surrounded by diapers and burped orange juice and you have a saggy body and couldn't give a damn how you look. Even if you dress up, there's always something that makes you feel dowdy—your hair's not fixed or your panty hose runs. I was going through a lot of personal turmoil. I had wanted babies and had them and still I didn't feel grown-up. Under this pressure, I lost interest in sex."

Penny's experience reflects many women's experiences after returning to work: "My life took on structure. I had an excuse to get up and fix myself up. I began to realize I could do something, I wasn't just a little gray wren that was the helpmeet at home. And gradually that began to spill over into sexual interest. At first, I was just pleased with myself. I felt attractive, and so I wanted attention. But that kind of sex was replaced by something deeper. I feel free now to express myself if I want sex. And I feel confident enough of myself to experiment."

The relation between a woman's sexuality and her work fits no simple equation. Going to work can have no effect at all. Or it can lead you to important changes.

HOW YOUR HUSBAND FEELS

Make no mistake, a husband who's behind you in your work, who truly appreciates the efforts you're making to help out with family finances and make it all work, is worth his weight in gold.

Most women say it simply: "I couldn't do it all without him. If he weren't with me in this all the way, I couldn't handle it."

Husbands who give this kind of support earn a wife's gratitude and loyalty, and are well repaid. Those who lend a hand, understand why a woman wants to work, and don't assume she's slighting him or the children, have taken a big step toward creating a new kind of family unit in which no member's needs are served at the expense of another's. These husbands express their feelings like this:

"I saw how unhappy she was when she was at home all the time. Things get pretty dusty around the house now, but we all seem to get along."

"She's very smart, and I'd be a fool to try to tie her down. So long as she's doing what she's good at, we'll get along."

"Sure I pay a price for her not being at home and doing all the things she could for my ease and convenience. And sometimes I get mad because she's tired or not with me when I want her to be. And I get jealous of how much she enjoys her office. But what I give up in return for having an active, involved wife is worth it."

CAN'T YOU SEE I'M TALKING TO YOUR MOTHER?

When you're pressed for time, you take it from the two people you know can take it—you and your husband.
—A WORKING MOTHER

A working wife describes her homecoming, that dangerous falling-apart of the household that occurs when mother's foot hits the doorstep: "The kids are all over me. My husband is already there and he's dying to tell me about his day. And the kids are dying to have me all to themselves. And it always ends up with me dancing around like a Marx brother trying to talk to everybody and then my husband shouts at us all, 'Will you be *quiet,* can't you see I'm talking to your mother?'

"And then I feel so guilty. Because he is an adult and he can hold it in and wait until later. But my kids are little and they don't know about 'later'; it's just 'now' and they want to be all over me. But he gets furious and it's a terrible problem. Who do I pay attention to?"

Working adds more tension to the pull between being both wife and mother. But don't forget that *all* mothers, working or not, must juggle a basic conflict in their double roles. Just as having a child forever alters your life, having a baby forever changes your marriage.

Having children is both the most uniting and the most divisive experience you and your husband can undergo. Alongside all the joy that children bring, most honest couples will also date their children's arrival as the beginning of the greatest strains in their marriage.

The conflict starts with pregnancy, when your body balloons from the young bride's he's loved to a new instrument housing another being. No matter how interested he is, no one can deny that childbearing is definitely your act, and normally you will be self-absorbed as you confront the cataclysmic physical and emotional changes of pregnancy.

After birth, the sensual joy you and your baby share in nursing or through simply touching each other shuts your attention off from your husband again. And your baby, equipped with keen survival instincts of his own, is sure to find other ways to thwart your turning your attention elsewhere. Couples are amazed at how uncannily the baby wakes up to howl in the middle of the night just at the moment when his parents began to make love. Some authorities even believe that sexual arousal stimulates an odor from the mother's breasts that rouses the baby to this threat. Danger! Mother is loving someone else!

Whatever the actual mechanism, husbands usually complain that a new sexual adjustment must be made with their wives.

And a different overall relationship emerges between you. Your husband must accept that from now on phrases like "the baby needs me" or "I want the children to have . . ." will forever be on your lips, reminding him that he's no longer first in your life. If he's skittish about responsibility, he may feel you're forcing him into a corner, tying him down and calculatingly looking on him as a breadwinner for your child.

Your job will be one more competitor for your time and attention. If your husband's been used to having his favorite dishes served on request, being greeted at the door by his loving wife with a drink in hand to wash away his day's labors, and commanding your full, wide-eyed attention whether he's pontificating on ball-game scores or the new tax laws, you can expect he won't adjust easily to having less of your time. This is true even of husbands who have been known to rustle up a plate of eggs for themselves, cheerfully take over the kids on the night you chair the PTA meeting, and loudly profess that they believe in women's rights.

Having time with you is *still* a problem. Mark, a twenty-eight-year-old civil-liberties lawyer married to a social worker, explains: "I couldn't be married to a woman without a mind of her own. I'm very proud of Jennifer. She's very good at her work, and I understand why it's important to her. But I feel left out a lot of the time. She comes home tired and upset. She's always busy with the children. We don't share enough together. I appreciate that she had to do what she's doing, but that doesn't make me feel any happier about it. I've begun to fantasize about a wife who'll just be interested in me."

The pressure of this-is-our-time-together can poison the time you do share. One man, married to a highly efficient woman who manages a pressured job and mothering three children, confesses: "I feel I'm just part of her program, even though she always finds time for me. We always have coffee after dinner on the patio, while the kids take their baths and get ready for bed. But I hear this clock ticking off in her mind while we talk. . . . 'In ten minutes, I'll go up and get the children to bed.' "

Women are used to juggling different sets of needs in their minds, but men can be upset by this wifely capacity. Making things even more difficult is the separate view of parental duties that most mothers and fathers possess. A husband has trouble understanding why his working wife can't just leave the children with a sitter and instantly turn back into the carefree creature he used to know and run off for a weekend of fun and sex together.

Finding Time Together.   Most working mothers do feel that their free time belongs first to the children, even though they admit that sometimes such an attitude is either selfish or foolhardy. The first step is to realize that intimacy requires an ongoing exchange of feelings, of being aware of the other person's thoughts and emotions, of being concerned about each other's moods, no matter how passing they may be.

Wives who have hectic schedules can sensitize themselves to a husband's "neglect signs." One woman knows her husband is feeling neglected when he accuses: "You're not spending enough time with the children."

Another wife of fifteen years knows her husband is angry when he starts planning outings they'd both enjoy without her. And, of course, many husbands stay in touch with their feelings well enough to simply let you know in no uncertain terms: "I never see you anymore," "You're too wrapped up in that job," or "I don't want to hear another word about what's going on in your office."

When that happens, says a woman realty agent, she forces herself to turn off work temporarily. "Once I even refused to handle the biggest house I'd ever been offered, but it turned out to be a white elephant, so I didn't lose a thing." She concentrates on her husband until the relationship restabilizes.

Short trips together can be a marvelous tonic. A boutique owner takes her husband along on business trips. "It's terrific—tax deductible and, since it's absolutely necessary, I don't have to feel guilty about leaving the children. We never had time like this alone before."

A Connecticut couple have her mother come for the weekend and check into a motel only two miles down the highway, guaranteeing forty-eight hours free from domestic duty.

Make the effort to find some unpressured time together, however artificial it seems, however disastrous the first try. (Says one young wife who took a weekend off with her husband: "I ended up crying and worrying obsessively about the children; he had too much to drink and spent all the second day in bed nursing a hangover.")

And don't confine your time together to weekend trips. You may get the same resurgence of the wonderful, unmatchable "us-two" bond from a half hour shared over a cup of coffee after work, or an hour driving around together after dinner. Not only your husband but you, too, may feel the warmth of Tender Loving Care if you manage to fix a tray and both enjoy breakfast in bed—or lock yourself off in a room separate from the children for a drink together.

It's easy to grow apart when you're pressed for time, when the moment you want to tell your husband something important, he's not around or you're rushing off to work. It's easy to have separate angers, separate hurts that never get faced. Keeping in touch requires great effort—though you may not want to go as far as the couple who told us they were having trouble but were too exhausted to quarrel at night. Instead, the husband set the alarm for 5 A.M. "so we could have time to argue before the children woke up. We had some roundhouse fights before dawn, and it wasn't long before we worked things out!"

Making sufficient time to feel that connection and to enjoy each other—which, after all, is why you got married in the first place—is one of the great open secrets of couples with self-renewing marriages. Investing energy in finding space for that will pay you back many times over.

Chapter Eleven
MAKING IT AS A SINGLE MOTHER

BUILDING A NEW SUPPORT SYSTEM

It's 8 P.M. on a sleety, pre-Christmas weekday in an Upper West Side apartment in Manhattan, the inconvenient hour appointed for a meeting of single working mothers who've never met. Sleet notwithstanding, the doorbell starts ringing promptly at 8, and the quiet apartment fills with ten women exchanging names and particulars. Molly, a soft-voiced twenty-eight-year-old nurse, has been sole parent to her eight-year-old since he was a baby, and recently landed an exciting job in cancer research at the hospital where she works. Josie is an editor who's supported her ten- and eight-year-old sons for the past seven years. Jane, a forty-four-year-old lawyer, had a husband die after divorce, cutting off all financial aid, a misfortune that didn't prevent her from going to law school. Ginny, thirty-one, divorced four years, a legal secretary and mother of a two- and eight-year old, is spunky and outgoing. As the women, all attractively dressed, sip their wine or coffee and begin to talk, they vibrate with a special openness and energy, an intriguing combination of vulnerability and strength.

This is the end of a long winter workday, crammed against the hour-and-a-half that each of these mothers had to rush home from work, juggle all the problems that collected for her homecoming, feed the children, gulp something down herself, and rush out again to grab a bus on the icy streets (few single mothers can afford to indulge in cabs) to a meeting called by two unknown women who announced on the phone that they were writing a book.

These lively women defy the expectations many people have of single mothers. Working mothers have a right to collapse under the strain of two full-time jobs. But single mothers must teeter along under the load of *three*—working and being two parents. How do these mothers seem so calm and together? Why do they all seem like such *individuals*— confident, but lacking the usual social defenses? We lost no time asking, Aren't you overworked? Isn't it terribly hard to be a single working mother?

As one, they answered: "Sure, but it's so much easier than being half of a bad marriage. When you don't get along with your husband, everything is always a big argument—disciplining the kids, arrangements, school. Your life is one long hassle."

Elka, thirty-nine, and a receptionist since she divorced her husband one year ago, enthuses, "When I rush home from work there's no longer that *lump of contention* sitting in front of the TV. Sure, I have three kids to raise and I'm the only human being in the world responsible for them, but at least it's not like when another adult was sitting around in the house not helping you one bit and you were mad all the time, resenting it because he was a dead weight."

Molly remembers she had much more to do when she was married: "I was taking care of two babies—my baby and my big-baby husband. When I came home, I had to feed three people and clean up for three and manage all these emotional needs. Things are *100 percent easier now*."

Ginny reveals another trigger that released her strength: "I thought: 'I can't *possibly* raise the children alone.' And then I suddenly realized— I've actually been making *all* the decisions about them for *years*. The only difference is now I make the decisions . . . and no one yells at me that I'm wrong."

All these women struck us as having the secret strength of survivors. The strength of people who had touched what they thought was bottom and declared: "Yes, I can come through." And the pearls they brought back from that perilous voyage were glowing. While coping with an amount of change that would probably send most men into a sanitarium, they were showing that admirable strength of women everywhere: grace under pressure. Given the responsibility of coming through for their children, they grew tremendously. And developed a new emotional resilience.

Their first message is clear: Doing it all by yourself is easier than doing it with a husband you're clashing with. But so is the second: Don't assume you *must* manage it all alone. The best strategy a single mother can adopt is to *establish a support system* to replace the traditional two-parent family. Over the years, most single mothers put together a support system of sorts. Save yourself a lot of wear and tear by *consciously* surveying your available resources and taking specific steps to integrate them into your life from the start.

No matter how indifferent your husband was, how inadequate as a parent, when you were married, you did have another adult in the house to test your opinions on. And you had another adult to back up your authority, even if he only shouted the kids down on occasion. ("Now there's never anyone," mourned one mother of three adolescent sons, "to just stand up and say, 'damn it, shut up.' I can say it, but they don't pay attention to good-hearted old Mom.") As a single parent, you'll discover that being one-on-one with your children twenty-four hours a day robs you of perspective. You can easily become overly protective or overly dependent on each other. As for your children, having no other stable adult in their lives except you can be frightening. Certainly it tends to put too much pressure on their relationship with you. They need other adults to trust in their world.

You won't find that other people fit naturally into your lives as though made to order. But with openness and determination, you'll establish a new "family" of friends or paid helpers who will enrich the lives of you and your children.

Find a Supportive Community.   Somehow the urge to get away from the world strikes many a newly divorced mother. She sees herself and the kids starting life all over on a Vermont apple farm (where, significantly, there will be no *people* to disturb their tranquillity). Before you plunge all your divorce settlement into a charming rural retreat, remember that there will also be no ready transportation for your children and baby-sitters, no superintendent to call when the furnace breaks down in a blizzard, and no corner movie to send the kids to when they're driving you up the wall.

Better to look for a place to live that will put you smack in a web of support services. If you've lived in the suburbs, moving to the city may simplify life. Your children won't have to be ferried around by a licensed driver. And in case of sickness, an urban working mother can usually dash home on her lunch hour. "I have a good neighbor just across the hall, so my five-year-old son only has to step outside our door to get help," says Beverly, who left a big suburban split-level with two acres of yard for a one-bedroom apartment near the hospital where she works as a clinical psychologist. "At our old house, he would have had to walk half a mile and cross the street, and I'd have been worried sick whenever I was delayed a half hour by a meeting at work."

Look, too, for a home that offers a pool of baby-sitting services. Locating near a college provides you with a wonderful, ready-made source of qualified young people eager for part-time work. Ask yourself, too, How far is the school? Or day-care center or family day care? Will you be able to come home at lunch in an emergency? How much time

ADVICE FOR THE NEWLY DIVORCED

Carolyn, twenty-seven, has been separated for seven months and living with her five-year-old daughter, Erica, in a small apartment. In that time, a friend helped Carolyn get her first job in six years—as a public relations assistant. Carolyn's glamorous-sounding job actually consists mostly of typing and Xeroxing pubilcity releases and calling up bored newspaper editors. Despite this progress, Carolyn wonders if she will ever be up to running her own life.

For the first months of her separation, Carolyn was so wrapped in a blanket of fatigue that she barely got up. Some days she simply lay in bed, unable even to order in groceries by phone. When she first got her job, she'd fall back into bed as soon as she got home, worrying over the past until the next morning. But one morning, she got up and dressed, met an attractive man, and exploded with restlessness. Since then, she's been going out three or four nights a week, leaving Erica with a succession of baby-sitters. Five-year-old Erica had regressed to babyish behavior, crying whenever her mother leaves in the morning and even harder in the evenings. Carolyn's mother, who comes over every single day, is convinced that her daughter is on dope and goes around peeking into the pill bottles when Carolyn's not looking.

Carolyn doesn't really enjoy the men she's seeing—the novelty has worn off. And hiring the sitters takes up a lot of her time at the office— something her boss is complaining about. Carolyn still feels in a fog, and while she knows she should protect her job, she somehow can't deal with it. When she has those awful middle-of-the-night awakenings, Carolyn feels a rush of consuming love for Erica and worries about losing her. But when they are together, she can't seem to pay attention to her daughter or cope with her demands for reassurance and love. Their evenings to-gether often end in tantrums and tears and a feeling of distance between them.

Is Carolyn crazy, weak, cracking up? No. She is going through stages of recovery that are universal enough to be predictable. If only she could find a wise friend, Carolyn might rouse herself from her circle of guilt, self-destructiveness, and self-pity to see ahead—and work toward the next stage. Try these simple but effective steps and you'll be on your way to recovery and establishing a new life.

1. *Expect to be a little crazy for a while.* Mary, an attractive thirty-nine-year-old auburn-haired woman who one year ago ended a twenty-one-year marriage to her high school sweetheart, says, "I went out four or five nights a week with a different man. I couldn't stay home." Carolyn's reaction of total collapse for a month or so is more typical. Says Betty, a teacher and mother of three daughters, "I hired a live-in sitter and then I collapsed. For eight months, I couldn't do anything." Expect a full year before you are really in shape to plan a new life. Realize that this is *natural* and *temporary.*

2. *Get out in the world.* The oldest advice in the world and still sound. No matter how dejected and worthless you feel, get dressed up, go out, meet friends. *Don't* put too high expectations on yourself or them—you're not likely to meet Mr. Right at the next turn. But putting yourself in motion and seeing that the world, despite your personal tragedy, is turning right along will help.

3. *Don't just get a job—find out what kind of work you want to do.* Two out of three divorced mothers work, and financial necessity makes it likely that you will, too. Even if you have to take a make-do job for the present, take the time to discover the work that you *want* to be doing. From now on, working is going to be an important dimension of your life. If you take the time to experiment and find something that you really like, your job will be a big part of your recovery.

4. *Make friends with women who've been divorced longer than you have.* No one can understand what you're going through better than women who've been through it. And if they are further along in making a new life for themselves than you, they can advise and inspire you better than all the therapists in the world.

5. *Be good to yourself.* Indulging yourself is not indulgence. If you feel you'll benefit from professional therapy, get it. If you've never borrowed money in your life and hate the idea of owing anyone, recognize that this is a time when you need help—and don't hesitate to ask your parents, sister, brother, or maybe a friend for it. Indulge some of your lighter whims as well—whether that means staying in bed until noon on Sunday, buying a frivolous dress, or eating crackers in bed—and enjoy the benefits of being on your own.

will you have to commute each day (there'll no longer be someone to put dinner on when you're late)? Can your children enjoy a social life in the neighborhood, or will all their friends have to be imported?

Your Family Can Help.   The first resource many single mothers turn to is their own families. As you and your children begin to function as a single-parent family, your own relatives may experience a deepened emotional commitment to you. A grandmother or aunt or uncle, instead of merely being an indulgent visitor, can become another central adult presence in your children's lives—someone who is an acceptable cover for you at school events or trusted enough to help your child weather an emotional crisis. A grandfather or brother can be a sustaining male figure in your female-headed family, one who can take your son and daughter on traditional outings to ball games, fishing, or on other activities you have no taste for.

Don't ever overlook support from *any* relative. Adopt early the rule of successful working mothers, single or married: *Get all the help you can.*

Alexandra, an artist who was left by the father of her baby one month before her son Jason was born, found an unexpected father substitute in her sister's husband, Tony, a self-made businessman whom she'd had little taste for. "I hardly ever saw my sister after college, except at family holidays, because she was such a typical suburban housewife, spending her days shopping and koffee-klatsching. But she and Tony have never been able to have children and they've become real second parents to Jason."

Through her son, Alexandra has also become close to her sister and Tony. "Tony is the stable male figure in my son's life, whereas he's seen his own father exactly twice, for an hour each time." Tony is old-fashioned and macho, and he and Alexandra disagree about politics, religion, and a host of other things, but they have never had a cross word over Jason. "Maybe because I can see how much Tony thinks of Jason, I can tolerate his views. If you told me four years ago that I'd let my son grow up influenced by Tony, I'd have said *never*. Now I wouldn't trade him for anything."

Emily, divorced from a gynecologist, sends her ten-year-old daughter for a month each summer to stay with her ex-husband's maiden aunt. "The two just happen to hit it off." Ann made friends with her mother-in-law *after* her divorce, and contentedly sends her two children off for a weekend with grandma once every month.

But before you rush back into the family bosom and arrange to live with or near them permanently, test out their reactions. Despite their love for you, parents can be angry at a daughter for "disappointing" them with a marital failure. They can be full of reproaches, of "I-told-you-never-to-marry-him." Or they may see your divorce as a *moral* failure and take your ex-husband's side. At a time in your life when your self-esteem is at its lowest ebb, the last thing you need is your mother delivering a running lecture on how you've let the whole family down.

Even if parents mask open anger, they can still deliver their resentments in subtle messages that just as efficiently drive you up the wall. They may overindulge your children, leaving all the nitty-gritty discipline to you.

Bonnie returned with her children to her family home after leaving a stifling seven-year marriage—and immediately started fighting with her mother over everything from how she dressed for a job interview to what time the children should be fed. "I didn't figure it out for a long time, but we were fighting over my right to have a new life. My marriage was miserable for nearly the whole time. But my mother invested everything in an unsatisfying marriage and she thinks I'm rejecting her whole way of life. Since I chose differently, she, along with my ex-husband, is praying I'll fall flat on my face."

Moral disapproval is sure to spur wounding fights between parents and an adult daughter who's in the uneasy position of having returned to her parents' protection. Bonnie, like many newly divorced women, went through an initial phase of seeing a different man every night. Her mother was ignorant of how common—and passing—this phase is. Shocked at what she saw as an outrageous sexual spree and convinced that her daughter needed to be saved from herself, she angrily screwed up phone messages from men and created awkward scenes when they came to pick Bonnie up. But she righteously felt she was only doing her duty as a mother.

Families can be wonderful sources of emotional, logistical, and financial support for the single mother. But it's up to you to set the terms on which you accept their help. Blaming, reproaches over your failure, or excessive meddling in your sexual life can't be part of the terms.

Help at Home. The smartest thing a single mother can do is to: (a) beg; (b) barter; or (c) pay through the nose for live-in help. For the first few months, when you aren't up to your usual energy level, having someone around twenty-four hours a day can be simply lifesaving.

Carla, a social worker, feels her live-in sitter made an enormous difference in her recovery in her first year alone. "Even though I'd instigated the divorce, for twelve months I was really so messed up that Susan was better with the kids than I was. I was locked in my bedroom wondering how the hell I was going to ever bring them up. Susan was really their mother and she gave them love, she was there for them all the time. I'll always love her for it."

Once your own motors are running, a live-in helper can free you from the prison of being the only adult on duty. Ginny, who struggled three years working and caring for two young children with only baby-sitter help, discovered new freedom when she hired a nineteen-year-old woman part-time student (who jumped at the chance to live with Ginny in New York City for a salary of $40 a week, room and board, and two nights off to attend classes). "I really have a wife," Ginny giggles, "which is what we all need. She takes care of everything the way I used to for my husband—the cleaning, the laundry, the dental appointments, taking the shoes to the repair shop. I've gotten rid of a whole world of strains. When I'm late at work, I don't have to worry. When one of the kids is sick, someone they know and trust is right there in the house. And I don't have the expense of a baby-sitter, so I can afford to go out a lot more."

Sara, a merchandise buyer who must travel regularly, likes the stability of having a live-in housekeeper, which allows her daughter to accept her frequent absences with equanimity. "I couldn't leave her with a succession of sitters. Of course, she'd much rather Mommy was at home, but she accepts Anita and I feel perfectly confident when I have to go off."

Living with Another Mother.　If your budget won't stretch to pay for live-in help, trade a room plus kitchen privileges for part-time baby-sitting—maybe to cover from after school to 10 P.M. on the evenings you'd like to be free to go out.

Or consider teaming up with another single mother to share an apartment for both families. Splitting the rent can help you afford a better apartment than either of you could manage alone. (But watch out for landlord prejudice. In a strange twist of logic, landlords are happy to lease a high-rent apartment to a flock of single stewardesses, but they may refuse to rent to two mothers unless one of them can afford the apartment on her own. They just assume the arrangement won't last long and that one or the other of the families will move out. Your best ammunition to fight this prejudice can be the local agency that handles housing discrimination.)

Having another grown-up there to share cooking and discipline and generally give weight to the adult side of the ongoing battle between Them and Us can be great. Annette, a teacher, who shares a sunny nine-room apartment in New Orleans with another divorced teacher, says, "It's wonderful to sit down at the dinner table and talk about something besides 'Starsky and Hutch.' And our kids like having each other to play with. I get much less of 'Mommy, I don't have anything to do; play with me.' "

If the idea of sharing your family life with another person doesn't seem your style, consider other combinations. Sue, a Houston cocktail hostess who's on duty from 7 P.M. to 3 A.M., happily lives with her son in an apartment shared with a secretary who works in the daytime. "We can't get on each other's nerves," says Sue, "because we only see each other for a half hour a day, from 6 to 6:30." But thanks to their opposite schedules, Sue has someone on the premises to get her son off to school and to sleep in while she's away at night. Her roommate can count on Sue to pick her twin sons up from nursery school in the afternoon and cover until she gets home.

You can arrange for more privacy but still get the support of sharing by renting two apartments in the same building or sharing a two-family house. Agree on alternating nights to cook dinner or be in charge of the children. Iris, a mother of four children who is divorced from a police officer, rents a two-family Queens home with another woman who has four children of *her* own. "With eight kids, there was *no way* we were going to share one house. But with upstairs and downstairs, and our own entrances and areas, we get along fine."

Women Friends. The most reliable source in your budding support system is likely to be women friends—particularly divorced women who are further along in making a new life. Invariably, women who've been there can be the most empathetic and selfless friends. But don't overdo this source of sympathy. Avoid using your friends as spectators at the ongoing soap opera of what-he-just-did and what-he-told-my-lawyer. Gain strength from their genuine concern—but don't cross that thin line where you turn sympathy into an exercise in self-pity. You can't afford it. Instead, use your friendship as an emotional support for moving on to new experiences.

When you take your kids on outings to the zoo, on a picnic, out to eat, you may be struck by that blow-to-the-stomach feeling that you're kidding yourself, that the whole world is a Noah's ark, with man and woman paired, two by two, two parents to a family. Instead of feeling sorry for yourself or inadequate as a one-parent family, use your women friends to build up new rituals in your family life. Betsy, a Chicago personnel-agency owner, gets together with her friend Sheila for their family dinner at an inexpensive restaurant every Thursday night. "Our kids are different ages, but they knew each other back when we all lived in the suburbs. So eating out is both a nice familiar link with the past and our own new ritual. Our kids have a family feeling for each other that cuts across the usual friendships between kids the same age. Her Jacqueline, who's twelve, plays big sister to my two-year-old. Her six-year-old son looks up to my ten-year-old-son as a big brother. The children get a real assurance from having this regularity in their lives."

Holidays can lose their we're-no-longer-a-real-family pall when you invite friends to share a pot-luck Thanksgiving feast. And you won't spend all your holiday trussing the turkey and making the mincemeat pies. These and other rituals can become enjoyable and valid on their own—not make-do substitutes for the old two-parent family Christmases and Sundays at the beach.

Married Friends. The usual script calls for a divorced woman's married friends to drop her as a Typhoid Mary, an agent of infection who'll spread the germ of marital infidelity among their content husbands. This is more often myth than fact. And there is a special value in cultivating and keeping up ties with married parents who can serve as models of normalcy to your children. "I moved into the city an hour and a half from the people I knew in the suburbs," says Greta, "but I've made a point of keeping up with them because I want my sons to know what life is like in a two-parent family. I make a huge effort to get my kids out to see them and to invite them to come with us to ball games at the city stadium. Some of the fathers continue to be very important and loving to my sons."

Support from Counseling. Your eleven-year-old daughter starts skipping school. Your son is driving you nuts with his negativism—he absolutely delights in dawdling while you shriek that it's his turn to do the dishes and your carefully worked out family-sharing chart might as well be a guide to the 1933 World Series.

Don't be hesitant to get professional counseling or family therapy when you and your children have emotional and disciplinary clashes. Lauren, a West Coast real estate salesperson, credits her good relationship with her ten-year-old son and twelve-year-old daughter to getting good professional help at crucial times. Lauren's family felt stress when her ex-husband remarried. "All of a sudden, things with my son got very rocky. Everything was my fault; if he lost something in his room, that was my fault too." Just as troubling were the constant fights that marred Lauren's daily homecoming.

"Being a single parent makes it damn tough to deal with these things, because there's no feedback from another loving parent to say, 'Oh, take it easy, you're worrying too much,' or 'Okay, you people, you're getting hysterical, go to your corners.' There's no one to help break the intensity of what's going on."

Lauren was surprised at the simplicity of the techniques her family counselor suggested. "Some of the techniques were so simple that they ran against my grain at first, but they worked. First, we set up that if the kids went for just ten minutes without fighting, they'd get a check mark on a piece of paper and a reward of a nickel each. I didn't like buying good behavior, but it didn't take more than a few days and all of a sudden we would forget to record it when a half hour went by with nobody fighting. It was so amazing!"

Next, Lauren's counselor concentrated on improving understanding among the family members. "Another fantastic technique was one our therapist called Stop. If an argument begins, or your kids escalate something and someone begins to take a potshot at someone else, you simply say to the other person, 'Stop.' That's the signal that the other person has to guess what you're feeling. They have to be precise—like you're feeling put down, or you're really angry, or really hurt. And keep coming up with adjectives that describe how they think you feel until you say, 'Yes, that's right.' Then the other person asks you to do it in reverse."

"When I'd get these teary calls at work, and Greg would be crying on the phone that Jennifer and her friends were doing such and such in the pool and wouldn't let him jump in, I would say, 'Greg, I think you ought to go play Stop.' "

Along with other techniques to end fighting, Stop quickly brought peace to Lauren's household. "The interesting thing was that although we used Stop a fair amount at first, we don't seem to need it anymore.

It's a way of forcing you to see how you're affecting the other person, to empathize and understand that, though you may be speaking out of pain, you're also hurting somebody else. It takes away the argument and focuses on the emotional interaction, which is what's really going on when you're fighting."

Lauren urges other single mothers not to feel self-conscious about getting objective professional help. "Mothers need to feel comfortable about getting help, and to get it early. Don't wait until the situation is really rough."

Elka's son Chris became a disturbed twelve-year-old when his father moved out of their home. Although Chris studied conscientiously every night, his grades went down. He became withdrawn and refused to discuss his study problems with his mother. Elka asked Chris's school counselor to administer the usual tests, and the counselor promptly reassured her that, while Chris's mind remained bright as ever, she should seek a therapist with whom Chris could work out his feelings.

"When I told him he was going to go someone to help him, he burst into tears—the first emotion he'd shown in months. As the months went by, I could see this terrible pressure lifting. I just wouldn't have been able to work it through by myself with him, because of his confused loyalty to my ex-husband and me. All the money I spent in those six months—I had to borrow every penny of it—was well worth it."

You don't have to spend a fortune to get good professional help. Lauren arranged for her family therapy at minimal cost through her religious group. Low-cost help is usually available from your local Family Service Association, church, clinics associated with a university, the outpatient clinic of teaching hospitals, and even your child's school. Ask for references from agencies like your local Family Service Association of America, Mental Health Association, or department of psychiatry at a teaching hospital.

Don't be afraid to shop around for a clinic or therapist that feels right for you. Counselors treat parents and kids separately and in groups. Or they may use the increasingly popular technique of family therapy, when all of you are treated together. (The idea is that a person doesn't develop his problems in isolation; they are reinforced by reactions of other family members). Warning: psychological counselors are not infallible, and some have even been known to harbor a grudge against working mothers. *Don't blindly follow orders from a counselor when they really go against your feelings.*

HOW MUCH PSYCHOLOGICAL SUPPORT
FROM EX-HUSBANDS?

Can your ex-husband be part of your new support system? Or will he hang around like a blot from the past, impossible to ignore and always guaranteed to leave you in a state of fury when you talk? One thing's for sure, as Melody, thirty-one, divorced three years, says sadly: "You *never* get rid of your ex-husband. I thought when I walked out that I was starting a whole new slate—you know, big Joan Crawford scene, walking off into the night. Instead, I'm talking on the phone to him four nights a week! When is he going to pick up the kids, where should they go to camp in the summer, can he afford braces for our son? I never expected life after divorce to go on just like it was before."

Like it or not, you and your children's father will most likely be involved for the next ten to fifteen years. Putting that involvement on a sharing basis that will do the most for you and your children will require yeoman effort from you. The *amount* of involvement you encourage your ex-husband to have in your life is crucial. We identify three different levels of involvement: no involvement, limited involvement, and full involvement. Each has strengths and problems, but one of them is probably best for you and your need for support.

1. Daddy Loves You, But He's Far Away Right Now. Josie, a vivacious thirty-four-year-old editor with a son, nine, and a daughter, eleven, left her husband eight years ago when he announced he was in love with a student from his college classes. "He was at the time an English instructor at a famous experimental girls' school in New England. The way he had his situation worked out so beautifully was that he didn't want me to work at all. He had his perfect family, ensconced in a beautiful old country house where I was baking bread and bringing up the kids. Only on too many of those long, snowed-in New England nights, he'd call to say he couldn't get home through the snow.

"I had no image of myself working, although I'd loved history in college and had planned to teach high school. But there were no openings up there in the country. I had nothing in the world to do, no one to talk to except nice country-neighbor ladies. He had a succession of affairs with students—all very pretty, very intelligent, very knocked out by him. When he finally decided he wanted to live with one, he gave me no choice. I had to get out.

"The only thing to do was put some space between him and me." Josie left her children with her mother in Iowa for three months and came to New York to search for a job and an apartment. She lived in an inexpensive hotel for women—a famous and famously depressing first stopover for New York newcomers—and one weekend, turned down for yet another job, she lost heart. She blew her savings on a plane ticket to Iowa and stayed a week, asking her mother, "Please mother *me* for a few days."

But since then, Josie's life has been all uphill. She landed a job as a secretary in a publishing house and moved up in double time. "I made a totally new career and life and I'm very proud of myself. Eric and Jennie are very together kids, and we get along better than most mothers and kids. I just moved into a new, better job where I'm making $19,000— more than my ex-husband *ever* brought in. We finally have a bigger apartment and some breathing space over money. But in all this time, he's had *nothing* to say about the way I bring them up, *nothing*. He sends very little money, so he has no claim.

"My marriage was obviously very bad psychologically for me and I couldn't have recovered if I'd been forced to talk to him every week or so, or even once a year. And since he was never an interested father, I don't have to worry about the kids missing him."

With such a traumatic marriage, Josie chose well to support herself and cut off all contact with her ex-husband. Only by submerging herself in a totally new environment, job, and city was she able to carve out a new life.

The advantages of going it alone are highly appealing to some mothers. They have all the responsibility—but they also have the freedom to make all the decisions. Without harassment. Without argument. Without the emotional trauma that can ensue from that neutral-sounding standard divorce agreement, Parents shall consult on matters of importance.

2. Daddy Will See You Sunday. A more common arrangement, one that exists in the majority of divorce settlements, is the Sunday Daddy. A future archaeologist, excavating among the exotic ruins of our McDonald's golden arches and Superdomes, might well theorize:

> In America in the late half of the twentieth century, fathers did not normally live with their biological off-

spring. Rather, the society set aside an entire day called "Daddy's Sunday," agreed to in a binding legal document, when the biological father would call on the home of the biological mother, and take the children out for a delightful day of fun, reckless eating, and undivided attention from the father. During this entire day, the mother could groom herself, clean her house, and indulge in social relations with women and men—becoming a carefree being for the day. Judging by the frequency of the custom, the system worked well.

Many a late-twentieth-century mother would greet this interpretation with a hollow laugh. Custody arrangements that grant Daddy Sunday visits don't necessarily lighten the mother's responsibility. Paula, an attractive forty-three-year-old woman who has been divorced for nine years (during which she founded and built an interior-design business) wearily reports: "I've had Sundays free from my two children—but *never* one whole weekend in nine years. I have a daughter who is a very demanding child, with many behavioral problems, and it was an unbelievable strain for me for a while, a terrific emotional drain. But my ex-husband said, 'I am not here to make *your* life easier.' Once a week, and he never misses. And what I've wanted for years is just *one* weekend to myself."

Some divorced fathers put in their Sundays with punctual regularity, determined no one's going to say *they're* welching on the bargain. They're just as determined as Paula's husband that their *wives* aren't going to get a break, either. But negotiating a more flexible arrangement for your husband's taking the children *can* be done. Even if your thoughts toward him are homicidal, even if his selfishness seems to be repeating the same pattern that drove you apart in the first place, it's worth the effort to try to make him more flexible. A good question to ask yourself is: do you really want him to be close to the kids? Or do you bemoan the heavy responsibilities thrust on you—while still not really wanting your children to enjoy being with him? This double desire is only natural. Recognizing your feelings may pave the way to a better arrangement.

Marian, a forty-six-year-old market researcher and mother of a six-year-old boy, points out the now-you-see-it, now-you-don't sense of responsibility of fathers limited to Sunday chores. She explains the uneasy background of their marriage: "Along about my late thirties, I decided I really wanted a baby, and I set out to find a man to give me one. Of course, I didn't realize it, but that's what brought me together with Matthew. It didn't last long—you might say I had a late marriage, and an early divorce."

After two years of marriage, when their son was only six months old, Marian and Matthew split. But Marian tries hard to keep the father-son relationship going. "I want our son to feel he has two parents and two homes, but it's damn hard. Last weekend, he was supposed to go to his father, and he didn't want to at the last minute—which was hurtful to his father and annoying to me, since I'd counted on having the time for myself. Every time he does this, his father withdraws emotionally."

At the same time, Marian sees herself working behind the scenes to make it appear to her son that his father does take an interest. "We still generate a remarkable amount of hostility over the most trivial matters," she says anxiously. "Last month, we got into a vicious argument over what our son should get for Christmas presents. Matthew hadn't bought a thing, but he didn't think I'd done my job because I hadn't bought presents for the two of us. But I try to keep up these efforts and keep putting these arguments out of my mind because I want him to be part of his son's life."

Hallowed by custom and legal tradition if nothing else, the Sunday-only visiting arrangement does have undeniable advantages for some mothers. They assume most of the control and spend most of the time with their children. But all of them are naggingly aware of the problems their children have in maintaining an emotional relationship with a father who appears once a week. Recently, two Brandeis University sociologists shed light on how the amount of time a father spends with his children affects his parenting. They compared parental competence and overall satisfaction expressed by four categories of fathers:

1. full-time or full-custody fathers
2. half-time or joint-custody fathers
3. quarter-time fathers (defined as those who spend between 7 and 13 days a month with their children)
4. fathers who visit one day a week at the most

The most satisfied fathers were the half-time group, as opposed to the week-end father and the full-time father. Week-end fathers tended to feel alienated from their children. Because they spend what time they

have with their children on unnatural, aren't-we-having-a-good-time entertainment, they had little chance to take an active parenting role or build experience in handling the emotional problems of their children.

Full-time fathers, on the other hand, felt overwhelmed by their responsibilities. No surprise to any single mother!

Half-time fathers felt more secure in their roles as parents; they tended to speak more confidently of their parental "rights," not "privileges," as the week-end fathers regarded their visits with their children.

Half-time fathers also managed to stay on better terms with their ex-wives. Both week-end and full-time fathers spoke of very hostile or mixed relations with their ex-wives. Those who shared the parenting more often described themselves as being "friendly" with ex-spouses. Which brings us to emerging arrangements that recognize the need of both parents to be actively involved in bringing up their children—variously called *split custody, joint custody,* or *co-parenting.*

3. Daddy's Always Around. At its most formal, sharing of parenting is legally arranged as *joint custody* or *split custody.* (For an enthusiastic look at co-parenting and the legal, financial and time-splitting arrangements to make it work, see *Co-parenting,* Miriam Galper, Running Press, 1978.) More informally, a mother may maintain legal custody but agree for the children to spend a significant amount of time with their father. They can carve up the time in half-week periods, giving one parent charge from Thursday through Sunday, the other, Monday through Wednesday. If the father lives far away, the mother and father may agree to six months with her, six with him. Parents may alternate weeks. Or, as one New York couple arranged in a new twist, the children stay in one spot and the parents move in and out every other week! (Both parents are architects with offices that double as living quarters.)

The obvious benefit of co-parenting is that you share the arduous responsibility of parenthood. You get time to yourself to develop your own life with adults, your ex-husband feels less isolated from his children, and the children benefit from having two actively involved parents.

On the negative side, some professionals still feel that having two homes is simply too confusing to a child, especially to one already beset by his parents' divorce. Joint custody is so new that most couples are still experimenting with the idea. About half the women we interviewed who were trying co-parenting found the arrangement was good on the whole. But they were frank about problems like jealousy.

Ruth, divorced from John, a high school teacher, reveals her efforts to deal with competition for her older daughter Patty's affections. "It used to tear me apart to see how eagerly Patty went with her dad every weekend. He really has the advantage because he has the girls on weekends when he's relaxed and there're no schedules to meet, no dressing for school on time. The days I spend with them are consumed with all these duties of homework and getting up in the morning and off to the baby-sitter and to bed—all these mother-do things.

"This bothered me for about a year. I'd be hurt if Patty didn't run

---

A TYPICAL JOINT-CUSTODY AGREEMENT

Financial and Custody Agreement for Miriam and Jeffry Galper

effective 3/1/76

Custody of Joshua:

We agree that we will have joint custody of Joshua. Who he lives with at what times will be jointly determined by us as we see fit. This includes vacation times, holidays, regular weekly schedule, and summers.

Financial agreement:

1. There will be no support paid by either person to the other. Joshua's costs will be arranged for in the following manner: Each of us will pay Joshua's costs, as they arise, for his food, shelter, entertainment, daily transportation, vacations taken with each of us, and any other regular costs that come up when he is living with that parent.

2. Other costs for Joshua, as listed, will be paid for by both of us in ratio to our base earnings (see below). These are:

(a) Doctors (including dental, psychiatric, medicines, hospitalization, Joshua's medical insurance)
(b) Joshua's after school baby sitter (budgeted at $45.00 per month as of this time)
(c) Joshua's camp, special trips
(d) school, tutorials, other lessons
(e) clothes

    (f) big toys (bikes, etc.)
    (g) college
    (h) allowance

We will each keep a record of our expenses on these items, share them with each other to arrive at who owes what to whom, each month, within the first five days of the business month.

    3. Our base earnings mean the basic earnings each has on his/her job. Does not include extra earnings from one shot consultations, book royalties, extra research jobs, and so on. We realize that this could be confusing if one or both of us makes a living from a combination of these odds and ends, but we will try to agree fairly and with good will what constitutes our regular earnings and what constitutes extras.

    4. If any one of us earns so little that he/she would have to pay less than 30% of Joshua's costs, she/he has to pay that 30% anyway.

    5. At whatever point we sell our stocks, bonds, mutual stocks, we split the proceeds equally.

    6. We agree to take control and payment of the other person's life insurance.

    7. Each of us has the right to see the other's paycheck upon request.

Dated: September, 1976

Signed: _____
       Jeffry Galper

_____
       Miriam Galper

Witnessed: _____

in and eagerly hug me when she got back Sunday night. And I'd come down on her real hard about discipline. Sometimes, she'd be overly loving, trying to manipulate me. Then, other times, she'd be stubborn about not helping in the mornings, especially when she just came back from her dad's. She'd complain that she was overworked, getting up and getting herself dressed and helping with the lunches. She never had to help clean up over at her father's because he had a maid.

"I talked it over with John and asked him not to make all their weekends such fun and games. He agreed that they should have chores at his place, too—mostly fun things, like helping him trim the hedge. But that helped. Their experiences with him now are pretty real."

Ruth is firmly committed to the principle of open communication with her children, and she finally solved the tension by talking it out with Patty. "I sat her down and told her, 'It's okay if you love Dad more than me. That is really okay. I know you love me. You don't have to feel guilty about that.'" Ruth's openness cleared the air and relieved her daughter's guilt over her ambivalance.

Would Ruth rather keep her daughters all the time? "Oh, no, this is best for all of us. The jealousy is just something I had to become aware of and stop acting out. I need this time by myself. And they need their father. It's a price I'm willing to pay."

Suzanne, a government career officer, and her husband John worked out an enlightened joint custody as part of their amicable divorce. Their eight-year-old daughter and four-year-old son spent four days with Suzanne, then packed their toys and schoolbooks to spend the next three days at their father's two-bedroom apartment across town.

"It worked out great for their father, me, and our daughter, who's very attached to her father. But the shuttling back and forth was too much for my son. All of a sudden, he wasn't sleeping or eating well, and he was obviously in distress, telling me he didn't want to go. They were used to John's traveling, so Michael got the idea when he went to Daddy's that I was off traveling. One day he asked me where I was going this week while he was at Daddy's, and when I told him nowhere, he was furious: *'You stay in the house and I have to go!'*"

That realization triggered an acting out of Michael's distress. "One day at nursery school," says Suzanne, "he got sick with a stomach virus and I left work to pick him up and stayed with him the afternoon. It was the twenty-four-hour kind, but the next day I got another call—Michael's having stomach cramps. As soon as I got him home again, the cramps disappeared. Then, on Friday, when I reminded him his daddy would be picking him up from nursery school, he got stomach cramps again."

Suzanne was alarmed enough to force a change in custody. "I had to threaten John with legal action to void our joint custody, because it was obviously detrimental to Michael. He finally agreed, though with a lot of anger. But Michael's settled down. Right now he needs one home."

Jan, a Tennessee social worker, came to an unusual sharing arrangement for her thirteen- and eleven-year-old sons. "I knew I'd never be able to take care of the house on alimony and my salary, and that Jim would never pay for us to live there. So I left the kids with him and moved to a small apartment a mile away. I'm not asking for alimony. The kids stay with me Monday through Thursday."

Jan has some anger because her husband is doing all the things she'd never have been able to afford. "He hired a housekeeper to help him. But she does free me from chores like doing the kids' laundry. And I'm still a suburban mommy. I drive them three nights a week to dancing class and Little League and Sunday School. I'm very much in their lives."

How does the arrangement work out? "We have perfect reciprocity. I went to Europe recently on a work trip and that happened to coincide with Jim's break from teaching. But he stayed home and kept the children. Then, at Christmas, I had a chance to go skiing and he kept them. If he wants to go away on a Sunday with his girl friend, there's no problem. I take them, so long as I have advance notice. He's a very good father, and although it sounds complicated, I think this is the next best thing to our all living together."

For women who've struggled for years shouldering the lion's share of parenting, who've sacrificed their personal lives to devote themselves to bringing up their children with only Sunday relief, co-parenting may sound like a dream—but, unfortunately, a trend that's come too late to help them. On the contrary. If you're to make your ex-husband part of your new support system, don't regard your present childcare arrangements as binding forever. As your children grow up, changes in your individual responsibilities may be in order, either because of their needs, your ex-husband's growing willingness to assume charge, or other pressing responsibilities in your life (like going to graduate school to get a better job).

Josie, for example, after managing solo for seven years, was amazed to get help from her ex-husband. "Now that the kids are older and more interesting as people he's gotten interested in them and wants to see them. We experimented last Thanksgiving, when they took the bus by themselves to spend three days with him. He has several motorcycles and cars that he's always working on, and my son thinks that's really neat. So they now visit regularly. I can even see, at some point, one of them announcing that they want to go and live with Daddy for a while. And I can see myself emancipated enough from the past to say okay, good-bye."

Formal co-parenting may not be wanted by many husbands. But without relinquishing your legal rights, you might agree to let a child spend an entire summer or other extended period with her father. And co-parents, as Suzanne and John discovered, also have to be flexible enough to change if children are confused or insecure in joint custody. Whatever the arrangement you started with, be open to experiment and change if you want to get maximum support from your children's father.

And whatever proportion of time your ex-husband shares with the children, here are a few areas of inevitable dispute, and tips on defusing them.

Winning More Flexibility. Paula, the interior designer whose husband refused to go beyond his once-a-week day with the children, finally got relief when their daughter's emotional problems threatened to become disabling. Paula, her ex-husband, and the children all went into family therapy. One outcome was the father's realization that he could easily arrange his schedule to trade two Sundays for one whole weekend—a block of time that, the counselor persuaded him, would give his daughter time to settle down and become accustomed to him, and for them to share better interaction. Paula finally got her weekends.

Creating a Helpful Setting for Visits. One of the chief complaints of single mothers is their thankless role as the disciplinarian. "Daddy appears for the fun and games. I'm there for the real-life times to say no, you can't, wipe your mouth, say please. I get tired of being the bad guy."

Innovate to give your children and ex-husband a chance to know each other in a natural parent-child situation. If your child is under two, having Daddy take him out for the day involves complicated logistics with diapers and food. And few toddlers can retain good temper under the stress of change. Instead, you might try getting out of the house yourself for the day and letting your ex-husband visit the child on his home turf, where daily courtesy and discipline are in order. Older children can benefit from the same at-home visiting. Their father gets to see them in their native milieu, and the firsthand encounter may make him sympathetic and supportive of your efforts in dealing with them.

Defusing Criticism of Your Parenting. Sue, an urban planner whose ex-husband lives nearby with his new wife, complains, "He was always criticizing the way I let our teenaged daughters dress. He'd say, 'For God's sake, why don't you buy them some decent clothes and shoes?' He didn't understand that that's the way girls dress these days. I can't get them out of jeans, and I don't try." Finally Sue invited her ex-husband to take the girls shopping. The trauma of this real-life experience "ended all his criticism on that score. The solution was so simple, I should have thought of it long ago."

Manipulation. No honest parent can ignore the reality that yes, those sweet innocents, those baby-cheeked progeny of ours do indeed possess the shrewdness and will to manipulate us. While parents will always idealize the purity of their relations with their children, few experienced parents would deny that power struggles and conflicts mar parent-child interchanges just as they do other relationships. If you're jealous of your ex-husband's hold on their affections, chances are your kids will find ways of using your emotion to get more of what they want. If you feel guilty because you prevent them from seeing him as much as he wants, chances are they'll use that, too. If you're still jealous of the women in his life, it's likely that the next time they resent your disciplining them they will remind you about "this nice lady Daddy lives with now who lets us do all these things you won't."

Instead of screaming, analyze what it is that tees you off during those uncomfortable transition times when they're either leaving your zone or coming back from his. Are the children using your distress to gain what they want? Examining the *utility* of what they're doing will help you remain more detached. And, of course, when the ploy doesn't work on you, it's likely to be abandoned.

Chapter Twelve
ESTABLISHING A NEW LIFE AS A SINGLE MOTHER

Part of establishing your new life is learning to handle yourself as a single parent. One of the happiest results of being single can be a deepened companionship with your children. Married mothers invariably feel the difference in their parental stance when their husbands are away for a while. Frances, married thirteen years, observes, "When my husband travels, I slip into a different relationship with the kids. We're less formal. They're less well behaved, but they help me more, too. Maybe I'm a little looser, too. When there's not two of us adults against them, I have to save my authority for when it really counts."

Single mothers often enjoy a greater comradeship with their children. Without another adult to share their problems, many single mothers discuss their thoughts more freely with their children. "My eight-year-old daughter loves to know just where I stand with my latest boyfriend," says Annie. "And you know, she has better instincts about them than my adult friends."

Children learn to share chores and responsibilities—after all, who else is there to go to the grocery store and help Mom lug home the heavy bag of groceries and that extra bag of kitty litter so they can all survive the weekend? Single mothers say the job of surviving together blurs the line between Responsible Adult and Carefree Child as well. "If we don't get it together, if they don't help me with the laundry in a responsible way, if I get sick, well, we're all in one big mess. Maybe I even count on them to be grown-up *too* much."

Here are common problems with children and solutions some single mothers have found.

Post-Divorce Anger. All children feel anger and guilt when their

250

parents are divorced. This is hard to deal with because of the difficulty children may have expressing how they feel to you. How can they be loyal both to you and to their father? One way to help them work through their emotions is to put them into contact with other children of divorce. Elka, whose twelve-year-old son Chris was disturbed by his father's departure, discovered real healing came from Chris discussing his thoughts and feelings with other teenaged boys whose parents were divorced. "I would slip around and hear them talking about these things—does your mom do so-and-so, does your dad have girl friends, do you think they'll get back together? They can talk to each other better than to any grown-up about things they could never, never bring up with you. I would advise any mother to see that her child has friends of the same sex whose parents are divorced."

Angers will be worked through faster if your children don't cling to any illusions about you and your ex-husband getting back together. If, after a day with Daddy, your daughter asks, "Are you and Daddy ever going to live together?" reply with a firm, "No we're not." Sometimes children dream of having their families reunited and never express the thought. Avoid any actions that might encourage the hope that everything can return to "normal."

And lest we worry unduly about the children's reactions, Dr. Lee Salk reminds us that divorce may even be emotionally liberating for some children. "Not *all* children love their parents," he writes. "Sometimes a divorce helps a child come to terms with his true feelings about a parent." If a man has in fact been a tyrant in his household, it's a good possibility that his child fears and resents him. If divorce rids him of the parent, "the child has a sense of relief and affirmation that he is not alone with these feelings." The notion of holding-the-marriage-together-for-the-children has long since disappeared from most people's thinking. But few of us take the next step to realize that divorce can be *good* for children in some cases.

Masculine Figures. *"My son is five years old, and between his older sister and me, I'm afraid he's overwhelmed by women. I asked him what he wanted to be when he grew up and he said, 'a girl. So I can boss people.' How can I provide a male figure in his life to model himself after?"* This mother's concern is not unusual.

Single mothers consistently worry about the absence of a steady male figure for their sons to pattern themselves after. Will he grow up homosexual if he only knows women? Will he have trouble getting along with other little boys? Who'll teach him to throw a baseball and those other American male things?

Scout around and enroll your son in those still scarce grammar and nursery schools which boast men teachers. "I've gone out of my way to find first a nursery school, then a kindergarten, and now a grade school with men teachers," reports a suburban California mother steeped in Freudian theory. "I didn't want my son to grow up in this hothouse of women only. He's adored all his men teachers and frankly they've responded by adoring him. I don't think he's suffering one bit. I think he's a healthy kid."

If male schoolteachers are missing in your community (though at least one mother we talked with got herself on the school board and changed that absence), try enrolling your sons in after-school recreational activities led by men. You'll find courses at the Y, your church group, or paid recreational groups that offer instruction in hockey, baseball, and many other sports.

Your own family may provide a strong male figure. Make the effort to stay in touch with married friends, too. Married fathers can show a special tenderness and interest in children who don't have a two-parent family. And they're likely to prove more permanent figures than men you are dating. In fact, unless you have a fairly stable, long-term relationship going, it's best not to count on men you're seeing as male role models for your son. That can lead to sticky situations where you're reluctant to stop seeing someone because he means so much to your children.

So long as your son is exposed to images of both women and men as authority figures, the chances for his healthy adjustment are fine. The pervading influence of movies, books, and the culture in general in driving home male behavior to your son ensure that your own role will be well balanced.

Overdependence. This is one of the knottiest problems that single mothers face. Here are some comments:

"When it comes down to the bottom line with my daughter, there's just me. We have a symbiotic relationship. It's very mutually dependent."

"Our relationship is very intense. He's an only child. I'm an only parent. We've been an island, the two of us."

"I was spending too much time with my kids—all the time, in fact. They were too dependent on me and the relationship between us was not good. I knew I had to do something to change it."

"After my divorce, I spent literally all my free time with my two sons," recalls Jane. "And we had and have a very close relationship. Most of the time, I think that's the way it should be, the best way I can make up for their father not being there. I want them to feel loved, that Mommy is always there for them. But at times, I worry. My younger little boy will never stay away from home as all the others in his class do. So I worry, am I making them cling to me?"

Emma, a thirty-year-old M.B.A., explained the symbiotic relationship between her and her daughter. "Mine was never a happy marriage, but when Jill came along, I hadn't yet really realized that. So I lavished all my emotions on her, and that intensity has never left our relationship. All her life, I've literally been up every night with her, even when I was in graduate school. My husband slept through everything. He has never been there for her in any way. Even now, my parents live very close, so you would think we have an extended family. But emotionally, it doesn't work that way. I never can leave her with them for very long. I know she counts just on me."

Emma is aware of the bad side effects that can result from this kind of symbiotic relationship and thinks she's making progress. "Jill is nine and she's only this year beginning to sleep through the night. It's no question that she's had a sleeping problem and other problems because I lavished all my time on her. But somehow I can't believe it's really destructive. I think we've helped each other survive."

Emma is wisely loosening the emotional bonds of what has been an unusually intense mother-daughter relationship. "I know I have to find a way for her to grow away from me. It's beautiful and satisfying now, but it won't be for her forever. I wanted her to go to camp this year and I talked it up big. But at the last minute, she decided she didn't want to, and I couldn't see forcing her. Better for her to stay at home than to think I don't want her with me."

After the shock of divorce, it's natural that you and your children draw together in your own tight emotional world to regroup yourselves. They will demand more of your time, love, and patience than ever before. And it's likely you'll feel pained and/or guilty for them having lost their father, whether that's reasonable or not. Still, there's a thin line between giving each other all the love and reassurance you feel welling up in you as you fashion a new life together, and becoming so tightly bound that you crowd out other relationships now and in the future.

There are three constructive things you can do to fight unhealthy clinging between you and your children. First, encourage your kids to develop a social life of their own. When they can draw love, continuity, and emotional response from their own friends, they will be less jealous of your adult social life—and create fewer of the screaming-at-the-door scenes and cries of "Mommy, don't leave" when you go out. Second, build up your support system so that other adults are part of their lives. And third, develop work and other interests that you enjoy and can express yourself through.

Being a single parent carries stresses and strains that are unique. Learning to trust yourself as sole disciplinarian and chief source of love takes time. But there's a good chance you were the primary parent when you were married; you may have had more practice than you realize.

RELATIONSHIPS WITH MEN—
ARE YOU READY FOR INVOLVEMENT?

I have a friend who said after my separation, "Joyce, you're one of the few people I know who was really sensible when she separated. You didn't go off on some wild, totally inappropriate kind of relationship. Everybody I know has gone off with a hippie or an artist who was totally irresponsible. I really admire the way you maintained your sense of perspective." And I looked at her and said, "Well, the truth is, nobody asked me."

—A DIVORCED MOTHER

Married mothers complain that they have to give up their social lives for their families, but single mothers lack time not only for friends but for social life with men. "If you're home every night after your children finally fall asleep, collapsed in front of the TV screen, you're not likely to meet any eligible men. Where are they? Maybe home collapsed before *their* TV sets," says one mother.

Not the least reason for lack of involvement for some women is that they put up their own blocks against too much intimacy—natural for a time, but a stage that can last for years in some women.

Jane, a forty-four-year-old Manhattan lawyer who's been divorced for sixteen years, brought up her son and daughter on her own. A few years after ending "a very destructive marriage," Jane pulled herself together and enrolled in law school. Only a few weeks later, her ex-husband suddenly died. Now Jane and her children were truly alone.

But her control of her life slowly increased. She progressed in her law-school work and began to date. One of the men, Robert, a divorced businessman, became important. Their relationship deepened into an arrangement as stable as marriage: he took her out on Wednesday and Saturday nights. She stayed at his place on Wednesday nights, when she had a sitter. Each summer, when the children went to camp, he moved in for two months. When the children returned on Labor Day, he moved out.

"After the wreckage of my marriage, which left me so broken, I can't tell you how much Robert has meant to me. But he always understood that I wouldn't marry him when the children were young.

"I wouldn't because I knew they were happier when they were the center of the house. If someone else comes in, they have to move over. My marriage was very disruptive and my ex-husband was a bad influence on the children, so I thought I owed it to them to have a place where it's peaceful and where they are central.

"Now my son is thirteen and my daughter is sixteen, and Robert is talking again about marriage. But I don't think I want to do it. Because I'm used to being independent now. God knows, I've worked hard to get to that state, professionally and personally. And while there's never any suggestion when we're together that I'm expected to do wife things, I know he's the kind of man that would expect to come in at 6:30 and have a beautiful meal on the table, and there's no way with my practice that I can do that."

Jane's determination not to let anything stand in the way of doing her best by her children is shared by many women. Her hesitation to marry, now that they're adolescent, is more unusual. Is she masking some other reason?

Jane says: "Am I just using that as an excuse to avoid the commitment—and possible pain—of marriage? I know I couldn't live through another divorce. And after all the energy I've put into developing myself, I couldn't see my career go down the drain. For a long time, I feared if I married Robert, I would give it up. But now I'm earning enough that no man can say your job is just secondary, we can get along without your salary. So I think essentially my decision is not made out of fear of that. I think it's an honest decision that I'm reasonably self-sufficient and I want to keep what I've worked for so hard."

By the time Jane felt free to marry, her pleasure in her own career and in her independence made marriage less appealing. Others are fully convinced that the prospective intimacy of a second marriage is too much for them to handle.

Lee, a forty-year-old divorcee, says, "I didn't unconsciously put marriage off; I was *consciously* scared of getting married. A lot of women really don't want to get married again. They seriously wonder whether they would have anything really to offer in the second marriage. You wonder if I'd done this or that would it have lasted. You feel guilty."

Other women stave off commitment by dating only unsuitable men. Annie, a vibrant twenty-eight-year-old photographer with a crown of curly brown hair, has been separated since her daughter was six months old. She admits frankly that she used her daughter to postpone intimacy with men. "I had this baby at home and it was a very good excuse for not doing anything that scared me, whether that meant going out with someone new, or taking a job. My husband was only the second man I'd ever slept with, and I knew I had a whole sexual life to discover, so what I did was go out with younger guys. We had really nice sexual relationships, but basically I couldn't get involved. They were like second children in the house. We would take my daughter on picnics and it was like three kids out together. I didn't feel guilty toward my daughter this way. It was just easier."

Choosing partners with whom you won't be deeply involved can be a stepping-stone to trusting yourself once more to survive emotional contact. And, as a way of keeping your hand in and avoiding feeling bereft and out of contact with all men, it can serve you well. Annie, for example, now feels ready to take her dating more seriously.

But no partners at all is a more familiar story. You're busy with your kids, you have limited social time, and many men shy away from women with responsibilities.

Joyce is a brilliant woman who, in her mid-thirties, has achieved an outstanding position in the academic world. She was married to a childhood sweetheart who fell short of her remarkable intellectual capacity and drive. When her husband, a Vietnam veteran, went to college, Joyce took a battery of vocational tests as a lark, and was surprised that the vocational counselor was excited. "These are the best test scores I've ever seen. You have too much to give," he told her, "to stay home and be nothing but a housewife." When her two children were old enough to go to nursery school, Joyce enrolled in college, and within five years, graduated with honors and won a coveted fellowship. Her marriage, however, was finished.

Since then, Joyce has established herself professionally and set up her single-mother family in a Western university town. She's weathered behavior problems with her children, and while devoting much time to them has launched a glittering career. She has not run off with a hippie. She has barely had any dates. She has some ideas why:

"Statistics for women with children who remarry are incredibly lower than for men. I had my children early, and the fellows who are about my age—mid-thirties—see this woman with a grown family, and it makes them feel as if you're older. And you *do* feel older; you've been through a lot. You're not the dewy-eyed happy-go-lucky young person that you would be if you hadn't had to cope with so much responsibility. I think when you've got kids, you really no longer feel comfortable in the social swim with a lot of men your age.

"And, of course, if you're working and raising a family, too, you've become tremendously independent, you are used to making your own decisions. One fellow who called me for a date was sort of concerned that I was going to wear a pants suit rather than a skirt. You think, where does this guy get off? You're not used to having to accommodate so much to someone else, you're used to making the decisions yourself, and maybe it makes you a little less pliable. . . .

"It's so lonely, the lack of companionship really breaks you up, but I think, realistically, you are much less eligible as a date because you're not seen as free—either emotionally or sexually. I mean, you're not just going to be able to take off for a weekend, as a childless woman could. And even if you could, there's so much logistics involved, it loses spontaneity."

Hurt . . . responsibility to your children . . . your own independence . . . the physically heavy load of working and parenting jointly —all these realities may make relationships with men so difficult that you're willing to declare a vow of chastity. It's a role that has some comforts. And with financial and emotional debts to work off every day, you may think it's all you can manage. Finding the emotional calm to start feeling for others is hard. As Annie described her five years of friendships with younger men: "Part of it was that I really didn't want my daughter to have a man who would take her away from me. Her father had abandoned us both, and I've made our lives go on. With all the pain it cost me, I didn't want some man waltzing in to take her affections back."

GETTING BACK INTO RELATIONSHIPS: FRIENDS AND MORE

Once you do start seeing men and feeling ready for emotional involvement, you will, of course, have a tricky new equation to manage in your household: (1) how he feels **about** the children, and (2) how they feel about him.

Josie, like many women, simplified her romantic life after dating a string of men who disliked or were indifferent to her children: "I'm not interested in a man who can't accept dealing with my children as part of being with me. For the next ten or twelve years, that's the way it's going to be. After that, maybe there'll be somebody who won't care that I have children nineteen or twenty years old. But for now, that's the way it has to be." She has her priorities firmly in place and feels better for it.

On the other hand, avoid pursuing perfect understanding between men and your children. Ginny warns: "One thing I've had to learn is to stop dreaming of the Perfect Family. I used to dream of Mr. Rich Texan, this handsome, understanding widower who would fall in love with my children, marry me, and take care of us. Stop thinking you're going to find this wonderful man who will love you and be a father to your poor little kids. *It is not going to happen.* No matter how great a guy he is, he is *not* going to be just like a father is. No stepfather is. So you try to date guys who like your children, but don't insist he *love* them."

The man in your life may turn out to be warm and loving toward your children; they may develop a terrific relationship. But *don't expect to produce a wonderful new father to heal your children's wounds and your guilt.* That's a fantasy, and not a very useful one. If you date with that ideal in the back of your head, it's going to distort from the start relationships with men you can like and enjoy being with. As stepparenting becomes more prevalent in our society, some of the illusions are being stripped away. Even the most loving stepparent rarely becomes as close as Mom or Dad. "There is always a difference," says a successful stepfather whose family consists of his own children from a previous marriage, his wife's two children, and their own baby. "You are always making tiny mental adjustments about 'her' kids and 'mine.' "

Any women who's planning to marry to give her children a new father should carefully reexamine just what she thinks "father" will entail. If she expects the same degree of responsibility toward the child that she feels, she's expecting too much. And if the children already have a father who's even moderately involved in their lives, her expectations become all the more inappropriate.

Here are some of the conflicts between your men and children you'll have to iron out.

Jealousy.   Your children will always eye the men you see as potential rivals. But soon after divorce, children have especially strong fears of abandonment and they react intensely.

Sandy, thirty and divorced for six months, did free-lance typing to supplement her salary and when she took along her son to deliver a job to the apartment of a client, Arthur, she was mortified that her son suddenly turned into a demon. He darted into the bedroom, dragged out a toy Arthur was saving for his own son, and promptly tore it to pieces. He calmed down only when Arthur picked him up and plopped him firmly on the sofa with an angry "*Sit* there." Sandy says, "I didn't understand why he was so bad until we were driving home and he asked, 'Is Arthur going to be my daddy?' " In the beginning, children will fear that every man who crosses your path is going to marry you and displace them. Handle their fears by saying firmly: "No, he's not your daddy. Your daddy will always be your daddy. He's Mommy's friend."

Some women keep children's resentments at bay by setting rules about how often they go out. They almost sound like high-schoolers on probation: "I can never go out two nights in a row." "I limit myself strictly to dates on weekends." These rules can be reassuring both for you and your children.

Another way to enjoy men's company without pushing your children to the background is to discover the joys of men as *friends*. Your whole family has fun if you're able to integrate men friends into your life. Elka spent the first few months after her divorce going out with a different man every night. "Then when I decided this *isn't* what I want to be doing, I discovered how nice it is to have men friends drop by." She thinks it's important for her children to see men not only as people who come and take her away. "One man friend of mine takes my son swimming. Another one comes by occasionally to take us all to the beach or a movie, and we have a great time. My kids used to be jealous because I kept all the men separate in our lives. Now I'm bringing them more into the family and it's working better."

Making time for your children to chat or visit with your date before you go out helps them feel more a part of your dating life. Leaping further along in a relationship, remarrying couples nowadays are asking their children to take part in the marriage ceremony. When children become an active part of the marriage, they are better able from the first to put aside jealousy and become part of a new living unit.

Sex Roles. "I almost die of embarrassment when Jim comes over," says Elaine. "My daughter is in his lap, all over him, Little Miss Coy dying for a daddy. She's only six, but she woos him, and he can't kiss her enough. While my son, who's eight, sits in the corner glaring at this man in the house."

If a child reacts negatively or with excessive affection, the motives may lie in his normal sexual development. Don't be too miffed or worried when your four-year-old daughter leaps into your boyfriend's lap—after all, she's trying to emulate *you,* in however crude a fashion. Youngsters in their teens, struggling to come to terms with their own sexual identities, can be particularly trying, running through the gamut of negative emotions from open disgust to insulting indifference. Before you and your man take offense, consider that their reactions are part and parcel of their own effort to come to terms with their own sexual lives.

Discipline. Few areas draw battle lines between mother and boyfriend more quickly than the discipline of her children. It may be fine for you to deal out smacks to misbehavers, but let your man do the same and you are likely to rush to protect them.

Keep the peace and a reasonable amount of order by setting firm guidelines for other adults. If a man is living with you, most of us agree that he has to have *some* disciplinary powers. "You can't have a man around the house and not have him interact," says one mother. "He has to exercise discipline and he has to be able to tell them when they're bothering him and to be quiet, turn down the TV, stop running around, and wipe their mouths and wash their hands. On their side, the kids have to feel free to tell him when they're tired of his teasing or whatever."

You may want to definitely draw the line at the physical discipline your friend exercises. Polly, who has a nine-year-old daughter and has lived for five years with Jim, complains that discipline is their biggest battleground. "My theory is that if a child requires disciplining, you handle it in a manner that is not repulsive to the child or yourself. Unless it's a life-or-death matter, handle it quietly, calmly. If it's something that requires definite action, I isolate her for a period of time or temporarily restrict her privileges. That's all that's needed, because if you make a child believe she's a good child, she *will* be good."

Jim is of the old spare-the-rod-spoil-the-child school. "He assumes children are bad, that they do bad things for their own sake or specifically to irritate him—like when my daughter chews with her mouth open, which he hates. The biggest hassle in our life is physical discipline, which I refuse to let him use. My father physically disciplined me and I hate him to this day. I don't believe spanking works. Sure, it may relieve your frustration for a moment. It does *nothing* for the child. Discipline is a real problem in our household, but I think we are painfully working it out because I insist on my way."

Insist on *your* way with your children. You are the person primarily committed to them, and your values—even if misguided—should be applied unquestioningly.

Your Own Sexual Life.   Sooner or later, you'll resume your own sexual life and face one of the more painful dilemmas that confront single mothers: How do you explain the strange man at the breakfast table? How open mothers are on this delicate subject is split right along a generation gap as clear as the San Andreas Fault.

Women over forty consistently told us they put a seal of secrecy over all their sexual lives. Samantha, forty-one, divorced ten years and mother of sixteen- and eleven-year-old boys, is typical. "I know these are the seventies and everything's much looser, but I would never, never have a man live with me. I know there are no more birds and bees anymore, the kids know more than we do. The other night my eleven-year-old was arguing that I should let him go see *Saturday Night Fever,* and he blurted out, 'Mom, I know all about screwing and sex.' And I gulped. But I think seeing their mother with a man in their own house would be destructive to my sons and I've never done it. I *have* arranged to go away on a weekend and I haven't hidden that I was going with a man."

At the other extreme, Francine, a twenty-four-year-old pediatric nurse well versed in child psychology, lives in a one-bedroom apartment and has frequently had a man stay over. "My four-year-old daughter has waked up to see me in bed with a man, and I think it's perfectly okay. She understands that when people like each other, you sleep together. But she doesn't understand just what that involves."

You should handle those aspects of your sexual life that affect your children in the way that feels most comfortable to you. Younger women, committed to great openness with their children, have fewer fears about letting their children know that they have sexual needs even though Daddy is no longer around. To a certain extent, their openness is merely realistic. As one young mother says, "Don't think they'll buy that old story about how he slept in the extra bedroom." True, children's sophistication nowadays guarantees that they will see through elaborate stories. As one forty-four-year-old divorced mother discovered to her chagrin, after years of fabricated excuses about why she had to be away at night, "My teenaged son blurted out one night when it turned icy outside, 'Joe, when are you going to stop this playacting with Mom? Why don't you just spend the night?' "

Most women distinguish between caring relationships and an indiscriminate parade of men. "I would only let a man stay over if I had a real feeling for him. I think it would frighten and confuse my children to see a number of men spending the night. And those are not the values I want to pass on to them, that you sleep with everyone."

We feel some precautions are not only prudent but essential. Be discreet. There's nothing wrong with a closed door to Mom's bedroom; letting your child in for a snuggle with you and a man in your bed may seem like innocent good fun on a Sunday morning, but even this could prove disturbing to young children.

Adolescents call for extra wariness and restraint in the physical affection you show with a man. A teenage son, working through normal Oedipal attractions to his mother or acutely aware of his own trigger-quick sexual responses, should not be exposed to the sight of his mother fondling another man. A teenage girl who sees her mother in physical intimacy with a man can easily misconstrue what is a normal, natural show of affection as an act of female rivalry. These are tinderbox times, and a little restraint need not cramp your own life.

SUCCESS AND YOU: I CAN DO IT!

If you're a single mother, chances are your paycheck is essential to your family's welfare. Only about 20 percent of all divorced, separated, or single women receive any regular financial assistance from the fathers of their children. Despite the fact that women are handicapped as earners in the job market, most single mothers must shoulder the support of their children.

As a result, almost half of all fatherless families remain poor by government standards—and many of these families are newly poor, having lived on a middle-class income before divorce. Louis B. Hays of the Department of Health, Education and Welfare (which, in an effort to stem rising welfare costs, recently required state welfare agencies to make efforts to enforce divorced fathers' payments to their children) offers this shocking assessment: "A fair amount of the children on welfare have fathers with fairly good incomes. Many welfare cases were formerly middle-class families but the father leaves, the mother is unskilled and unemployable, and is forced to go on public assistance."

For all the grim financial problems faced by mother-headed families, there *can* be a positive spin-off from the money squeeze. Necessity galvanizes many a single mother into a career she would have put off until the kids were grown or maybe never have had at all.

And many women make the decision early on that being financially responsible for herself and her children is going to mean more security and peace of mind than waiting for a check or haggling over it every month. Emma's husband decided he wanted to drop out of corporate life, and his checks dried up overnight. Her decision: "I sat down and considered my options. I could go to the courts, scream, cry, or get aggravated. No, I thought, it's easier to do without."

With family courts set up as they are—"a shrine to bureaucracy and injustice," said one woman bitterly after seeing her husband, a $50,000-a-year man, walk out from the fifth court appearance without coughing up a penny of the two years of child support he owed—your decision to become financially independent just may be the one that sets you on your way to success. And you will be in good company: Many single mothers decide to seize financial fate in their own hands.

Says Annie, the photographer: "My husband announced he was reducing my child support from $100 a week to $25. I decided not to fight him because I'd be better off spending my energies getting another client and finding another job. And it was only then, that moment, that I truly accepted that *I* was going to be financially responsible for me and my child. . . . And I can tell you, it was the greatest motive to succeed a woman ever felt."

Your work will probably have even more urgent meaning for you than for a woman who can count on her husband's paycheck. And even if you're currently provided for by your ex-husband, don't forget that circumstances change—if he loses his job for whatever reason or if he remarries and has other children, your children are likely to be squeezed out. Here are some special tips for the single mother whose job will be vital to her family's security and to her identity in her new life.

1. Take Yourself Seriously. You're going to be working for a long time. Take this investment of your time and life seriously. Many women say that being a breadwinner forced them for the first time to think realistically about their career options and to set goals and ways to work toward them. Use the upheaval in your life to reexamine what you *want* to be doing.

Don't expect to find the answer to your vocational problems overnight. Lynn remembers: "I spent two years after the divorce in the playground with my daughter trying to figure out what I wanted to do. My ex-husband was starring in a Broadway show and I'd pass his picture on a poster every time I wheeled our daughter along and think there he is fulfilling his dreams, what do I want to do with *my* life? Finally I decided I'd been having such a hard time deciding because I was fighting the fact that I wanted to be a writer. That was the one thing I liked to do in life and was good at. I had worked at a publishing house as an editorial assistant when I was married but it was like I was just playing —I didn't take it seriously. Now I got down to work and persuaded a new paperback house to let me read books for them free-lance. I don't think they ever read the reports—they were very flakey—but I got my toe in the door and said let me write your advertising, I can do it!"

Lynn's first step led three years later to a copywriting job in an advertising agency where she's making $25,000 a year and loves her work.

If the career you want requires that you go back to school, *do it!* Don't be afraid of the commitment, if you can possibly swing the finances. Divorced women who have clearly focused goals are surprised when their concentration puts them ahead of younger students. As Aline, a single mother who began law school in her late twenties, recalls:

"You go back to school with a whole different attitude. I had been out of college five years, three of which I spent at home taking care of an infant. So naturally I had a different attitude from someone who goes directly from college. I had a goal and I wanted to succeed at it desperately. I was surprised when I discovered I could do it and it wasn't even that hard."

Says Louise, who earned her master's in urban planning at thirty-six, "I went back to school at thirty-two, when everyone else was twenty-two. I was very much aware of the generation gap and very nervous about it. But I found I was a much better student, more able to concentrate than the younger students. And because urban planning is a very realistic, real-politik field, I had life experiences to draw on that the kids didn't. The whole experience of studying and thinking was richer for me than for them."

2. Believe in Yourself. This simple bromide is the key to success for many a single mother. And the first step to achieving this is simply to *act* as if you do. Present yourself confidently to employers. Keep in mind that your experience, maturity, and ability to handle responsibility make you an attractive candidate for many sought-after jobs. Summon the will power to start seeking jobs that will offer you the personal and financial rewards you deserve.

Learn to value yourself and how to convey that feeling to the world. You don't have to come across as an aggressive go-getter; simple enthusiasm and quiet confidence can do the trick. Molly, soft-spoken and gentle, had put in three years of nursing night shifts, and her young son was tired of kissing his mother good-bye every night at 6:30 P.M. as she left for work. When she learned of a daytime opening in the research department of her hospital, she nervously scouted it out. Qualifications were fuzzy—the job seemed to call for an intern or nurse practitioner, but that requirement wasn't stated. She recalls, "I had been carrying out duties similar to those of a nurse practitioner on the skeleton night staff, though I didn't have that actual title. But I steamed myself up and went in to the director and was very enthusiastic about his project. I asked a lot of questions and I said, 'I can do this job.' And they hired me!"

Molly underscores a good strategy for any woman looking to move ahead fast: Pick a new occupation where qualifications aren't rigidly established and say, "I can do it."

For Ginny, a legal secretary, positive thinking helped her put together a totally new job image. "I'd always felt inadequate because I never got a college degree, and, of course, my resume revealed that. It didn't even seem worthwhile putting down that I was enrolled in a night course at Columbia. I'll never forget one personnel director for a big company who yawned over my resume and told me they had no openings." One year later, feeling stronger about herself in the work world, Ginny redid her resume, "omitting all mention of marital status and children. And I listed at the very top: Enrolled in Columbia University. Then I put down all the five colleges I'd attended all through my checkered educational career, without once mentioning dates. And this very same personnel director—he didn't remember me at all—looked at it and said, 'I can see you're a very educated person!' And he wanted to hire me."

No matter what your job level, going armed with a well-written resume will put you a step ahead in conveying the image you want. Often, with a resume, you won't have to fill out an application form at all, and that's in your favor. Remember that old lawyer's rule: Avoid answering other people's questions. It's better to make up your own questions to put yourself in a favorable light.

3. Is Your Business Your Pleasure? The time pressures on a single mother narrow her world down to two horizons: home and work. Your work life is not only your livelihood, but the source of most of your companionship and social life.

That is, if you're lucky. Co-workers don't necessarily become bosom buddies and they may not even share similar interests beyond work. Paula, an interior designer, got her first job after her divorce in an office populated by happily married people. She felt stimulated being around busy, talented people and enjoyed her work and colleagues so much that she voluntarily worked late at night, loving the congenial after-work atmosphere when they sent out for coffee and sandwiches and chatted amiably.

"But on Fridays, everybody went home for the happy weekend to their families and I would go home alone, feeling really down and really separated from them, like an abandoned child. I didn't feel I could presume on our business friendship to push myself into their suburban lives."

Paula discovered a divorced man in the office who had two children and was also alone on weekends. They chatted about similar problems—

her loneliness, his guilt at not being with his children. "He was one of my bosses and I would never have gotten involved with him sexually, but he was a very good person for me to talk to. I felt shy about identifying myself as a single woman with the others. They were all such family people—jokes about their wives and kids and mortgages. But between the office comradeship and the understanding of the divorced man, I got through a very rocky first year of divorce. They were my family, my therapy group, my friends."

Some women deliberately pick jobs that will provide a social life. Nona had been a New Jersey housewife until age thirty-two, when her husband woke up one morning and announced he needed "more joy in life." For him, that spelled leaving her. She reentered the work world by first taking a secretarial course, then finding a job as secretary at a busy literary and movie agency where parties promoting clients were frequent and brought her into contact with a wide assortment of men from the entertainment and media worlds. Within a year, Nona's efficiency and skill in social interaction had made such an impression on her bosses that she was promoted to handling a few accounts of her own. Now a full-fledged agent, she moves in a business world that provides her with social pleasures. "All my lunching and cocktail parties and so on during the day give me more social contacts in a week than I had in ten years of marriage. So I rush home to my kids every single evening and I'm very content to spend every nonbusiness hour with them. When I'm seeing a man regularly, we eat dinner at my place and spend just about all our time there. I can't think of a more ideal combination of work and pleasure. This is the only way I can work and still have enough time for my children."

HELPFUL BOOKS ON MONEY

How to Be a Financially Secure Woman, Mary Elizabeth Schlayer and Marilyn H. Cooley (Rawson Books, 1978).

Everyone's Money Book, Jane Bryant Quinn (Delacorte, 1979).

Sylvia Porter's Money Book, Sylvia Porter (Doubleday, 1975).

4. Set Financial Goals. Now that you're the chief breadwinner don't drift. Take control of your financial future. You will want to take out adequate life and medical insurance—without going to the other extreme

---

LIFE INSURANCE BASICS

Life insurance has long been ignored by women. Single mothers can't afford to. When you wake up at night worrying "what would happen to them if something happened to me?" you can reassure yourself by answering: "they'd be covered by life insurance." Here's a checklist of basics you should know.

What is life insurance? It's a plan by which you pay monthly sums to guarantee that your beneficiaries will receive a certain sum upon your death.

What kinds are there? Two basic kinds of insurance exist: term and cash value (also known as whole life, ordinary life, twenty-pay life, thirty-pay life). Term insurance offers the most coverage for the least money. It can be bought for any term up to ninety-nine years, and benefits are paid only in the event of your death. Cash-valued insurance is a mixture of life insurance and a savings account. As time goes on, the policy accrues in value and you can cash it in should you need the money. Payments are naturally higher for cash-valued insurance, and if you are disciplined enough to save on your own, you'll earn higher interest on your money in an ordinary savings account.

How much insurance should you carry? One rule of thumb is that you should carry an amount equal to your annual income. Another equally quoted rule is that a family should be insured for four or five times its annual income. But your decision will depend on how many other people your children could count on in the event of your death and how much you realistically can afford. Don't let an insurance agent pressure you into something you can't afford.

What's the best buy? Assess your personal needs and then shop around. Usually your best bet is to take out insurance through your employer, since group rates are cheaper. If you have substantial debts, you may want to take out extra insurance.

What traps do you look for? Be sure to read your contract, which, by law, must be in understandable English. Two points to check: be sure your policy is *renewable* (can be renewed after five years at higher rates agreed upon at the time of your original contract) and *convertible* (allowing you to change to another form of insurance should you choose to).

---

of being insurance poor. You may want to invest in a home—if so, bone up on credit antidiscrimination laws before you go to the bank. Some lenders regard single mothers as poor risks. Increasing your understanding of money can help you find unsuspected fat in your earnings or help you invest or work toward a financial goal. And while you're learning, don't hesitate to seek professional advice—good old brother Bill may have your best interests at heart, but that doesn't make him an expert on financial juggling. Try a reputable accounting firm or the trust department of a bank if you have a sizable settlement (over $10,000). If you have a smaller nest egg, the bank officer where you have a checking account can help you set financial priorities, arrange for a loan, or otherwise help you untangle your budget. Or you can get reasonably good counsel from some free agencies run by Parents Without Partners, church, or government groups. Cover yourself by getting advice from several sources.

One typical money hang-up: many women feel uneasy about borrowing and owing money. If you insist on paying every bill on the first of the month, you may not be getting the most leverage from your money. A professional adviser or a good book on money management can help you figure out how much credit you can handle.

There's no mystery about money. And no reason you can't take charge of your financial future along with the rest of your own life.

LIVING ALONE AND LIKING IT

"I get mad at myself for wanting a man sometimes. Why can't I just accept that this is my family, my kids and I, and that we love each other, and that's enough?"

Every single mother knows moments like these—moments when she feels lonely, unable to cope, longs for Mr. Rich Texan to come bail her out . . . and at the same moment, hates herself for feeling that way.

For some of us, it's hard because it's our first chance to experience that scary yet quintessentially human condition of being alone. Bonnie realized how little preparation she'd ever had to be alone a moment in her life. At first, she hated being by herself, especially sleeping in her big king-size bed after she and her husband split. "There was a point when I felt I couldn't deal with being alone. I would have moved in with a man if there'd been anybody around. I really thought: I'll never do well alone."

Bonnie realized she'd never been on her own in her entire life. After growing up in a close two-parent family, she moved directly into a college dormitory with two close friends. She married on the day of graduation, and since then "never slept more than two nights alone. But now I no longer wake up in the middle of every night in a panic; I'm determined to hang on and find out what it's like. There are things I want to do that I don't want anyone to tell me I can't, like dancing all night or buying a pair of $65 jeans. Utterly impractical. But I'm finding out about myself."

Given time and space, most women discover that the pleasures of being alone are real—and they're not eager to give them up. A single mother can pick her own friends—no more seeing people because of "couple ties." Lynn, who divorced after twelve years of marriage to a well-known Broadway actor, realized, "All our friends came to us through him. Afterward they *stayed* with him. But it was good for me. I have a different kind of people in my life now, people I like much better and who are better for *me*. I was always trying to fit myself to his world and people. I had no idea what a strain it was."

Your children, too, can sometimes pick friends that Dad didn't approve of. And without another adult questioning your values, your child-rearing methods, or your wants, you can come to treasure the sense of being in control that you've worked so hard to achieve.

Being single calls forth a daily churn of emotions: loneliness, fright, joy at succeeding on your own, relief that you're still able to keep going. But as you establish a new life, you'll enjoy more and more moments of feeling high, charged with the confidence you've earned from being on the line—and coming through. Being alone, you're forced to become your own judge of your worth, instead of getting self-esteem from a husband or other men who tell you whether you're smart, attractive, or worthy of love. And when a woman reaches that happy state of independence when she can decide herself how she's doing in the world and what she wants, she's reached a heady new freedom.

These are the good moments, and they're worth fighting for.

Chapter Thirteen
GUILT AND OTHER MISERIES: SUCCEEDING WITH YOURSELF

Scratch a working mother and what will you find festering right under the skin?

Guilt.

You may have an acute case that makes you bring home your brief-case loaded with gifts, spurs you to shelve discipline and spend your time with your children doing only fun things "because after all, we're only together a little while." Or guilt may bury itself, gnawing quietly and only rarely flaming into consciousness. A Boston mother, asked how she got rid of guilt during her ten years of working, confesses: "I don't think I have. I've just learned how to dam it back and block it out of mind better."

Even the most confident mother suffers self-doubt when her child develops a reading problem or has a small accident. Then she may share the anguish of Connie, a successful academic who's refused chances for career advancement, yet still feels guilty about not being home with her nine-year-old: "I worry," she says, "because he seems to attach himself to people so desperately. I keep saying it's because he never got enough mothering and so he's emotionally needy and he will be at twenty-five, and forty, and even when he's seventy." Poor mother, who sees her failures making her child miserable sixty years hence! What a painful load of anxious self-blame to shoulder!

Will you ever achieve that blissful state depicted in magazine stories where superorganized Mom trots off to work coping so well that she never feels a pang of guilt? Just as at-home mothers often feel guilty for not filling all their chldren's needs, so you as a working mother will probably feels stabs of self-blame. The best question to ask yourself is *how reasonable is my guilt?*

WHAT THE RESEARCHERS SAY

One way to answer that is to see the effects of maternal employment on a large population. If we examine the confused and often contradictory research findings available, we are likely to be reassured, though data are still scant and ambiguous. Interestingly, as more women join the work force, studies are turning up more positive effects on their children!

SOME OF THE THINGS YOU MAY FEEL GUILTY ABOUT

- missing your child in the middle of a business meeting
- not missing your child at all
- forgetting to bring a birthday present for your daughter to take to a party
- watching TV when you feel you should be making a big hearty stew
- falling asleep at a PTA meeting
- your child's toes turning in because you haven't had time to shop for new shoes
- being too tired for sex with your husband
- not having a clean tablecloth when your mother comes to dinner
- not having the beds made for two weeks
- going to your office when your child lies in bed with a 102° fever

Do children of working mothers develop more social and school problems? To start with worst fears first, studies do not support that old theory of the "experts": The mother works, so the children get in trouble. "There is no evidence that the children of working mothers are more likely to be delinquent," say Hoffman and Nye, who sift through a mass of findings in their definitive *Working Mothers*. And no evidence suggests that children perform less well in school when their mothers work. Indeed, some studies indicate that children of working mothers have higher academic aspirations (usually measured by desire to go to college) and that many seem to be more highly motivated to achieve, particularly at the grade-school level. More controlled studies are needed to probe the validity of these findings.

The impact on daughters is more definite. Hoffman and Nye report, "There is evidence that college-educated daughters of working mothers have higher career aspirations and achievements than do college-educated daughters of nonworking mothers." As we observed from our interviews, children of working mothers fail algebra and so do kids whose mothers are home all day. The nine-year-old whose mother works may be apprehensive at school, but so may his classmate whose mother waits for him at home with milk and cookies. Recent studies also show no difference in school attendance between children of working and nonworking mothers, an impression that was certainly confirmed by our interviews. In fact, while an at-home mother may allow her child to take an occasional day off for "rest and recreation," working mothers are understandably disinclined to do so.

Do working mothers' children have more emotional problems? Pediatrician Mary Howell, in her authoritative article "Effects of Maternal Employment on the Child," points out that the emotional problems of Children *"have been found repeatedly to be related not to the mother's employment, but to her own emotional state."* Studies in England also have found no difference between working and nonworking mothers' children in emotional problems, school achievement, or social adjustment.

Do children raised with the help of caregivers grow up to be unresponsive adults, unable to relate warmly to others? Probably the keenest fear working mothers experience is worrying about the effect that having a surrogate mother will have on a young child. But in Harvard psychologist Jerome Kagan's intensive six-year study of the effects of day care, he has found no important differences—in attachment, separation anxiety, social and emotional development—between babies cared for in a day-care center and those being raised at home. Although the center where Kagan's research was conducted was far superior to the average (highly trained personnel, low child–caregiver ratios, etc.), he still draws encouraging conclusions about the outcome: "The results of these investigations suggest that if the child comes from a relatively stable family and if the day care is of good quality, the child's development seems to be normal."

With infants, the growing body of psychological opinion is that a child can "attach" successfully to a number of people, and indeed that this variety is normal and desirable. (See pages 121–122 for the meaning of attachment.) Rudolph Schaffer, professor of psychology at the University of Strathclyde, Glasgow, and author of *Mothering* (Harvard University Press, The Developing Child series, 1977), found that children can make multiple attachments by the age of eighteen months. And Schaffer adds this reassurance on the meaning of such multiple attachments: "Being attached to several people does not necessarily imply a shallower feeling toward each one, for an infant's capacity for attachment is not like a cake that has to be shared out. Love, even in babies, has no limits."

DAUGHTERS AND SONS

Most gratifying to many mothers is the effect working has on their children's concepts of sex roles—of what men and women do in life. Hoffman and Nye offer four important findings.

1. *"The effect of maternal employment was to raise the estimation of one's own sex—that is, each sex added positive traits usually associated with the opposite sex; daughters of working mothers saw women as competent and effective, while sons of working mothers saw men as warm and expressive."* The sharing of child-rearing and housekeeping tasks that usually result when a mother is working helps break down the stereotypes of passive mother/breadwinning father for children of both sexes. For those of us committed to nonsexist child-raising, this is indeed heartening.

2. *"Elementary-school daughters of working mothers see women as less restricted to their homes and more active in the world."* Allied to this finding is a more surprising one: When asked to describe which activities they thought women liked or disliked, the daughters of working mothers report more liking and less disliking of all activities—household, work, and recreation! This suggests that these children come to feel that working contributes to a woman's sense of self-esteem and pleasure in *all* activities in life.

3. *"Daughters of working mothers view work as something they will want to do when they are mothers."* If the mother enjoys her job, it is not surprising that her daughter will want to

emulate her. But, report several women we spoke to, many young girls need to see themselves as mothers before they can even envision themselves as having a career. "I'd ask her, 'What do you think you'll want to be when you grow up?' " one woman recalled. "And she'd always say, 'A mother.' I'd feel very disappointed, and I'd try to tell her about all the professions a girl can have nowadays. But finally I realized that she had to deal first with the basic need to be a mommy."

4. *"For girls, maternal employment seems to contribute to a greater admiration of the mother, a concept of the female role that includes less restriction and a wider range of activities, and a self-concept that incorporates these aspects of the female role."* For boys, the results are not that clear. "Maternal employment might influence their concept of the female role, but what the effects are on their attitudes toward their father and themselves depends very much on the circumstances surrounding the mother's employment."

How does the parenting of working mothers stack up? May Howell notes that homemaker-mothers report they spend six-plus hours a day in childcare, compared to employed mothers, who spend four-plus hours. While two hours a day may seem like a lot, Howell estimates that the difference in "attentive care" is probably not significant.

By the time children reach adolescence, even time differences disappear. Working mothers spend the same amount of time with their teenage children as do at-home mothers. And significantly, adolescent daughters of employed women are more likely to name their mothers as "the person I most admire."

Hoffman and Nye point out that the middle-class mother and many a lower-class one tend to make a deliberate effort to compensate the child for her employment. In fact, "if a mother's work is gratifying, if she does not feel unduly hassled, or if she deliberately sets about to do so, she may even spend *more time in positive interaction with the child than does a nonworking mother.*"

Probably the one finding that most mothers will back up from their own experience is the overriding effect of *a mother's own attitude and satisfaction in her work.* Hoffman and Nye concur with the women we talked to in concluding that when a mother enjoys her work, "she does a better job" as a mother. They cite studies that indicate that the satisfied working mother is often a better parent than the dissatisfied nonworking mother. Indeed, in one study, the full-time mother who avoids employment because of her "duty" to her child obtained the lowest scores on "adequacy of mothering." In another study comparing professional women with college graduates who had chosen to be full-time homemakers, the stay-at-home women viewed themselves as less competent in most areas, *including that of childcare.*

"The data, on the whole, suggest that the working mother who obtains personal satisfactions from employment, does not have excessive guilt, and has adequate household arrangements is likely to perform as well as the nonworking mother or better; and the mother's emotional state is an important mediating variable." Hoffman and Nye warn: "Mothers of young children . . . may mar employment satisfaction by too much guilt."

And so we come full circle. How we feel about what we do—and thus about ourselves—has a profound effect on our children. If we are anxious or unhappy about working, we communicate this dissatisfaction to our children, just as the dissatisfied housewife sends out danger signals about her boredom and depression to her children. Excessive guilt can wreck the very benefits that a working mother hopes to bring to her family.

Handling guilt, then, is a matter of more urgency than your mental comfort. This nagging anxiety calls for two strategies so universal they can be set down flatly as rules.

> *Rule 1.* If you really are guilty of something, stop doing it. If your child truly is suffering under your present childcare arrangement, perhaps you should consider lowering your life-style and paying for better care. If your child is undergoing hardship that you can clearly trace to your absence, maybe you should consider working part-time.
>
> *Rule 2.* Don't instantly jump to the conclusion that your working is the cause of every problem that occurs. Guilt has a way of blinkering us, bottling in our normal sensitivity, so that difficulties seem insoluble.

HANDLING GUILT

Alas, when your child has trouble at school or the neighbors complain that he's making noise, your husband, you, and other interested parties are likely to immediately blame what is still seen as unnatural: the mother works. Lucie, a twenty-nine-year-old financial analyst, agonized for a whole year when her only child, Linda, went off to nursery school and Lucie got reports of behavior problems from her teachers.

"She couldn't stand to stay in line or wait for anything," Lucie remembers with lingering embarrassment. "She bit and hit the other children. I'll never forget the first meeting at the school—the teacher leaned over and gently asked: 'Do you think it's because you work?' "

Like most of us, Lucie's own conviction wavered when faced with authority. "After all, the teacher had seen hundreds of kids; what did I know? Even my own mother—who supported my working—asked me the same thing. Well, the truth was we'd done the classic only-child thing— we'd spoiled Linda rotten. She had only to say something and we adults immediately interrupted ourselves to hear her words. If she wanted her shoelace tied, I'd throw down whatever I was doing that second to tie it."

Lucie's failure in child-rearing was much more painful to face than the easy solution of quitting her job. She and her husband reexamined all their behavior. "We worked it through very painfully and consciously changed our child-rearing program. We had our hands full to undo it, but Linda's come round. Still, every teacher Linda has had always comes down to saying to me: do you think you should work, do you think that's a problem for this particular child?"

Lucie spoke with the satisfaction of one who's worked through a problem. "For a long time, my answer was a guilty yes, maybe it is. My answer now is God, no, it has *nothing* to do with anything."

Mothers we talked with had been through any number of problems with their children: a son who stole small amounts of money at school, a three-year-old boy who suddenly stopped talking, an incommunicative teenage daughter. Not one of the problems, when resolved, appeared related to the mother's absence during part of the day.

This is not to say that side effects of a mother's working—her tension or her fatigue, for example—can't be part of a larger picture in which behavior problems develop. But the simpleminded equation of mother works = child's-in-trouble, is simply not true.

WHO MAKES YOU FEEL GUILTY?

If you feel your childcare arrangement is satisfactory and you're in touch with your children, yet you still suffer frequently from guilt, one of the most useful things you can do is explore the emotion. Analyze what triggers it. Try to understand, in precise detail, what it is you think you're doing wrong. Whose ideals are you not living up to? Your own? Authority's? Your husband's?

Mothers and Mothers-in-Law.   Of all the garden varieties of guilt, the most poisonous is guilt fed by someone else. Rosa, a warm, twenty-eight-year-old brunette who manages a popular beauty salon in a California shopping center, has worked since she was eighteen, when the oldest of her three daughters was six months old. For five of those years, Rosa left her daughter in her mother's household—an arrangement which she thought was the best for her child . . . but instead darkened her relations with her daughter.

"My mother created problems with the kids that I didn't see for years," says Rosa. "Coming from the old country and always having stayed home with us, my mother just thinks the family's all a woman should have. She's never taken my working seriously."

Rosa's first daughter was unusually prone to minor childhood infections. But when Rosa would drop her off for the day, her mother would say to her daughter, "Well, your mother shouldn't be taking you out, you should be home in bed. And my daughter would take it up—'How come you're leaving me when I'm *so* sick?' when really I knew she was okay."

Rosa felt all kinds of demands to compensate for her absence. "My mother told her, 'If your mother didn't work and she was a good mother, you'd be able to take dancing lessons.' That really had me running around. My daughter was only three, too little to practice, and she'd go down to class and just fool around. But I put myself on a crazy schedule to leave work at 1:00, pick her up and take her to dancing lessons at 1:30, rush back to do my comb-outs and pick her up at 2:30. I was a nervous wreck. Even though I should have been able to see my daughter wasn't even enjoying it, I thought I *had* to do it."

Rosa discovered that no one can make us feel quite so agonizingly guilty as our mothers. The situation became serious enough to force her to action. "It got to the point where my daughter had a fit every time I went to work. So I made a big decision and put her in a nursery school two days a week so she could play with other kids. And overnight it *all* changed. They have such a small world at that age, she had thought she was the only kid in the world whose mother worked. But when I put her in the day-care center with other kids whose mothers worked, she saw that it was normal. That changed the way she felt about it. When I realized the resistance wasn't really coming from my kids, I felt as though a great weight had come off and it's been wonderful for us all."

Mothers and mothers-in-law often become protectors of their grandchildren. They see themselves as combining the infallible wisdom of experience with the seasoned judgment of distance ("after all, my daughter's never had a child before, she can't see what she's doing, leaving that child").

Combined with a mother's power over our consciences, the effect on you can be devastating. If the disapproving mother baby-sits for you, she has a double-whammy hold. First, there's the martyrdom of doing your job—"My daughter works, so I keep her children," these willing do-gooders sigh to friends. And second, she becomes the expert on your child—and you can be sure she'll report all the bad news. Kathryn, returning to graduate school at twenty-nine, asked her mother to take over at home. To her distress, "When I'd get home, my mother would say, 'Jonathan has been sitting at the door waiting for you for the past hour.' Maybe he was, but *she* should have been doing something to amuse him. Of course, I didn't see it that way for a long time. She made me feel guilty as hell."

Learning to trust your own instincts with your kids is an essential step in your growth as a mother.

NONWORKING MOTHERS

Mothers who don't hold jobs outside the home are next in line in making a coping working mother suddenly feel she's been deluding herself. You may meet open hostility ("I love my children too much to let someone else bring them up," accuses the busy mother of four glaring at you at the PTA meeting. Or "If you want to work, why did you ever have children?"). Or you may be wounded more by perfectly sincere, well-meant queries about the effects on your child.

Taking a good, hard look at what stay-at-home mothers really do, how many hours they spend with their children, can refresh your viewpoint. Julia, a thirty-one-year-old Chicago medical writer, moved with her doctor-husband and young daughter to a suburb and was thrust into a virulently antiworking group of women. "They came right out and demanded, What are you trying to prove? Are you trying to be better than other women? To compete with men? Aren't you afraid your daughter will never know you?"

Julia shakily reexamined her mothering over the next six months. "Then I started really seeing what they did with all this time they were supposedly devoting to their children. They served their kids cold tuna fish sandwiches for supper. And they let them watch TV all afternoon instead of taking them to a museum. And they had their husbands take them out three nights a week because they're so bored. I make it a point to organize a trip into the city once a month to take my daughter to the museums. And we all bake our bread together. I think our relations are just dandy."

As we worked our way through interviews with dozens of women, we were amazed to discover that most working mothers had never shared their problems and worries with others. Isolation can quickly lead to self-doubt . . . while sharing worries with other mothers (particularly older ones who've lived through it) can be a wonderful catharsis.

Starting a small rap group where you and other working mothers share your problems in a sympathetic, nonjudgmental atmosphere can yield wonderful insight and confidence. Knowing that you are not alone, that other women suffer the same agonizing doubts, helps you distinguish between needless guilt and conscience. There *may* be times when you are actually neglecting your child, and it would be harmful to bury those feelings. But chances are that, like the majority of mothers who work, both you and your children are managing just fine. Sharing your feelings and experiences with others is an excellent way to help you realize just that.

BUT AM I A GOOD WOMAN?

Many stereotypes about women are being shattered, but one that still has more power than we would have guessed is that of the barren career woman. Only a decade ago, the woman who pursued a career was regarded as a sexual oddity, known by such special terms as a "professional woman" or coyly as a "career gal" (read, unmarried). She was presumed to be deficient in some womanly way: physically ugly, frigid, or (the whispers went) lesbian. Today the woman who loves her work may still harbor inner doubts about whether that means she's deficient in womanly qualities, whether she's lacking some fundamental female trait.

When a woman has fears about being a "good" woman, she may errone-
ously read personal failure into the fact of her working.

We first noticed this excessive guilt in Connie, a highly conflicted
mother who is a brilliant professor, with sons nine years and six months
old. Connie finds motherhood far more difficult than her academic career, which has soared almost in spite of herself. She has limited her
career to part-time—"otherwise I'd be eaten alive by guilt." Nonetheless
she is, at thirty-three, the youngest and only female professor in her
department in a prestigious East Coast university.

Connie experiences the conflicts about her success that many gifted
women do. "I always excelled in male-type areas, and I had great fears
about my womanliness. I wasn't popular, and never dated much. I married very young—at twenty—because I was anxious to have that confirmation of my womanhood, that I was okay as a woman. I was very
fearful about pregnancy when that happened. It didn't seem possible
that *I* could have conceived. So I was delighted to discover when my
first son was born that I loved caring for a baby! That was contrary to
all expectations, since I hate cooking and housework.

"But after the first year, my son became much harder to cope with,
we had power struggles. I would walk around the house thinking I can't
stand ten more minutes of this, I'm going to beat that kid to a pulp!
I was not Supermother.

"I knew I had to get out of the house, but I couldn't work full-time.
I would have been eaten alive by guilt. I still can't accept the thought
of being a full-time employee and a mother, so I work part-time, although, to be honest, all my avocational interests take me out of the
house as much as a full-time job. I feel I'm deficient as a nurturer, and
that grieves me deeply. Why should my sons pay for that?"

The side of her life that Connie sees as "masculine" is quite different. "I'm totally in control in a classroom or dealing with 'male' intellectual things. I rarely meet my match. I guess that keeps my ego going."

Connie has fears of being like her mother. "My mother was a brilliant physicist who quit work to tutor my sister and me. Her great fear
was not being able to give, although she gave up her career to be with us
and spent hours teaching us to read at age four, listening to music, painting, and writing poetry. But she worried that she couldn't give warmth,
physical affection, generosity of spirit. I am more physically expressive
than my mother—I can hug and spank my child spontaneously. But I
have the same flaws. And it bears in on me horribly that I'll never be

a good mother. I'll never be able to give to my children the way a lot of women do."

We wondered how Connie might have felt if her brilliant mother had continued her career at least part-time instead of turning all her energies into being home and dosing her children with learning. Despite her image of herself, Connie appeared to be an exceptionally warm, nurturing person, and as her nine-year-old son is turning out well, even to her critical eyes, her guilt seems less related to her hours of work than to her worries about being an adequate woman.

Many successful women agree that their feelings of guilt over working are intertwined with secret fears about being a "good woman."

Alice, forty, is a state judge in Massachusetts. In her quiet, oak-paneled chambers directly behind the courtroom, Alice, clad in a stylish pants suit, studies cases with her feet propped on the oak desk. Fragile and redheaded, she looks like a TV actress playing the role of judge. But behind her fashionable image and crisp professionalism lies a deeply concerned mother.

"I didn't marry until twenty-nine, after I established myself as a lawyer. My husband is a successful architect and, as a childless working couple, we had an exciting first four years of marriage, free to travel or work all weekend if we wanted to. Then we decided that if we were ever going to have a child, we should go ahead—my doctor advised me not to wait—and I had a child at age thirty-four, just before the biological deadline. My son is six now and a great kid. But I have these black times when I wonder if I'm capable of being a mother to him. I feel totally in control in my courtroom. I can handle insubordinate lawyers; the harder the case, the more stimulated I get. Then I leave my office to go home and Robert's waiting there with all these problems. And no matter how I handle them, I feel inadequate and never sure I'm doing the right thing. I really feel guilty about my mothering, no matter how hard I try. There are times when I feel I have no business being a mother. Am I doing him a service to be his mother?"

Alice gave a start of recognition when we mentioned the fear of not being a "good woman." "Worrying over my mothering prompted me to go to a psychiatrist last year. And what we're discovering is that this guilt over my son and how I mother him isn't really the trouble. It goes back much further to how I feel about being a woman."

Doubts like these come as a painful shock to women who have spent major energies during their lives demonstrating that they have minds as good as men's and capabilities perfectly undeterred by the monthly hormonal rages that a White House doctor recently claimed would make any woman pilot behind the wheel of a 747 a public menace. On the face of it, their doubts seem like a betrayal of the ideal of equality they've fought for. Many of us, in the first flush of feminist confidence, assumed that simply recognizing how cleverly we had been conditioned to passivity, pleasing others, and playing secondary serving roles would make it possible for us to change. But we need to recognize how deeply embedded in our consciousness are the traditional sexual roles of women: "Good women" are instinctive nurturers. They mysteriously know how to handle babies. They have many dates in adolescence and much experience dealing with the opposite sex. Most important, their babies are the center of their lives—there's never any conflict. Good women instinctively want to do the things their babies need.

This view of good womanly qualities is more powerful than most of us realize. High-achieving women like Connie and Alice can be particularly vulnerable to feeling inadequate when measured up to this mythic image. Indeed, to achieve, they may have consciously discarded what they regarded as "female qualities." When they become mothers, they suddenly are faced with feelings of inadequacy at handling this biological event which is an irrefutable sign of growing up female. And despite their success in work, they feel guilty over not being successful as "women." The result is that they transfer their fears and guilt to their mothering. They start with the fear that they can't possibly measure up —and every normal failure confirms their miserable lacks as "good women." But instead of facing these older, deeper fears, their guilt instead focuses on the conflict between working and mothering—even though none may exist.

We look forward to the time when being a "good woman" has no relation to a set of prescribed characteristics, biological urges, or personality type. Until then, we must recognize the contradictions and difficulties that beset us along the way. And recognize that good mothering need not come only from women who have tracked the usual course of female experience.

SETTLING UP

In the final reckoning, the antidote to guilt that mothers find most reliable is their belief that working helps them be *better* mothers than they would be if they stayed at home full-time. The great majority of mothers we interviewed believed this to be true:

A head nurse: "Staying home all the time would not be good for my relationship with my children. I would get frustrated and not really be loving and caring with them."

A junior-college teacher: "I'm doing her a favor by giving her someone else to spend time with. The lady who looks after her is a mother-earth sort, and she gives her a lot of the simple, repetitive kind of care that drives me batty."

A *computer programmer for a banking system*: "I come to my children mentally refreshed and dying to see them. When we spend time together, it's quality time."

A majority of mothers come to feel that less intensive mothering is a benefit to both them and their children. We all get caught up in the Best Mother Competition. We anxiously watch our children's peers, eager that our children walk earlier, behave better, and share with us the most loving, understanding mother-child relationship in the world. Of course, our love is likely to color our judgment, and we do see our own genetic creation as indeed smarter, more sensitive, and better adjusted by miles than Cousin Peggy's noisy, undisciplined brood or the nine-year-old semidelinquent next door who likes to cut cats' tails off. But focusing your whole sense of worth on your children's progress in life can be less satisfactory for both of you than having other sources feeding your self-esteem and energy. Some mothers plainly fear that they would worry obsessively over their children if they didn't have outside work into which to channel their energies. Certainly the identification of a woman's success with her children's success that occurs in exclusive motherhood is calculated to produce an overinvestment of mother in child (much as a man's overinvestment in success at work is bound to produce a narrowed life experience). But perfect mothers do not necessarily produce perfect children, as many a mother discovers.

Says Sandra, a thirty-four-year-old Kansas lawyer: "I think my children were relieved when I went to law school and wasn't hovering around them every day, organizing their playtimes and naps. Whatever kind of craziness I pass on to my children, at least it won't be like my mother's. She was the classic smothering mother, who made me feel I had to excel at things for her sake and if I didn't, she wouldn't love me. I'm proud of my kids, but they don't feel they have to do things for me."

Paula, a South Carolina teacher, thinks, on the other hand, that her staying at home full-time created a too idyllic and protected environment for her son to grow up in. "I stayed home with my older child and I can honestly say that I was *too good* a mother. I really was. His life was too easy. His expectations of life and of people were unrealistically high. If I invest all my energies in my children, then I have to be a perfectionist with them, and that's not good for them. My son remains shy, withdrawn, not ready to accept life. My daughter's much more outgoing because she's been in nursery school since she was two."

Some mothers even find their working reduces tensions in the household by teaching them how to handle their authority. Marjorie, an office manager for a midwestern utility company, says she's learned to cope with her sons' behavior much better since learning how to manage at work. "One morning last week, my husband couldn't walk our younger son to first grade as he usually does. So I got my older son to agree to leave later and walk his little brother. But Jimmy started screaming that he wanted Daddy. Before, I would have been in a dither, not knowing what was right. Now I said, 'Listen, Jimmy, you get Daddy to walk you to school *every single morning,* and you can walk with your brother just this once.' And he saw the sense of that. Children recognize, when it comes down to it, when you're being fair." She adds: "I've learned that when you're in charge, you have to make decisions and stick to them. The kids, like the people I supervise, may get mad or resist, but I have to see that they do it."

Not to be forgotten as well are the financial benefits that your working gives your family.

"Guilty? How could I be," asks Faye, a Denver factory worker. "My husband works hard, but we could barely scrape by on what he made. Now that I'm making money, I can take us all out on a Saturday night, even if it's only to McDonald's. But it's important to the kids to feel their parents can do things for them like other kids' parents. I'm doing so much more for my family by working than I ever did staying home and seeing that everybody had their socks washed."

Finally, you'll come to terms with guilt only in time and through your own experience. When you see your children thriving without you at their elbows, you can relax and trust your feelings. Like Ellen, who at thirty-six had waited a long time for a baby, having suffered a series of miscarriages. She joyfully quit her job when she had a healthy daughter. To her dismay—and overwhelming guilt—she felt bored at home, anxious, depressed. In the next eighteen months, she ate compulsively, gaining twenty-five pounds. At her doctor's advice, she took a part-time job. "I had been depressed for months, crying for no reason and unable to lose even one of the twenty-five pounds I had gained. I loved my baby dearly and even loved taking care of her. But something was missing. The first week back at work, I lost four pounds and found myself smiling for no reason. My daughter missed me, but somehow even she seemed relieved at my decision. Now we both had found her place in my life—special, central, but not the only sun. Now she didn't have to be the only source of my life satisfaction."

THE BALANCING ACT

For each of us trying to carve out a life that combines achieving and loving, nurturing our children and our own selves means a constant struggle to balance. There are no givens, no guarantees. You have to trust your own instincts and fly by the seat of your pants. "You're always trying to strike a balance," said a woman lawyer as we talked over coffee. "And you're never quite sure it's struck." Tears welled up in the eyes of this controlled woman, who habitually freezes opposing lawyers with her calm self-assurance.

Supermom may have passed her ideological vogue—as a recent *Ms.* suggests, "having it all" requires a woman to possess unflagging energy and the determination of a dictator—but many of us still end up on a compulsive treadmill. A divorced mother wearily explains the pressures she puts on herself: "After a terrible week at work, I got myself together and took my daughter to a school picnic, and guess who the other parents were who showed up: seven other working mothers, all divorced like me. We had a great day, but I asked the teacher, 'What are you running, a school experiment in divorced working mothers?' I wondered where all these other mothers were who had husbands or who stayed at home all day and she didn't know. Still, I'd rather fall in bed too tired to sleep and know I've been doing good things for my children."

The cog that lies hidden in our compulsive treadmill may be our basic uneasiness about our right to play what many of us still see as a male role—holding a job. The only way a woman can justify working is to be as good in her "woman's" jobs as possible—so good that *no one* can criticize her. The trouble is, of course, that with her unresolved conflict about having both work and traditional feminine rewards, she goes on questioning herself.

Nothing but some hard thought can help you here. But not every woman has this problem. Many working mothers simply bring to their homes the same urge to do things well that they feel at work. Just as they like to be efficient and good at the office, they want to be successful as

THINGS TO DO FOR YOU

Don't neglect your own friendships. Hard as it may be to squeeze in, making a little time for your own women friends is a necessary tonic to refresh your spirits. An ideal way to combine two pleasures is to exercise with a woman friend. Make a weekly date to exercise at a health club (schmoozing while you stretch makes it easier anyway). Or meet a close friend for a three-times weekly evening run.

Create a transition zone for switching from the office to home. Get off the bus a block early and walk alone for a few minutes. Decompress from office tensions by walking briskly. Or take a slower bus or train that allows you to sit and read the paper before plunging into your evening round of feeding and mothering. Even ten minutes of "your" time can give you the second wind you need.

Train yourself to recognize your personal signs of stress and over-work. Whether it's a neck pain or a cold that puts you in bed for three days, know your stress signs. Learn to pick them up *early,* then slow down for a day or two and avert the big sickness. Sleeplessness . . . an extra measure of fatigue . . . listlessness . . . all are common early body warnings of overwork.

Analyze your day. When is the most stressful time? Is it the morning, when you're trying to get your army fed, uniformed, and out to meet the school bus, the car pool, or the 8:05 commuter train? Is it bedtime, when the house is still disorganized, the children clamoring to stay up? Major reorganizational changes may be the only solution. You might de-cide to get up an hour earlier—the relief of stress can make it worth the effort. Or you may decide your husband must help with bedtime frenzies.

Teach yourself a quick tension-reliever. Ten minutes with your feet up in a dark room . . . yoga breathing . . . a warm bath with the bath-room door locked against all comers—these proven relaxers can be adopted by every working mother. If you have an office with a door, try closing it and using your yoga breathing at the end of the day before you plunge into home routines.

mothers. They don't like to do a half-baked job on either front. And they'd rather push themselves to the limit than fail.

To balance yourself, the conventional advice is that you must set new priorities. "So we eat off paper plates on week nights, and I sent my two kids to camp without name tags on their underwear," reports a Brooklyn mother. "How low can your priorities get?" But besides relegating housekeeping to the backseat, you'll probably pare down your social life. You're more likely to be found spending Saturday afternoon taking your children to the park than sitting in the beauty parlor curling your hair for a big night out alone with your husband. And a lot of family togetherness can be packed into nights and weekends. Babies get toted in mother's backpack right to the A & P. And children share their parents' social life instead of being packed off to bed for the usual adults-only dinner parties.

But while you keep on the go sixteen hours a day, while you use weekends to catch up on your family, when you haul yourself out of bed on Sunday morning to take the kids on an outing when you'd love to just lie there, you probably remind yourself that working mothers, statistically, enjoy better health than nonworking mothers. And that you are less likely to have severe emotional problems than housewives.

Don't take that for granted. You'll find all your jobs will go smoother if you take a little time for yourself. A little time for you—for your own friendships, to put some space in your day, to relax.

A Good Mother Is . . . But the most basic change in priorities for working mothers is realizing that there is no one right, natural way to mother. (Each culture tends to pattern mothering to produce the kind of person who is thought successful in *that* culture). And, despite our cultural ideal of exclusive mothering, working mothers believe that "mother" does not necessarily mean handling each of your child's physical needs, from morning bath to tying shoes at the playground. It does not mean assuming that every problem, every unhappiness that your child undergoes, must be personally managed by you. The fact that your child's day-care teacher can soothe his tears or quiet him when his aggressive impulses get out of hand does not mean you are losing your place in his life as mother.

"Mother" does mean being available when your child really needs you. Myrna, a political-party officer who keeps a hectic day-and-night schedule, reflects: "I don't feel guilty because I know that at the times when my kids have needed me, I've put in large blocks of extremely concentrated time and energy. Like the year my son was eight and turned up with a writing problem related to his ambidextrousness, I dropped every political commitment to solve it. After twenty specialists, I finally discovered that he had a nutritional problem—he had to eat every two or three hours. And I spent the rest of that whole year tutoring him until he got up to his grade level." For a real and acute need, Myrna was there.

"Mother" does mean showing your unwavering love and concern by staying in touch with your children's feelings. It means showing your children the model of a mother who respects herself and is working to lead a full life. "Mother" can mean living new roles for women so that our daughters and sons will not be caught in the same shoulds and can'ts that we have grown up with. We are the products of our past, but our children—as every mother dreams—need not be products of that same past.

Being a mother implies not only love and the sharing of personal values with our children. "Mother" also means passing along values and commitment that stretch to a larger world than that immediately around us. Many mothers hope to inspire their children with a vision, however misty or incomplete, of how the world might be better for women, men, and children, and that such a vision will be part of the legacy they leave their children. And they are convinced, as Betty Friedan has written, that only by participating in the mainstream of society, will women and mothers reap the training and experience and skills to understand the complex society we call home.

To Each Season . . . No matter how well you manage, you're bound to end up busy and harassed some of the time. Most of us accept this pressure as simply a part of the motherhood season of our lives. And we are aware that a modern woman's life will span many seasons. Says a marketing executive who works long hours yet still manages to spend lots of time with her fourteen- and thirteen-year-old daughters whose values she has worked hard to help shape, "I'm so busy now, I wonder myself how I keep such a pressured schedule without collapsing. But my own inner psychology is that there's plenty of time ahead just for me. I am thirty-nine, and in four years, both girls will be out of the house. There will be a whole other life then, when the kids are gone, and plenty of time for reading poetry and making strawberry preserves, long before there'll be any grandchildren."

She enthusiastically adds: "Forty-three is young these days, and my husband will be forty-six and into the new career he's preparing for. I don't know exactly what it will be like when our child-rearing ends. But I know it will be better and more exciting because of this season being full and rich. And because I haven't been tied down for twenty years driving the kids around in a station wagon and doing nothing else."

This season may be one that takes more stamina and energy than any other. But if you're like most women, you'll look ahead to a more relaxed time when your children leave the nest—a future that will be less lonely and not find you feeling abandoned and purposeless.

I'M A SUCCESS!

Not so long ago, Margaret Mead could speak of an ambitious woman being faced with the grim choice between becoming either "a loved object" or "an achieving individual." Some choice.

And in *Passages,* Gail Sheehy direly concluded that women simply can't integrate marriage and career before the age of thirty at best, and probably not until thirty-five. Until then, she felt, a woman hadn't had time for the *personal* integration to direct two different spheres in her life. Her words struck an apprehensive chord in the hearts of already apprehensive working mothers. Many told us, "I read in *Passages* about all these late-baby superachievers—Margaret Mead, Barbara Walters, and Sophia Loren—who didn't have babies until almost forty. And I wonder am I just kidding myself that I'm managing them both. Maybe I'm short-changing my children and myself?"

We found that women—single and married, committed to feminism or indifferent to it, from seventeen to fifty—*are* changing these realities. We don't want to skate over the difficulties you must overcome in a social and political climate that is, at best, ambivalent to working mothers, sometimes hostile. With no public commitment to childcare, with a child-rearing philosophy that emphasizes the mother's sole responsibility to rear a happy, socially useful child, many mothers feel they are scaling a glass mountain—climbing one step up, sliding two steps back down.

Not all of us make it. And not all families of working mothers adjust.

But the more of us who attempt, the easier it gets. Just in the span of time from when we began this book to when we finished the last page, the women's magazines have begun to fill with stories of working mothers and how to cope. For many a woman, the deep satisfactions she gets—no matter the hassle—convince her she's on the right track.

"Believe me, I would work without the paycheck," says a head nurse who loves her work. "I get emotional and psychological rewards every day. I wouldn't think much of myself if I didn't get those things."

And another woman says: "I am a wife and mother. That's about 82 percent of who I am. But there's this other 18 percent that's just me alone, and if I didn't do something with that, I'd feel I was failing myself. To me, working means the difference between being a success and not being a success."

Take time to look over what you *are* accomplishing. Chances are, when you add up the pluses and minuses, the things you do and the things you *wish* you could get done, you'll come to a conclusion that makes it worthwhile: I'm a success!

Epilogue
WHAT WE NEED

Throughout this book, we've focused on the realities of managing, of how working mothers can cope with things as they are. We've saved for last one of our basic concerns: what working mothers need to ease the strains of their lives.

Every woman we talked to had a secret dream of *one* change that could make her life easier. For some, it was after-6 P.M. childcare. For some, a job that would not be so rigidly locked into a 9 A.M. starting hour. But few moved beyond wistful longing to the firm conviction that working mothers have a *right* to expect help from their employer and government.

We believe that the changes needed to support working mothers and their children and their families are not revolutionary but right in the line of traditional American ideals. After all, Jimmy Carter announced as the keystone of his administration his commitment to the family as the fiber of our society. He is not alone. Male politicians have long ritually proclaimed their dedication to the preservation of the family— and just as ritually bemoaned the death of that institution. We feel it's time for them to put their money where their mouths are. And to re-examine what national commitment to support of the family means. Doesn't it mean that we all have a stake in the care of future generations? Doesn't it mean that a society concerned about its future is obliged to make the atmosphere in which its youth comes to maturity as good as we can make it? And since more than half of all the school-age children in this country have mothers who work, isn't it time to realize that there is an overwhelming constituency whose needs we can no longer afford to ignore?

Employers, too, have an obligation to see their workers as part of families—and that should include their male employees as well as their women workers.

What do we need? Not programs with billion-dollar price tags. Just some sensitive, responsive changes like these—

ON THE JOB

Flexible working hours.   The rising number of firms experimenting with alternatives to the rigid nine-to-five day are learning that greater productivity and less absenteeism and tardiness are their rewards. For a mother juggling home and work needs, the chance to plan her week with some flexibility would be a godsend.

Maternity and paternity leave as standard inalienable benefits.   Not only mothers but fathers should have the opportunity to care for a new baby without fear of job loss. This simple recognition of the need to support family life merely affirms the principles of humanistic management that influential business leaders are adopting.

Part-time work that is decently paid and respected.   For business, an investment in developing part-time work plans can mean cost savings and the retention of valuable, experienced employees. For mothers, a part-time job that is neither dead-end nor viewed as trivial could ease the harsh choice between suffering a career setback and not having the time she wants to spend with her children. And in a time of high un- employment, when part-time jobs could mean more jobs for more individuals, government should provide tax incentives for companies that are willing to sponsor meaningful part-time work.

Job sharing between husbands and wives.   We think this modern up-date of the traditional Mom-Pop business has great potential. A couple might share a sixty-hour week on a factory shift, for example, with the wife working twenty-five hours, the husband thirty-five. Job sharing for couples could give employers the benefits of less-fatigued workers and less time lost to illness (if a husband is sick one day, his wife can work a longer week to fill the sixty-hour commitment). And only one set of fringe benefits for the family would have to be paid by the employer.

End to nepotism restrictions in companies and institutions.   Well-intentioned in origin, the banning of wives and husbands being employed by the same company needlessly limits mobility and opportunity for working couples. A realistic recognition of the growing incidence of two-career families should prompt a sensible lifting of these bans where they are clearly not abused. And, in compensation, a business that can successfully employ both husband and wife is much less likely to lose them to other firms.

Transfers as an employee's option, not obligation. Refusal to uproot one's family and hie off to a new part of the country according to the corporation's need has long been considered tantamount to disloyalty . . . and a fearful lack of ambition. But a business that looks upon its employees as members of families and communities, not as mere sets of hands or brains for hire, is going to win greater loyalty, less expense in employee turnover, greater worker productivity, and an overall community of stability that will reduce operating costs for the business.

FOR OUR CHILDREN

A thorough, publicly funded exploration of the viability and desirability of various childcare options. Some thoughtful observers believe that day care, no matter how well funded, is not the panacea we need to provide quality care for all children. The scandal is that our government, faced with rising numbers of employed mothers, is not really exploring the options. To our minds, what's most likely is that a *variety* of childcare facilities—public day care, private day care, family day care, tax support for individual caregivers—will offer the choices we need so that each individual child and family can find the best situation.

Full-time use of schools. Despite the sizable amount of public capital sunk into school real estate, and the shrinking school population that's making many an expensive school structure a white elephant, our schools continue to be utilized only part-time, a waste that would horrify any factory manager charged with optimizing his equipment time. Schools need to become more sensitive to working mothers' needs, using their ready-made facilities to offer after-school play programs for students, summer day care, and any of a dozen obvious, badly needed programs that would increase their service to the community.

After-hours childcare. Day-care centers that keep children after the usual 6 P.M. closing are rare or nonexistent in many communities. Many working women—nurses, computer programmers on night shifts, others who start the workday early—are often stuck for off-hours childcare and have to manage elaborate fill-in arrangements.

On-the-Job childcare. More talked-about than practiced, childcare facilities on factory sites so far prove to be a limited fancy of employers. In some cases, employers use the bait of dependable, onsite childcare facilities to lure mothers to underpaid work. But we see this option as potentially helpful and workable.

Childcare facilities staffed by senior citizens. Many a lonely, financially pinched retired person could earn wages *and* bring to children the enriching experience of another generation if we could unite kids and the underused contributions of retired people.

Childcare clearing houses. A reliable, central fund of information on childcare facilities for each community seems so obvious a need that it's surprising how few exist. San Francisco's Child Care Switchboard and New York's Preschool Association of the West Side, both of which provide, without charge, information on childcare centers, locations, openings, and cost, are inspiring examples of how childcare clearinghouses support their communities.

FOR US ALL

Shared parenting. No one loses by shared parenting. Kids enjoy the emotional resources of two people instead of one. Mothers are able to avoid investing all their energies and expectations in their children—to the detriment of their children, who have to perform for Mom's sake. Fathers learn the joy of nurturing another human life. Why, then, does the omnipresent script of all television commercials show every husband a klutz in the kitchen, every wife winning her husband's love with the latest cake mix, and every child turning to Mommy for clean clothes?

We offer the prize title of Forward-Looking Human Citizen of the World to the first big-time copywriter who dares to show a man competently diapering a baby, a working mother rushing home to find her children nonchalantly putting a cake made from the latest mix on the table, or—who knows—a father driving the station wagon that used to be reserved for the suburban housewife "because it helps me get my grocery shopping done in no time."

For us all, a new openness from pediatricians and other professionals to the burgeoning evidence that a mother who spends nine hours at work does not automatically produce children primed for juvenile delinquency or lifelong neurosis.

And finally, the recognition by all of us that our children, the future of the human race, are too precious, too important, to be left solely on the shoulders of one sex, unsupported by the rest of society.

Index